Teaching for Cognitive Engagement

Teaching for Cognitive Engagement offers a bold yet accessible vision for K–12 teaching and learning rooted in reliable principles from cognitive science. Schools today have put their trust into trends like excessive differentiation, self-paced personalization, and "student-led" learning, but are these models misrepresenting how learners learn and how teachers should teach? This book outlines a reinvigoration of evidence-informed instruction that prioritizes memory, knowledge-building, explicit teaching, and other strategies proven to raise achievement and equity across K–12 education contexts. Authentic scenarios, lesson structures, interventions, success criteria, and other recurring features show how these approaches can flourish in real classrooms. Provocative and highly practical, this book will help educators refocus their efforts on what students truly need to learn: clarity, knowledge, practice, and expertly designed instruction. In-service teachers, teacher-leaders, instructional leaders, curriculum developers, and other school staff will find an essential professional development resource that draws on the latest educational, psychological, and brain-based research.

Rebecca A. Huggins is an Instructional Systems Specialist for Grades 6–12 Literacy at the Department of Defense Education Activity, where she collaborates with teachers and leaders to strengthen instructional practice and advance district-wide improvement initiatives.

Also Available from Routledge Eye On Education
(www.routledge.com/eyeoneducation)

The Brain-Based Classroom:
Accessing Every Child's Potential Through Educational Neuroscience
Kieran O'Mahony

The Neural Teaching Guide:
Authentic Strategies from Brain-Based Classrooms
Kieran O'Mahony

Cultivating Behavioral Change in K–12 Students:
Team-Based Intervention and Support Strategies
Marty Huitt & Gail Tolbert

The Teacher's Guide to Scratch – Beginner:
Professional Development for Coding Education
Kai Hutchence

Harnessing Formative Data for K-12 Teachers:
Real-time Classroom Strategies
Stepan Mekhitarian

The K-12 Educator's Data Guidebook:
Reimagining Practical Data Use in Schools
Ryan A. Estrellado

Teaching for Cognitive Engagement

Nine High-Impact, Myth-Busting Strategies for K–12 Instruction

Rebecca A. Huggins

Routledge
Taylor & Francis Group
NEW YORK AND LONDON

Designed cover image: Getty Images

First published 2026
by Routledge
605 Third Avenue, New York, NY 10158

and by Routledge
4 Park Square, Milton Park, Abingdon, Oxon, OX14 4RN

Routledge is an imprint of the Taylor & Francis Group, an informa business

© 2026 Rebecca A. Huggins

The right of Rebecca A. Huggins to be identified as author of this work has been asserted in accordance with sections 77 and 78 of the Copyright, Designs and Patents Act 1988.

All rights reserved. No part of this book may be reprinted or reproduced or utilised in any form or by any electronic, mechanical, or other means, now known or hereafter invented, including photocopying and recording, or in any information storage or retrieval system, without permission in writing from the publishers.

For Product Safety Concerns and Information please contact our EU representative GPSR@taylorandfrancis.com. Taylor & Francis Verlag GmbH, Kaufingerstraße 24, 80331 München, Germany.

Trademark notice: Product or corporate names may be trademarks or registered trademarks, and are used only for identification and explanation without intent to infringe.

ISBN: 978-1-041-24211-6 (hbk)
ISBN: 978-1-041-24209-3 (pbk)
ISBN: 978-1-003-74071-1 (ebk)

DOI: 10.4324/9781003740711

Typeset in Palatino
by SPi Technologies India Pvt Ltd (Straive)

Contents

Meet the Author......vi
Acknowledgements vii

Introduction: Where We Are Going Wrong in American Schools......1

1 **Explicit Teaching** 34

2 **Building Knowledge**......74

3 **Setting Clear Learning Intentions** 100

4 **Teacher Clarity and Credibility**......113

5 **Scaffolding and Worked Examples**......139

6 **Formative Assessments and Checks for Understanding** 183

7 **The Power of Feedback**......196

8 **Retrieval, Interleaving and Spaced Practice**......209

9 **Deliberate Practice**......234

10 **A Call to Action: Why Cognitive and Progressive Teaching Models Can't Cohabit** 253

Meet the Author

Rebecca A. Huggins, M.A.T., M.Ed., is a secondary literacy leader, instructional designer, and professional development facilitator with more than 15 years of experience in classroom teaching, curriculum leadership, and educator coaching. She currently serves as an Instructional Systems Specialist for Grades 6–12 Literacy at the Department of Defense Education Activity (DoDEA), where she collaborates with teachers and leaders to strengthen instructional practice and advance district-wide improvement initiatives. Previously, she led literacy transformation efforts as a district-level coordinator in North Carolina, designing coherent curricula, supporting teachers, and implementing large-scale professional learning programs. *Teaching for Cognitive Engagement* reflects her commitment to bridging research and practice to design instruction aligned with how the brain learns best.

Acknowledgements

I would like to acknowledge the many cognitive scientists, psychologists, educational researchers, and practitioners whose work has informed and inspired this book. Their insights into learning, memory, and instruction have provided the foundation for the strategies and frameworks presented here. I also recognize that education research is constantly evolving; the ideas and practices presented here are part of an ongoing conversation, and I remain grateful to the scholars, educators, and students whose work continues to inspire reflection, learning, and growth. I am also grateful to my commissioning editor, Daniel Schwartz, for his guidance, encouragement, and thoughtful feedback throughout the development of the manuscript of this book.

Introduction

Where We Are Going Wrong in American Schools

An Example of the Student-Centered Learning Model

In Mrs. M's first-grade classroom, students are engaged in literacy workstations. At a half-moon table, she has called two students to join her for small-group instruction, using carefully chosen texts that match their instructional level. This is her "above grade-level" or "enrichment" group—students who read fluently at grade level, comprehend text with ease, and display the skills that we typically associate with proficient readers. They join her table eagerly, knowing that for the next ten minutes, her undivided attention will be theirs. Meanwhile, the other 15 students work independently at stations, most of which are located at their table groups. Activities include listening exercises through the district's literacy program, flipping through books stored in plastic baggies, or completing vocabulary work with brightly colored cardstock word cards. Words such as "modern" and "classic" are paired with a picture of a black-and-white skyscraper, and students are provided a Frayer Model to help them learn these terms.

Michael, one student, struggles to make sense of the cards. He hands them to me and explains each as if they are unrelated: modern, classic, and city. Without background knowledge of skyscrapers, he can't infer the intended connection. Growing up in a small suburban neighborhood and attending school in a city without skyscrapers, he has never seen one in person. Across the room, Johnny flips through a *Little Critter* book, chuckling at the illustrations. When I ask what's so funny, he points to the picture and says, "Look at the mess they are making!" But when I ask him to read a page, he stares at me as if I've grown three heads: "No. But you can go help someone else." Meanwhile, Mrs. M continues working diligently with her group of three.

Once that group's time is up, she calls her "lower-level" readers—Johnny and Michael among them—to the half-moon table. This time, the text is noticeably different. She begins by having them read the title and predict the book's topic. One student proudly reads aloud the title, which the other two repeat. Their excitement earns a quick redirection from Mrs. M before she moves on: "Can any of you tell me who you think is on the cover of this book?" The image is a well-known side profile of Susan B. Anthony, the abolitionist and women's suffrage leader. None of the students recognizes her. Notably, the whole-group lesson prior to workstation time had no connection to the activities under way. When the observers and I leave, the conversation focuses almost entirely on Mrs. M's use of "guided reading." By many measures, she is following the expected playbook: differentiating instruction, personalizing learning, grouping flexibly, and providing materials tailored to students' levels. (These terms will be familiar buzzwords to many educators; for those who are new to them, we'll unpack them over the course of this book.) On the walkthrough form, her lesson earns checkmarks in all the right boxes. Yet one glaring problem remains: most of her students are not truly learning. Even the two groups she met with received only about ten minutes of her time.

The scene I just described in Mrs. M's classroom may feel familiar—especially if you're an elementary school teacher. What she was attempting to model were "literacy centers." According to Daniels and Bizar (1998), effective literacy centers "allow for student choice and have explicit and ongoing routines." These centers, proponents argue, "promote student collaboration, facilitate student motivation, and provide targeted practice for students." Sounds great, right? The purpose of these centers is to provide meaningful learning opportunities for the rest of the class while the teacher works with a small group to develop reading skills and strategies—typically on texts at their "instructional reading level." (We'll look more closely at leveled texts—and the assumptions behind them—in Chapter 1.)

Since it wouldn't have been fair for me to give Mrs. M the unfiltered feedback I wanted to, I focused instead on ways she might encourage more peer interaction during workstation time. This seemed important, given that she would be working with only 5 of her 22 students while the rest were largely left to manage on their own in the name of personalized, differentiated learning. Unfortunately, many of her students were not strong enough readers to make peer engagement especially beneficial. Still, as is so often the case in education right now, the teacher was not truly the one at fault.

The Student-Centered Approach

According to the U.S. Department of Education (2010), student-centered learning is most simply defined as an approach in which learners choose not only what to study but also how and why that topic might be of interest. In this model, responsibility and activity lie with the learner, in contrast to the instructor control and coverage of academic content characteristic of much conventional, didactic teaching. The roots of student-centered learning run deep in constructivism—an educational theory strongly shaped by Jean Piaget and Lev Vygotsky. Constructivism views reality as (1) socially constructed, (2) constituted through language, and (3) organized and maintained through narrative (Matthews, 2003). Both Piaget and Vygotsky saw children as active participants in their own learning, with development driven by cognitive conflicts or discrepancies. While they shared this core belief, their emphases differed: Piaget positioned teachers as facilitators of discovery learning, whereas Vygotsky viewed teachers as guides and mediators, emphasizing social interaction and scaffolding. Despite their differences, the two agreed that children actively construct understanding rather than passively receive knowledge.

In the United States—and in many other parts of the world—few have had a greater and more lasting influence than John Dewey. Dewey championed "hands-on learning," arguing that children learn best through direct experience rather than passive absorption of information. For him, education was an interactive process tied to real-life situations, intended to prepare individuals to fully participate in a democratic society. He believed that teaching should provide "the context for the child in which his or her naturally occurring developmental processes" could unfold (Matthews, 2003). While Dewey trusted experience as a more powerful educator than the teacher, he still saw teachers as essential guides who shape and direct that experience. His work, though rooted more in common sense and anecdote than empirical research, has fueled the progressive approach to education—now a cornerstone of schools of education and, ultimately, K–12 systems in the United States and in other countries around the world.

Yet despite its philosophical appeal, student-centered instruction (or learner-centered instruction) faces a significant problem: there is limited empirical evidence of its effectiveness. A study by Sakata, Bremner, and Cameron (2022) found that while the strategy can yield "positive results," there is "currently little objective evidence to prove its effectiveness." In their review of 62 journal articles (2001–2020) on learner-centered models in low- to middle-income countries, only 9 reported objective evidence of improved academic outcomes. Most studies were more subjective than scientific, focusing on teacher and student perceptions of learner-centered practices rather than measurable gains in learning. Similarly, syntheses of John Hattie's *Visible Learning* research indicate that student-centered or inquiry-based teaching approaches yield an average effect size of about 0.35, which falls slightly below his 0.40 hinge point for one year's expected growth (Hattie, 2023). Cuccolo and DeBruler (2023) found similar results in their research on the impact of student-centered learning on K–12 achievement. The authors argue that with the limited studies that currently exist, the findings may be limited in their generalizability, in part because the research that does exist focuses primarily on "attitudes, motivation and perceptions" rather than how student-centered learning can address the gaps in student achievement (Cuccolo & DeBruler, 2023). This is interesting, considering that this school of thought has been a driving focus in most colleges of education and classrooms across the country in the 20th and now 21st century. And while this data could certainly be skewed by variations in implementation of student-centered learning, it is interesting how a theory could persist with so little evidence that the educative system in the United States is improving.

Mrs. M exemplifies aspects of a progressive learning environment through her child-centered approach, in which students engage with leveled texts while she differentiates instruction using flexible groupings. Much of this practice is rooted in developmentalism—a view that "an individual's social, emotional, and cognitive development is the result of a progression of natural tendencies that have occurred through natural selection and evolution" (Matthews, 2003). In such a framework, teachers may feel less compelled to take direct responsibility for students' learning, operating under the assumption that students possess the innate ability, through evolutionary means, to "pick up" essential skills such as reading and math or can somehow interpret reading, math, and writing, through environmental factors, as opposed to explicit instruction. However, while language development in children has been shown to occur through immersion, there is no evolutionary or scientific evidence to suggest the same is true for the acquisition of complex skills such as writing, reading, or mathematics (Matthews, 2003).

The Un-Science of Learning

Conceptions of active, student-centered learning have shaped the vision of "effective" instruction in schools nationwide. The prevailing idea is that students should be active participants—using "voice" and "choice" to tailor experiences to their "unique needs." Yet research shows that lower-aptitude students often select, or are placed in, unguided approaches and that less-able learners tend to choose less-structured tasks—resulting in reduced learning, as evidenced by lower posttest performance (Kirschner et al., 2006). In this model, teachers become facilitators, tasked with "tailoring learning experiences" to individual "learning styles" or, even more ambitiously, creating pathways for students to "discover" their own learning.

Differentiation: Just the "Right Size" for Learning

Since the inception of Carol Ann Tomlinson's work on differentiated instruction, educators across the United States have been encouraged to meet students' "individual needs." Tomlinson—an American educator, author, and speaker—is widely recognized for her seminal work in this area. She defines differentiated instruction as the "process of identifying students' individual learning strengths, needs, and interests, and adapting lessons to match them" (Sparks, 2015). According to Tomlinson, there are four primary ways to differentiate teaching: (1) process, (2) product, (3) content, and (4) learning environment. A core tenet of her work is that today's classrooms are too diverse for a "one-size-fits-all" approach. In its 2010 National Education Technology Plan, the U.S. Department of Education placed differentiation under the broader umbrella of "personalized learning," defined as instruction tailored to students' individual needs, preferences, and interests (Sparks, 2015).

While personalized learning and differentiation have many similarities, they differ in two key ways: the focus of personalization and the method of adaptation. In a heterogeneous classroom, students may share the same overall learning goals, but individualized instruction breaks content into smaller steps, allowing students to progress at different paces. Technology has made it even easier today for students to be placed on an "individual pathway" in reading or in math, with an adaptive program that essentially gives students *more practice* on "key skills." Differentiation, on the other hand, focuses on varying how instruction is delivered. This philosophy draws heavily on Vygotsky's research on the Zone of Proximal Development (ZPD), which describes the range in which a child "cannot successfully function alone but can succeed with scaffolding or support." In this framework, new learning occurs when a teacher pushes a child just beyond their current abilities, providing coaching and support for a task slightly more complex than they could manage independently (Tomlinson et al., 2003). The goal is for students to work within a level of "moderate challenge," avoiding both boredom and frustration. Building on Vygotsky's ideas of the zone of proximal development, Jerome Bruner and colleagues (Wood et al., 1976) described "scaffolding" as the temporary supports provided by a teacher that are gradually removed as learners gain independence.

While Vygotsky's ZPD remains highly influential in education and psychology, its direct scientific proof is complex and often debated, with research relying more on observation and application than on strict experimental validation (Palincsar, 1998). By contrast, scaffolding has been more robustly supported by empirical studies—particularly in science and STEM (science, technology, engineering, and mathematics) fields—where it has been shown to improve learning outcomes and facilitate the transfer of knowledge (Paci et al., 2025). Differentiated instruction evolved in part from strategies designed for gifted students and as an alternative to academic tracking, which separates students of different ability levels into distinct groups or classes (Sparks, 2015). In theory, differentiation "does not involve creating separate lesson plans for individual students for a given unit" (Grant & Basye, 2014; Reis & Renzulli, 2018; Sparks, 2015). Instead, teachers identify overarching themes, vocabulary, or concepts and then offer individual and group assignments of varying complexity, enabling students to demonstrate understanding in multiple ways. In the 1990s, when differentiation first gained traction, teachers were also encouraged to align instruction with students' "learning styles"—visual, auditory, or kinesthetic—a theory now largely debunked (but persistent nonetheless).

Perhaps because the conception of differentiation is so complex, it has proven difficult to implement in classrooms and to study empirically. In a 2010 report by McREL, Bryan Goodwin noted that

> to date, no empirical evidence exists to confirm that the total package—conducting ongoing assessments of student abilities, identifying appropriate content based on those abilities, using flexible grouping arrangements, and varying how students can demonstrate proficiency—has a positive impact on student achievement.
>
> (Sparks, 2015)

Similarly, a 2017 RAND study conducted in partnership with the Bill & Melinda Gates Foundation found that personalized learning "seemed" promising but lacked convincing evidence to determine which practices were most effective. In their one- to two-year study, Pane and colleagues reported only a 3-percentile-point gain in math compared with a control group, with similar but statistically insignificant results in reading (Pane et al., 2017).

In personalized learning, the student plays a central role in creating learning activities, with the assumption that "personal interest and innate curiosity" drive learning (Grant & Basye, 2014). Tetzlaff and colleagues (2021) define personalized learning as "data-based adjustments of any aspect of instructional practice to relevant characteristics of the learner." They reject the notion that "learners know what is best for them," instead arguing that the degree of learner control should be determined by the teacher "in accordance with the learning prerequisites and the learning goals." With the rise of artificial intelligence and adaptive technology, personalized learning has surfaced as the latest in a long line of progressive trends. Yet, as Zhang and colleagues (2020) point out, there is still no strong empirical evidence supporting its effectiveness as a whole-school initiative. Much of the existing research is deeply tied to implementation details and local contexts, making it too limited to justify sweeping conclusions.

Michael Petrilli, head of the Thomas B. Fordham Institute, cautions that some personalized learning models risk promoting "a reductionist type of education" that fragments learning into isolated skills, stripping it of an inspiring, coherent whole (Herold, 2017). Research has echoed this concern, finding that when students were allowed to progress entirely at their own pace, many "went too slow" (Herold, 2017). Similarly, studies have repeatedly concluded that true differentiation is multifaceted and challenging to implement effectively (Sparks, 2015). These difficulties are compounded by a shrinking pipeline of qualified educators: the proportion of students earning education degrees fell from 21% of all degrees in 1970–71 to just 4% in 2019–20 (Perna, 2024; Schaeffer, 2022). A large-scale study by The New Teacher Project (TNTP) further found that many students "spend most of their time in school without access to four key resources: grade-appropriate assignments, strong instruction, deep engagement, and teachers who hold high expectations" (TNTP, 2018). Taken together, these trends raise a pressing question: can American schools still deliver a robust, high-quality education, or are they drifting toward systemic failure?

Many education graduates today are introduced in teacher-preparation programs to the dominant psychological perspectives of behaviorism, constructivism, humanism, and information processing. Often presented in a "pick-a-tool" fashion, these theories can lead new teachers to believe they can simply choose whichever style best matches their personal teaching preferences (Willingham, 2017). The danger, as Willingham notes, is that such an approach may leave them unprepared for the realities of how children actually learn. Worse still, it misrepresents some theories as "evidence-based approaches" when, in fact, they are based on teacher and student perceptions (Cuccolo & DeBruler, 2023).

This lack of appropriate educator preparation may explain why nearly half of new educators leave the profession within their first five years (Duval & Frick, 2025).

Multiple Learning Styles

In 1983, Howard Gardner proposed his theory of multiple intelligences, arguing that humans possess not a single, general intelligence but several relatively independent ones: linguistic, logical–mathematical, musical, spatial, bodily–kinesthetic, interpersonal, intrapersonal, and naturalistic. Although Gardner's theory was often conflated with the notion of "learning styles," he himself rejected that interpretation. Nonetheless, the framework encouraged educators to consider individual differences in how students learn and demonstrate understanding. This broader attention to learner diversity aligns with Tomlinson's influential model of differentiation, which she describes as anticipating variations in students' readiness, interests, and learning profiles and designing varied learning paths so students can learn as much—and as deeply—as possible without "undue anxiety" or boredom from tasks that are too easy or too difficult (Tomlinson, 1997). These ideas have also informed more recent frameworks such as Universal Design for Learning (UDL), which emphasizes proactively designing flexible learning experiences for all students, regardless of individual differences. UDL promotes presenting information in multiple formats, providing varied ways for students to demonstrate learning, and fostering engagement through choice and relevance.

Yet the learner differences emphasized by these frameworks may not be as pronounced as they suggest. Recent research in cognitive science and education has shown that, while individuals naturally display distinct strengths, weaknesses, and preferences, the fundamental processes of human learning are remarkably consistent. Studies in developmental psychology, neuroscience, and cognitive science indicate that all learners rely on core mechanisms such as prediction and error correction, reinforcement and feedback, hierarchical structuring of knowledge, and social learning (Eckstein & Collins, 2020). Core learning mechanisms are consistent for all humans; it is life experience, not fundamentally different "styles," that shapes the brain's unique pathways and connections (Bretz, 2017; Whitman, 2023).

Cognitive Learning and Educational Theories

It seems contradictory to ask students to write research papers supported by evidence when many teachers graduate from schools of education steeped more in philosophical teaching ideologies than in empirically supported practices. While it is beneficial for teachers to understand various learning theories to build a mental model of the learner, what they really need are practical, evidence-based teaching strategies that directly translate into classroom action that improve student learning. The problem with many theories is that they often generate untested or even misleading predictions (Willingham, 2017). Indeed, some of the ideas that students encounter in schools of education remain untested, as reflected in persistent educational beliefs that often lack strong scientific support. Take, for example, learner-centered teaching methods, an umbrella term encompassing approaches like problem-based and inquiry-based learning. These approaches promote students taking an active role in decision-making and their own education, often without strict adherence to a predetermined curriculum. Despite their widespread adoption and significant investment worldwide, rigorous research on the implementation and outcomes of learner-centered pedagogy remains limited or context-dependent (Bremner et al., 2022).

Interestingly, schools of education often devote little attention to how memory works—specifically how we learn, retain, and retrieve information in long-term memory—and which techniques best support students in accessing and applying this stored knowledge during learning. Young, hopeful teachers might be surprised to learn that students can actively engage in problem-solving or investigations without truly learning key concepts. Activity alone—even successful activity—does not guarantee learning (Ashman, 2023). This is supported by cognitive load theory, introduced by John Sweller in the mid-1980s, which highlights that human working memory has a limited capacity and duration, whereas learning involves changes to long-term memory, which is effectively unlimited. For information to move into long-term storage, it must first be processed and retrieved by working memory. Neuroplasticity plays a crucial role in learning, involving the brain's rewiring and strengthening of connections between neurons—the fundamental cells for learning (Cunnington, 2019). Learning and memory are deeply intertwined; without storing new information, learning cannot occur. However, learning is not a "set-and-forget" process. Newly acquired knowledge and skills must be actively maintained, or they risk being forgotten—often quite rapidly. German psychologist Hermann Ebbinghaus's research on the forgetting curve shows that students forget the vast majority of what they learn, sometimes within a single day of first exposure (Swain, 2024).

Progressive theorists often emphasize that memorization is not synonymous with learning. They argue that deep learning arises from constructing knowledge through experience, inquiry, and reflection. Dewey's philosophy of "learning by doing" is a prime example of student-centered, experiential approaches. However, cognitive load theory suggests that novices benefit most from direct or guided instruction, while experts—having developed relevant schemas—can often handle problem-solving or inquiry more independently, though even experts may require guidance for unfamiliar or complex tasks (Swain, 2024; Sweller et al., 2011b). What works best therefore depends largely on whether students are relative novices or experts in the task or domain at hand. For example, a middle-school student learning algebra benefits more from structured worked examples, whereas a mathematics major can explore complex proofs with less direct guidance. Crucial to deep or transfer learning is a student's ability to retrieve new information from working memory and consolidate it into long-term memory.

John Hattie's research provides strong empirical support for key principles of cognitive load theory, especially in early learning stages. Hattie, a New Zealand education researcher renowned for his Visible Learning program, synthesizes findings from over 2,100 meta-analyses involving millions of students worldwide, creating one of the largest bodies of evidence on effective teaching. In his latest synthesis, Hattie highlights that while many teaching methods exist, educators should focus primarily on maximizing their impact on student learning (Hattie, 2023). According to Hattie, direct instruction has an effect size of approximately 0.59—considered "above average" in the Visible Learning research (Hattie, 2023). He clarifies that these terms do not imply didactic teaching or scripted lessons; rather, they describe a structured, sequenced approach that includes (1) clear learning intentions and success criteria, (2) fostering learner commitment to engage, (3) modeling and guided practice, (4) checking for understanding, (5) feedback, and (6) gradual release of responsibility (Hattie, 2023). He further stresses the importance of independent practice embedded within this gradual release, enabling students to move from surface to deep learning, consolidate knowledge, develop fluency, and transfer skills to new contexts—once they have acquired sufficient long-term knowledge and built the necessary schemas to avoid overloading working memory (Sweller et al., 2011b).

Effective teaching hinges on a teacher's ability to carefully select instructional strategies based on the phase of learning students are in—whether they are acquiring "knowing-that" (factual knowledge), "knowing-how" (procedural skills), or "knowing-with" (collaborative or applied understanding) (Hattie, 2023). This selection also depends on understanding how students have already built relevant schemas and they are ready to move toward transferring their learning—from acquiring and consolidating new knowledge to applying it in novel contexts (Hattie, 2023). Cognitive load theory supports this approach, particularly through the worked example effect, which demonstrates that novices learn more effectively by studying well-structured, fully solved example problems rather than struggling through tasks unguided (Swain, 2024). As students gain proficiency, they can gradually shift toward more independent learning—but only after mastering foundational skills and knowledge (Kalyuga, 2007; Kalyuga et al., 2003).

Teacher-led learning experiences are often viewed as antiprogressive because they appear to conflict with core values of progressive education—student agency, inquiry, collaboration, and relevance to 21st-century skills. These teacher-centered models are sometimes seen as opposing student voice, equity, and shared power. However, even progressive icons like Dewey and Vygotsky emphasized the teacher's vital role as facilitator and guide—not as an absentee figure. Research generally shows that excessive student choice for novices can reduce learning efficiency, increase fatigue, and impose extraneous cognitive load. Similarly, instructional methods such as project-based learning, which aim to foster relevance and engagement, show modest effect sizes (~0.15–0.33) unless students already possess strong background knowledge. Collaborative learning is most effective when carefully structured and accompanied by clear accountability (Hattie, 2023).

Cognitive science and evidence-based research often stand in contrast to widely accepted progressive practices and remain poorly understood or accepted in mainstream American education. However, an increasing number of countries, school systems, and networks are moving away from discovery-based or progressive methods toward evidence-based, cognitively informed instruction—with impressive gains in literacy, math, and equity. Australia, where cognitive load theory originated, has been at the forefront of this shift. For example, New South Wales promotes explicit instruction, phonics-based literacy, and knowledge-rich curricula. Their "Best in Class" initiative documented improved student outcomes through widespread adoption of explicit teaching, teacher clarity, worked examples, and structured curricula across sectors.

While evidence-based instruction has made meaningful inroads in elementary education worldwide and in some pockets of the United States, progress has been slower and less consistent in secondary schools. Many high school teachers are trained primarily in their subject areas rather than in learning science. There is often a pervasive belief that students "should already know how to learn" by the time they reach high school—a notion not supported by research. Consequently, key strategies such as metacognition, retrieval practice, and cognitive load principles are often underutilized in secondary classrooms. Instead, many secondary classrooms emphasize open-ended approaches, project-based learning, student autonomy, and real-world relevance—even in contexts where research favors more structured instructional methods.

Motivation and Student Success

Progressive education theorists argue that students are naturally curious and thus schools should tap into intrinsic interests to make learning personally meaningful—encouraging open inquiry, project-based learning, choice-driven tasks, and student agency. They emphasize that motivation is deeply rooted in emotions, identity, and relationships, often prioritizing autonomy over mastery (Ryan & Deci, 2000). However, progressive models frequently avoid difficulty to protect motivation, which can unintentionally widen achievement gaps by denying students the challenges needed to build competence, knowledge, and confidence (Bjork & Bjork, 2011; TNTP, 2018; Willingham, 2009). Tasks focused on "fun," high-interest topics, open-ended projects, and student choice often benefit only students who are already high-achieving—those who (1) have ample background knowledge, (2) can self-regulate their learning, and (3) are comfortable with vague or abstract tasks (Kirschner et al., 2006; Willingham, 2009; Willingham, 2017). Meanwhile, struggling students may flounder without sufficient structure, fall further behind, and appear disengaged, reinforcing misconceptions that they lack motivation. Assuming that some students can't handle rigor becomes a self-fulfilling prophecy: they miss out on building essential schemas, skills, and confidence, and the gap widens.

True motivation arises not from making tasks easy but from helping students succeed at challenges that initially felt difficult. Structured difficulty combined with support—such as scaffolding, timely feedback, and worked examples—helps all students experience real success, fueling motivation and narrowing achievement gaps. While relevance can enhance engagement, it is not a prerequisite for learning. Overemphasizing personal alignment may delay access to core content, allowing knowledge gaps to compound. Without exposure to rigorous material, students' background knowledge stagnates, hindering reading comprehension and academic vocabulary development. As Daniel Willingham aptly states, "Motivation is a consequence of learning, not a prerequisite for it."

Defining the Novice Student

Because instructional design in secondary education often favors exploration and inquiry, there is a common assumption that leading with a "discovery first" approach—also known as inductive learning—is ideal. This approach is grounded in the idea that students should grapple with a problem before receiving formal instruction (Hiebert & Grouws, 2007; Lombrozo et al., 2007; Schwartz & Bransford, 1998). The belief is that learners who attempt to generate explanations, hypotheses, or struggle with solutions prior to explicit teaching engage in desirable difficulties that ultimately lead to deeper learning. However, explicit instruction research challenges this assumption. Novice learners—those new to a field or skill and lacking experience or expertise—typically rely on foundational knowledge and external guidance to navigate tasks and solve problems (Malamed, 2023). Expert learners, in contrast, are motivated, strategic, and resourceful; they possess a deep understanding of their own learning processes and actively adapt strategies to meet goals (SWIFT, 2025). Importantly, simply being older or in middle or high school does not make a student an expert in a discipline. Learners who appear motivated and strategic may still lack a deep understanding of complex content, which often requires specialized knowledge and skills used by practitioners within that field (Shanahan & Shanahan, 2012). As a result, novice learners exist at every grade level and across all disciplines, with background knowledge varying widely depending on how much prior learning has been effectively transferred from short- to long-term memory in previous schooling (Deans for Impact, 2015; Sweller et al., 2011a; Willingham, 2009; Willingham, 2017).

It is crucial to understand that an explicit-first instructional sequence does not preclude students from engaging in problem-solving or inquiry. Rather, it acknowledges that students cannot effectively participate in rich problem-solving, analytical writing, or inquiry without a foundational knowledge base (Kirschner et al., 2006; Sweller et al., 2011). Instructional models that prioritize explicit teaching ensure that learners lacking secure background knowledge receive adequate support and

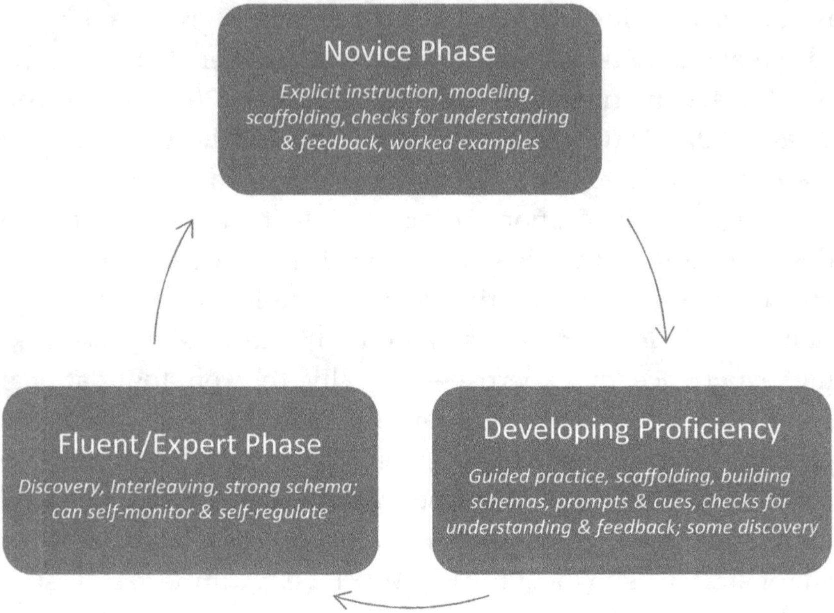

18 ◆ Teaching for Cognitive Engagement

Novice Phase
Explicit instruction, modeling, scaffolding, checks for understanding & feedback, worked examples

Developing Proficiency
Guided practice, scaffolding, building schemas, prompts & cues, checks for understanding & feedback; some discovery

Fluent/Expert Phase
Discovery, Interleaving, strong schema; can self-monitor & self-regulate

FIGURE I.1 The learning cycle.

guidance. Moreover, students may revert to the novice phase whenever introduced to new or unfamiliar concepts, underscoring the need for ongoing scaffolding throughout the learning process (see Figure I.1).

Teachers also need to recognize when a student has reached the fluent or expert learner stage and no longer requires scaffolding or support. Indicators of mastery include demonstrated knowledge, cognitive flexibility, metacognitive skills, independence, quality output, and the ability to teach or explain the task to others (de Groot, 1978; Chi et al., 1988; Bransford et al., 2000; Barnett & Ceci, 2002; Zimmerman, 2002; Sweller et al., 2011; Willingham, 2009). Effective instructional design protects working memory, making success—and thus motivation—more likely. Novice learners exist at every grade level and require clear goals, success criteria, and structured steps to build confidence and sustain engagement. When students track their own progress, their sense of efficacy grows. Frequent feedback and retrieval practice make learning visible and reinforce growth (Hattie, 2023). While making material "relevant" can capture students' attention, it is insufficient to sustain motivation or learning on its own. What truly maintains engagement is cognitive success—achieving mastery—even in subjects a student initially thought uninteresting (Hidi & Renninger, 2006; Willingham, 2009; Hattie, 2023).

This perspective challenges some assumptions behind Tomlinson's differentiation model, which advocates individualized learning paths based on learner profiles. Differentiation, while widely embraced, has only moderate empirical support, is logistically complex, and is frequently implemented in ways that do not effectively enhance student learning. With a relatively modest effect size (~0.46), differentiation can backfire if poorly implemented, leading to fragmented instruction and lowered expectations for struggling students rather than equipping them to meet rigorous goals (Hattie, 2023). Much of differentiation's foundation rests on beliefs in learning styles and preferences—concepts not supported by scientific evidence (Pashler et al., 2007).

Instead, targeted, responsive teaching practices grounded in formative assessment (effect size 0.68), scaffolding (0.75), timely feedback (0.70), and acceleration strategies (greater than 0.40) have demonstrated greater positive impact—especially for struggling learners. These approaches provide access to grade-level content with appropriate support, avoiding the pitfalls of simplified or watered-down instruction (Hattie, 2023; Lemov et al., 2016; McLeskey & Waldron, 2011; TNTP, 2018).

Leveling Texts and Dumbing Down Expectations

You may recall Mrs. M, from the first-grade teacher example I mentioned above. In her literacy stations, she provided students with leveled texts, another means to differentiate learning for her students. Students—including struggling readers—actually benefit *more* from working with grade-level (or complex) texts with appropriate scaffolding, than from being limited to easier "leveled" texts (ACT, 2006; Fisher & Frey, 2012; Shanahan, 2020). Students need exposure to complex, meaningful language to build reading comprehension, vocabulary, and background knowledge. Avoiding complexity starves working memory and long-term memory of the input it needs to grow. Using leveled texts to "match ability" might feel supportive, but in reality, it limits cognitive growth.

Instead, students need grade-level content with scaffolding, not simplified content with lowered expectations. In Shanahan's reviews of research from 2012 to the present, there is virtually "no empirical evidence that matching texts to reading levels improves outcomes—and in some cases, students made more progress with harder texts that were scaffolded." Using leveled texts assumes that students must master easier texts before tackling harder ones, which is not how reading development or brain plasticity actually works (Castles et al., 2018; Lesaux & Galloway, 2012; Shanahan, 2020; Wexler, 2019). Reading is not natural; reading involves "recycling" neural networks originally designed for speech, vision, and pattern recognition (Dehaene, 2009). This means that kids don't just pick up reading the way they do oral language—they need structured instruction to map letters (graphemes) to sounds (phonemes). When students practice reading with accuracy and effort, the brain rewires itself, strengthening the neural "circuit" for reading. This takes time and high-quality, deliberate practice—not just exposure. Plasticity means that late bloomers can catch up—but not without effort. Targeted, explicit instruction can dramatically improve reading even in older struggling readers (Torgesen et al., 2001). When it comes to actual skill development (reading fluency, vocabulary, decoding or comprehension strategies), there is little direct evidence that representation alone leads to better outcomes, and domain knowledge and language proficiency largely drive reading comprehension (not identity or interest) or leveled texts.

What We Know Works in Teaching Practice—and Why More People Aren't Doing it

What we know works in teaching practice, and what is actually happening in classrooms across the country and in schools of education, often is contradictory. While many progressive ideologies in education are well intentioned, their continued influence has often more to do with values, politics, and culture than with what research actually says about how learning works. Progressive ideals appeal to core educational values that may seem morally or emotionally compelling. Many progressive approaches are tied to equity discourse, but, ironically, avoiding challenge to protect students can widen achievement gaps; meeting students "where they are" can mean leaving them there; and student-centered learning often favors those with the most background knowledge and home support. Progressive strategies produce high levels of student enjoyment, appealing classroom "buzz," and the illusion of deep learning, but cognitive science shows that effortful practice and retrieval—which feel harder— lead to better retention and transfer.

So, what actually works in teaching practice? Table I.1 shows the key tenants of an evidence-based, empirical approach to instruction, which can easily be implemented in both elementary and secondary schools. This list isn't exhaustive, and there are certainly other strategies that accompany the list below, which we will discuss in more detail in the upcoming chapters.

TABLE I.1 Evidence-Based Teaching

Evidence-Based Teaching Practices Backed by Cognitive Science

Strategy	What is It?	Instructional Implications	Effect Sizes and Cognitive Load Theory (CLT) Principles
Explicit Instruction	Clear, direct teaching of new content, in small, manageable steps; highly interactive between teacher and students	• Break down complex tasks to reduce cognitive load. • Ensure that students are not left to "discover" essential ideas on their own.	Hattie Effect Size: ~0.59 CLT Principle: Minimizes extraneous load, supports schema acquisition
Building and Activating Prior Knowledge	Connect new content to what students already know	• Use advance organizers, pre-teach vocabulary, and use concept maps.	Hattie Effect Size: ~0.60–0.70 CLT Principle: Helps integrate new ideas into long-term memory
Clear Intentions and Success Criteria	Make goals and expectations explicit before and during lessons	• Students should know what they're learning and how they'll know they've learned it.	Hattie Effect Size: ~0.75 CLT Principle: Reduces ambiguity and focuses attention
Teacher Clarity and Credibility	Teacher clarity is the ability of a teacher to clearly communicate learning goals, explanations and instructions and expectations in ways that students can understand and can act on. Teacher presence refers to the teacher's ability to project confidence, authenticity, and connection in the classroom, making students feel engaged, seen, and safe to learn.	• Be organized, coherent, and intentional in explanations. • Have a plan and work the plan. • Maintain strong teacher–student relationships and classroom presence.	Hattie Effect Sizes: Teacher Clarity: ~0.84 Teacher–Student Relationships: ~0.72 CLT Principle: Reduces extraneous load and helps students stay focused and on task for essential, effortful thinking

Scaffolding and Worked Examples	Providing structured models and step-by-step demonstrations before independent work	♦ Embed a gradual release model of responsibility in instruction and fade support as students gain competence.	Hattie Effect Size: ~0.75 CLT Principle: Helps build schemas without overloading working memory
Formative Assessment and Checks for Understanding	The process of gathering evidence about student learning during instruction in order to inform teaching decisions and provide feedback to help students improve; checks for understanding are a subset of formative assessment, and happens during a lesson, sometimes multiple times, to ensure that students are "getting it"	♦ Use frequent, low-stakes assessments to gather real-time feedback and adjust instruction based on student needs.	Hattie Effect Size: ~0.77 CLT Principle: Helps pace instruction to match readiness and prevent overload
Effective and Timely Feedback	Feedback should be specific, actionable, and timely	♦ Helps students understand errors and improve strategies, not just scores	Hattie Effect Size: ~0.70 CLT Principle: Promotes germane load (processing that builds understanding)

(Continued)

TABLE I.1 (Continued)

Evidence-Based Teaching Practices Backed by Cognitive Science

Strategy	What is It?	Instructional Implications	Effect Sizes and Cognitive Load Theory (CLT) Principles
Retrieval Practice (Active Recall), Interleaving, and Spaced/Distributed Practice	Retrieval Practice: Deliberately pulling information out of memory—not just reviewing or re-reading but actively trying to recall what you've learned Interleaving: Mixing up topics, problem types, or skills during a study session or practice set, rather than doing one type all at once (i.e., blocked practice) Spaced Practice: Studying or practicing material over time, rather than cramming all at once	◆ Have students actively recall information (i.e., quizzes, low-stakes tests, brain dumps, concept reviews/skill reviews). Strengthens and reveals learning gaps ◆ Revisit material multiple times with gaps in between to create "desirable difficulty" which strengthens memory. ◆ Forces students to switch between concepts and recognize which strategy applies to which problem	Retrieval Practice: 0.61–0.80 (Dunlosky et al., 2013; Hattie, 2023) CLT Principle: Reduces extraneous load, builds germane load, supports automation of core knowledge Spaced/Distributed Practice: 0.65 (Cepeda et al., 2006; Hattie, 2023) CLT Principle: Allows forgetting and relearning, creating desirable difficulties; reduces cognitive overload and reinforces long-term schema building Interleaving: 0.44–0.75 (Dunlosky et al., 2013; Rohrer et al., 2015)

Introduction ◆ 25

Deliberate Practice	Highly focused, goal-directed practice designed to improve performance, based on feedback, repetition, and increasing challenge	◆ Give students focused, purposeful practice with feedback. ◆ Emphasize quality over quantity and avoid busywork.	CLT Principle: Helps chunk and discriminate between similar ideas; enhances transfer through varied practice and boosts germane load via deeper cognitive engagement Hattie Effect Size: ~0.79 CLT Principle: Builds fluency and automaticity, essential for freeing up working memory and builds long-term memory, while strengthening retrieval pathways

Key instructional strategies supported by cognitive science, with explanations, classroom implications, and research-based effect sizes. Includes principles from CLT and recommendations for practical implementation.

If We Know What Works, What's the Problem?

The paradox is that we know what works—but we don't always do it. What's effective is not often flashy or trendy—we don't necessarily see it on Pinterest or Teacher Pay Teacher—teachers often don't find it as appealing as easy-to-implement strategies that *feel* like they are making impactful changes to learning when really they are not leading to deep learning. Many evidenced-based strategies, like explicit teaching, retrieval practice, spaced repetition, and worked examples, are structured and repetitive and can be cognitively demanding. This can be perceived as boring or rote or "old-school," especially when compared with engaging tech tools, authentic projects, and creative discovery learning. As a result, more effort often goes into student motivation through entertainment than learning through memory-building. Desirable difficulties—a key concept in cognitive science—just don't *look* exciting from the outside. To add to the conundrum, teacher education programs today still promote constructivist, student-led or discovery-based models, despite limited evidence that they work for novices. Phrases like "guide on the side" are common mantras and, though philosophically appealing, don't reliably lead to learning gains—especially for disadvantaged students. Evidence-based strategies often require skillful design, knowing when to scaffold, and patience as well as consistency. This requires concerted efforts on the part of districts and school-level leadership to devote impactful, effective, ongoing professional learning and coaching support to new and veteran teachers alike. Efforts to increase engagement and equity sometimes interpret structured instruction as rigid or "culturally oppressive," and leveled texts, project-based learning, and student choice are prioritized under the assumption that they're more inclusive or respectful of diversity—despite limited evidence they close achievement gaps. High expectations and explicit support are actually critical for equity—especially for students who haven't had access to academic language or background knowledge at home.

New programs do not always help address all of the barriers impacting effective instruction, either. They often need to look innovative to get funding or attention, and leaders may adopt what is new or popular, not what is proven. Curricular and pedagogical decisions are often made without grounding in cognitive science or metaanalyses, and are subject to waves of social critiques, based on political forces. Education in the United States is heavily influenced by federal priorities and shifts dramatically depending on the philosophy, party, and priorities of each presidential administration, affecting funding and accountability systems, curriculum and standards, testing, school choice, teacher evaluation, and areas of focus. A prime example is George W. Bush's No Child Left Behind Act (2002), which was designed to ensure equity through accountability and emphasized standards-based instruction and testing. Barack Obama's Race to the Top and Every Student Succeeds Act (ESSA) (2015) similarly was test-centered, but focused on equity and innovation, by creating Common Core State Standards, data systems to track student growth, and teacher evaluations tied to test scores. And while these policies ultimately were put into place to improve learning outcomes for students, they mostly have had mixed results on overall student achievement. While they have raised awareness and pushed accountability, success depends heavily on how states, districts, and schools implement policies—especially whether they use evidence-based instructional practices to support teaching and learning.

At the end of the day, learning is and should always be about the *learner*. It is important that those in education, and those making policy decisions for education, remember that. Not recognizing needed shifts in our schools and in our colleges and universities risks deepening inequities, stagnating outcomes, and undermining public education. School choice policies, such as those promoted by the Donald Trump administration (2025–), aim to address some of these issues through market-driven approaches, but it also leaves states to address complex issues of teacher quality, infrastructure, and curriculum independently, with wide variance. While countries like Finland and Singapore invest heavily in teacher training and professional respect and have tightly sequenced curricula grounded in cognitive science, US curricula vary widely by state and district. Additionally, evidence-based teaching is more consistently implemented in high-performing countries. The need to adopt evidence-based instructional strategies, invest in teacher development and support, and create a more coherent curriculum—so that the impact of instructional shifts can be felt by students and truly puts students first—ought to be the focus of education reform in America.

References

ACT. (2006). *Reading between the lines: What the ACT reveals about college readiness in reading*. ACT.

Ashman, G. (2023). *A little guide for teachers: Cognitive load theory* (1st ed.). Corwin UK.

Barnett, S. M., & Ceci, S. J. (2002). When and where do we apply what we learn? A taxonomy for far transfer. *Psychological Bulletin*, *128*(4), 612–637. https://doi.org/10.1037/0033-2909.128.4.612

Bjork, R. A., & Bjork, E. L. (2011). Making things hard on yourself, but in a good way: Creating desirable difficulties to enhance learning. In M. A. Gernsbacher & R. W. Pew (Eds.), *Psychology and the real world: Essays illustrating fundamental contributions to society* (pp. 56–64). Worth Publishers.

Bransford, J. D., Brown, A. L., & Cocking, R. R. (Eds.) (2000). *How people learn: Brain, mind, experience, and school* (Expanded ed.). National Academy Press.

Bremner, N., Sakata, N., & Cameron, L. (2022). The outcomes of learner-centered pedagogy: A systematic review. *Educational Research Review*, *35*, 100399. https://doi.org/10.1016/j.ijedudev.2022.102649

Bretz, S. L. (2017). Finding no evidence for learning styles. *Journal of Chemical Education*, *49*(7), 825–826. https://doi.org/10.1021/acs.jchemed.7b00424

Castles, A., Rastle, K., & Nation, K. (2018). Ending the Reading wars: Reading acquisition from novice to expert. *Psychological Science in the Public Interest, 19*(1), 5–51. https://doi.org/10.1177/1529100618772271

Cepeda, N. J., Pashler, H., Vul, E., Wixted, J. T., & Rohrer, D. (2006). Distributed practice in verbal recall tasks: A review and quantitative synthesis. *Psychological Bulletin, 132*(3), 354–380. https://doi.org/10.1037/0033-2909.132.3.354

Chi, M. T. H., Glaser, R., & Farr, M. J. (Eds.) (1988). *The nature of expertise*. Lawrence Erlbaum Associates, Inc.

Cuccolo, K., & DeBruler, K. (2023). *Insights into the effectiveness of student-centered learning in K-12 education*. Michigan Virtual Research Institute.

Cunnington, R. (2019, September 18). Neuroplasticity: How the brain changes with learning. *Science of Learning Portal*. https://solportal.ibe-unesco.org/articles/neuroplasticity-how-the-brain-changes-with-learning/

Daniels, H., & Bizar, M. (1998). *Methods that matter: Six structures for best practice classrooms*. Stenhouse Publishers.

de Groot, A. D. (1978). *Thought and choice in chess* (2nd ed., reprint). Mouton.

Deans for Impact. (2015). *The Science of Learning*. https://deansforimpact.org/resources/the-science-of-learning/

Dehaene, S. (2009). *Reading in the brain: The new science of how we read*. Viking.

Dunlosky, J., Rawson, K. A., Marsh, E. J., Nathan, M. J., & Willingham, D. T. (2013). Improving students' learning with effective learning techniques: Promising directions from cognitive and educational psychology. *Psychological Science in the Public Interest, 14*(1), 4–58. https://doi.org/10.1177/1529100612453266

Duval, T., & Frick, L. (2025, May 22). *Beyond the exit interview: Practical solutions for teacher retention in 2025*. Leader 2 Leader Blog. Florida Association of School Administrators. https://www.fasa.net/Leader2Leader/beyond-the-exit-interview-practical-solutions-for-teacher-retention-in-2025

Eckstein, M. K., & Collins, A. G. E. (2020). Computational evidence for hierarchically structured reinforcement learning in humans. *Proceedings.*

National Academy of Sciences. United States of America, 117(47), 29381–29389. https://doi.org/10.1073/pnas.1912330117

Fisher, D., & Frey, N. (2012). *Better learning through structured teaching: A framework for the gradual release of responsibility* (1st ed.). ASCD.

Gardner, H. (1983). *Frames of mind: The theory of multiple intelligences*. Basic Books.

Grant, P., & Basye, D. (2014). *Personalized learning: A guide for engaging students with technology*. International Society for Technology in Education (ISTE).

Hattie, J. (2023). *Visible learning: The sequel: A synthesis of over 2,100 meta-analyses relating to achievement*. Routledge.

Herold, B. (2017, October 16). The problem with 'broken' education: Why piecemeal skills instruction doesn't work. *Education Week*. https://www.edweek.org/teaching-learning/the-problem-with-broken-education-why-piecemeal-skills-instruction-doesnt-work/2017/10

Hidi, S., & Renninger, K. A. (2006). The four-phase model of interest development. *Educational Psychologist, 41*(2), 111–127. https://doi.org/10.1207/s15326985ep4102_4

Hiebert, J., & Grouws, D. A. (2007). The effects of classroom mathematics teaching on students' learning. In F. K. Lester, Jr. (Ed.), *Second handbook of research on mathematics teaching and learning* (pp. 371–404). Information Age Publishing.

Kalyuga, S. (2007). Expertise reversal effect and its implications for learner-tailored instruction. *Educational Psychology Review, 19*(4), 509–539. https://doi.org/10.1007/s10648-007-9054-3

Kalyuga, S., Ayres, P., Chandler, P., & Sweller, J. (2003). The expertise reversal effect. *Educational Psychologist, 38*(1), 23–31. https://doi.org/10.1207/S15326985EP3801_4

Kirschner, P. A., Sweller, J., & Clark, R. E. (2006). Why minimal guidance during instruction does not work: An analysis of the failure of constructivist, discovery, problem-based, experiential, and inquiry-based teaching. *Educational Psychologist, 41*(2), 75–86. https://doi.org/10.1207/s15326985ep4102_1

Lemov, D., Driggs, A., & Woolway, E. (2016). *Teach like a champion 2.0: 62 techniques that put students on the path to college*. Jossey-Bass.

Lesaux, N. K., & Galloway, E. P. (2012). Teaching advanced literacy skills to struggling readers: Critical issues and promising approaches. In S. E. Israel & G. G. Duffy (Eds.), *Handbook of research on reading comprehension* (pp. 307–337). Routledge

Lombrozo, T., Zacks, J., & Hasher, L. (2007). The effect of structure and explanation on memory for categories. *Memory & Cognition, 35*(5), 1160–1170. https://doi.org/10.3758/BF03193677

Malamed, C. (2023). The novice brain: Characteristics of the novice learner. *The Learning Coach*, https://theelearningcoach.com/learning/the-novice-brain/

Matthews, M. R. (2003). Constructivism in the classroom: Epistemology, history, and empirical evidence. *Science & Education, 12*(1), 1–23. https://eric.ed.gov/?id=EJ852364

McLeskey, J., & Waldron, N. L. (2011). Educational programs for elementary students with learning disabilities: Can they be both effective and inclusive? *Learning Disabilities Research & Practice, 26*(1), 48–57. https://doi.org/10.1111/j.1540-5826.2010.00324.x

Paci, E., Swainson, A., & Cerminara, N. L. (2025). Facing the fear: A scaffolding approach to teaching life sciences undergraduates R coding. *Frontiers in Education, 9*. https://doi.org/10.3389/feduc.2024.1504877

Palincsar, A. S. (1998). Keeping the metaphor of scaffolding fresh—A response to C. Addison stone's "the metaphor of scaffolding: Its utility for the field of learning disabilities". *Journal of Learning Disabilities, 31*(4), 370–373. https://doi.org/10.1177/002221949803100408

Pane, J. F., Steiner, E. D., Baird, M. D., & Hamilton, L. S. (2017). *Continued progress: Promising evidence on personalized learning*. RAND Corporation.

Pashler, H., Bain, P. M., Bottge, B. A., Graesser, A., Koedinger, K., McDaniel, M., & Metcalfe, J. (2007). *Organizing instruction and study to improve student learning (NCER 2007–2004)*. National Center for Education Research, Institute of Education Sciences, U.S. Department of Education.

Perna, M. C. (2024, January 3). No more teachers: The epic crisis facing education in 2024. *Forbes.* https://www.forbes.com/sites/markcperna/2024/01/03/no-more-teachers-the-epic-crisis-facing-education-in-2024/

Reis, S. M., & Renzulli, J. S. (2018). The five dimensions of differentiation. *International Journal for Talent Development and Creativity, 6*(1), 87–94.

Rohrer, D., Dedrick, R. F., & Stershic, S. (2015). Interleaved practice improves mathematics learning. *Journal of Educational Psychology, 107*(3), 900–908. https://doi.org/10.1037/edu0000001

Ryan, R. M., & Deci, E. L. (2000). Self-determination theory and the facilitation of intrinsic motivation, social development, and well-being. *American Psychologist, 55*(1), 68–78.

Sakata, N., Bremner, N., & Cameron, L. (2022). A systematic review of the implementation of learner-centered pedagogy in low- and middle-income countries. *Review of Education*, *10*(3). https://doi.org/10.1002/rev3.3365

Schaeffer, K. (2022, September 27). A dwindling number of new U.S. college graduates have a degree in education. *Pew Research Center*. https://www.pewresearch.org/short-reads/2022/09/27/a-dwindling-number-of-new-u-s-college-graduates-have-a-degree-in-education/

Schwartz, D. L., & Bransford, J. D. (1998). A time for telling. *Cognition and Instruction*, *16*(4), 475–522.

Shanahan, T. (2020, January 11). Who's right about text complexity, you or the Institute of Education Sciences? *Shanahan on Literacy*. https://www.shanahanonliteracy.com/blog/whos-right-on-text-complexity

Shanahan, T., & Shanahan, C. (2012). What is disciplinary literacy and why does it matter? *Topics in Language Disorders*, *32*(1), 7–18. https://doi.org/10.1097/TLD.0b013e318244557a

Sparks, S. D. (2015, January 28). Differentiated instruction: A primer. *Education Week*. https://www.edweek.org/teaching-learning/differentiated-instruction-a-primer/2015/01

Swain, N. (2024). *Harnessing the science of learning: Success stories to help kickstart your school improvement*. Routledge.

Sweller, J., Ayres, P., & Kalyuga, S. (2011a). *Cognitive load theory*. Springer. https://doi.org/10.1007/978-1-4419-8126-4

Sweller, J., van Merriënboer, J. J. G., & Paas, F. G. W. C. (2011b). Cognitive architecture and instructional design: 20 years later. *Educational Psychology Review*, *23*(3), 247–270.

SWIFT. (2025). *Creating expert learners in every classroom*. SWIFT Education Center.

Tetzlaff, L., Schmiedek, F., & Brod, G. (2021). Developing personalized education: A dynamic framework. *Educational Psychology Review*, *33*, 863–882. https://doi.org/10.1007/s10648-020-09570-w

The New Teacher Project (TNTP). (2018). *The opportunity myth: What students can show us about how school is letting them down and how to fix it*. https://tntp.org/our-work

Tomlinson, C. A. (1997). *How to differentiate instruction in mixed-ability classrooms*. Association for Supervision and Curriculum Development (ASCD).

Tomlinson, C. A., Brighton, C., Hertberg, H., Callahan, C. M., Moon, T. R., Brimijoin, K., Conover, L. A., & Reynolds, T. (2003). Differentiating instruction in response to student readiness, interest, and learning profile in academically diverse classrooms: A review of literature. *Journal for the Education of the Gifted, 27*(2/3), 119–145.

Torgesen, J. K., Alexander, A. W., Wagner, R. K., Rashotte, C. A., Voeller, K. K., & Conway, T. (2001). Intensive remedial instruction for children with severe reading disabilities: immediate and long-term outcomes from two instructional approaches. *Journal of learning disabilities, 34*(1), 33–78. https://doi.org/10.1177/002221940103400104

U.S. Department of Education. (2010). *Student-centered learning* (TEAL Center Fact Sheet No. 6). https://lincs.ed.gov/sites/default/files/6%20_TEAL_Student-Centered.pdf

Wexler, J. (2019). *The knowledge gap: The hidden cause of America's broken education system—And how to fix it*. Avery.

Whitman, G. M. (2023). Learning styles: Lack of research-based evidence. *The Clearing House: A Journal of Educational Strategies, Issues and Ideas, 96*(4), 111–115. https://doi.org/10.1080/00098655.2023.2203891

Willingham, D. T. (2009). *Why don't students like school? A cognitive scientist answers questions about how the mind works and what it means for the classroom*. Jossey-Bass.

Willingham, D. T. (2017). *The Reading mind: A cognitive approach to understanding how the mind reads*. Jossey-Bass.

Wood, D., Bruner, J. S., & Ross, G. (1976). The role of tutoring in problem solving. *Journal of Child Psychology and Psychiatry, 17*(2), 89–100. https://doi.org/10.1111/j.1469-7610.1976.tb00381.x

Zhang, J., Liu, X., Zhao, F., & Liu, Z. (2020). Understanding the implementation of personalized learning: A research synthesis. *Journal of Educational Technology & Society, 23*(1), 154–168. http://dx.doi.org/10.1016/j.edurev.2020.100339

Zimmerman, B. J. (2002). Becoming a self-regulated learner: An overview. *Theory Into Practice, 41*(2), 64–70. https://doi.org/10.1207/s15430421tip4102_2

1

Explicit Teaching

Explicit teaching often gets a bad rap. Many educators associate it with rote drills, teacher lectures, and stifled creativity. Yet decades of research in cognitive science suggest that structured, well-guided instruction—done thoughtfully—can actually empower learners, build confidence, and support deep understanding. Explicit instruction works by guiding learners through a scaffolded, clearly sequenced set of steps. It honors what we know about working memory and our limited capacity for processing new information at any given time. By breaking content into small, manageable steps, providing models, and guiding practice, explicit instruction reduces cognitive overload and helps students retain and organize knowledge (Kirschner et al., 2006). When lessons are carefully sequenced from foundational concepts to more complex skills, learning aligns with how the brain naturally builds understanding (Sweller, 1988; Sweller et al., 2011; Willingham, 2009). Explicit instruction also removes some of the unpredictability inherent in minimally guided or inquiry-based approaches. In purely exploratory models, students may spend significant time on paths that lead nowhere or misunderstand core concepts. Explicit teaching prioritizes efficiency and mastery, ensuring that foundational knowledge is solid before students move on to independent or inquiry-driven tasks.

As a structured, research-based approach, explicit teaching has gained strong empirical and theoretical support since the 1970s, and its evidence base has grown with advances in cognitive science, meta-analysis, and large-scale classroom implementations. Often associated with direct instruction, explicit instruction is an umbrella term for teacher-led, clear, and goal-driven lessons. Yet unlike traditional, didactic methods, these lessons are modeled, scaffolded, and adaptable across grade levels and disciplines. They generally follow a gradual release of responsibility and incorporate plenty of guided practice, feedback, and frequent checks for understanding. Contrary to common misconceptions of teacher-led instruction, explicit teaching is highly interactive and responsive, involving frequent exchanges between teacher and student as well as student-to-student.

Nearly all the tenets of explicit teaching can be found in Barak Rosenshine's "Principles of Instruction" (Rosenshine, 2012), which examines ten key principles of effective instruction:

1. Begin a lesson with a short review of previous learning.
2. Present new material in small steps with student practice after each step.
3. Ask a large number of questions and check the responses of all students.
4. Provide models and worked examples.
5. Guide student practice.
6. Check for student understanding.
7. Obtain high success rate before moving on.
8. Provide scaffolds for difficult tasks.
9. Require and monitor independent practice.
10. Engage students in weekly and monthly review.

As Kirschner et al. (2006) put it, "any instructional procedure that ignores the structures that constitute human cognitive architecture is not likely to be effective." Almost everything in working memory that isn't rehearsed is forgotten within about 30 seconds, and it can handle only a small number of elements at a time (Kirschner et al., 2006). Because of this, working memory can easily become overloaded, especially when learners are tackling unfamiliar or complex material. Learning happens when information moves from working memory into long-term memory, where it can be stored and retrieved later. If working memory gets overwhelmed, learning breaks down. This is especially true for novices, who lack the schemas—mental frameworks that organize information into meaningful chunks—needed to ease cognitive effort and interpret new material. Explicit instruction helps alleviate some of the cognitive load of working memory. It breaks instruction into small, manageable steps, that are introduced gradually to the learner. It uses modeling, worked examples, and guided practice to reduce the need for the learner to "figure it out" themselves. By focusing working memory on the right things (essential concepts and procedures), explicit instruction helps students form accurate mental models, and once schemas are stored, future learning becomes faster and more automatic—freeing up working memory.

Decades of research in cognitive science, meta-analyses, and large classroom studies suggest that explicit teaching is generally more effective than many progressive teaching models—especially for building foundational knowledge, supporting novice learners, and closing achievement gaps. Instruction that offers little guidance is usually less effective and less efficient than approaches that actively guide students through the learning process (Kirschner et al., 2006). This stands in contrast to inquiry-based or project-based learning methods, which prioritize student-led learning environments. Novice learners with weak prior knowledge are particularly vulnerable to ineffective inquiry-based learning methods that emphasize minimal feedback, opportunities for scaffolding, and teacher-led guidance (Lazonder & Harmsen, 2016). Even students who are relatively experienced in a subject can benefit from guidance when they encounter new material.

While educators often accept that younger elementary students benefit more from a guided approach, we are quick to assume that older students are more capable of less-guided methods of instruction. The "expert error" often occurs when we assume that age and expertise are the same thing. Just because a student is older doesn't mean they have expert schemas in a particular subject. This is particularly true for students in secondary schools. For example, a high schooler might be "expert" at texting or video game strategy but still be a novice in algebra, chemistry, or Shakespeare. Kirschner and colleagues (2006) make this point directly: when faced with new content, *everyone* starts as a novice. Disciplinary knowledge takes *time* and is associated with a deep and specialized knowledge. Experts in a field don't just "know many facts"—they organize knowledge differently. Novices tend to store information as disconnected bits; their understanding is often surface-level and context-dependent. In contrast, experts organize knowledge into larger, meaningful patterns (or "chunks") that allow them to see relationship principles flexibly and retrieve information efficiently (Chi et al., 1988).

For example, when solving problems, novices often focus on the surface features (i.e., numbers in a math word problem), whereas experts attend to the underlying structures and principles (i.e., proportional reasoning). This difference is often referred to as the development of schemas. Schema theory, developed through the work of Anderson (1977) and extended by Sweller's (1988) cognitive load theory, shows that experts' schemas allow them to process complex tasks with less strain on working memory, because information is organized and stored in ways that reduce cognitive load. High schoolers, even advanced ones, don't yet have enough exposure and practice to form these schemas, so they are often still operating with lots of unconnected bits of knowledge (Altindis et al., 2024; Petersen et al., 2020). They may have surface-level knowledge but not the breadth or depth to connect ideas across units or subjects. Mastery requires repeated practice, retrieval, and reinforcement over time (Kirschner et al., 2006; Sweller, 1988), and semester-based pacing limits opportunities for this. Even if instruction is explicit, students may encounter a topic only once or twice before moving on. Many high school courses are organized around semester or block schedules, and students may spend only half a year on a subject. Within that time, teachers must cover a large amount of material, often at a faster pace. Consequently, students may get only surface-level exposure to concepts, without having time to revisit, connect, or practice them in depth.

Moreover, experts are more likely to engage in metacognition—monitoring their thinking, recognizing when they've misunderstood something, and selecting strategies for solving problems (National Research Council, 2001). This self-regulation is part of what makes expertise transferable to new, complex contexts. These findings explain why novices often struggle when given little guidance: they lack the organized knowledge structures to navigate complexity. These limitations are further compounded by ongoing brain development. Adolescents' executive functions—planning, attention, and working memory regulation—are still maturing well into their mid-20s (Casey et al., 2005), making it even more challenging to master complex content without repeated, guided practice. Older students still struggle with self-regulation, sustaining attention, and managing cognitive load—especially when material is novel or complex. For information to enter long-term storage, rehearsal, chunking, practice, and connection to prior knowledge are necessary (Baddeley, 1992; Willingham, 2009). Without rehearsal, retrieval, practice, and feedback, even older learners forget new content quickly. Inquiry-based and project-based methods assume that students can organize their own learning pathways. It often takes for granted how complex disciplinary knowledge truly is, and it leaves learners with weak mental schemas that do not transfer to new learning situations. Cepeda and colleagues (2006) and Roediger and Butler (2011) show that repeated retrieval practice, spaced over time, is one of the most robust ways to transfer knowledge to long-term memory, but this too takes *explicit* exposure.

Given these developmental and cognitive constraints, it's clear that novice learners (regardless of age) benefit most from instruction that is structured, guided, and reinforced over time. Meta-analytic research supports this, highlighting specific elements of explicit instruction that have the largest impact on student learning outcomes. John Hattie's meta-analyses highlight components of explicit instruction as some of the most powerful strategies for improving student achievement. Among over 300 influences, strategies like teacher clarity (0.84), ongoing feedback and corrective guidance (0.70), direct instruction (0.59), spaced practice (0.65), mastery learning (0.58), worked examples (0.57), scaffolding (0.57), and breaking complex tasks into smaller steps, or cognitive task analysis (~0.50–0.60), stand out as highly effective (Hattie, 2023). Forcing novice learners to "search for problem solutions" with minimal guidance or using pure discovery methods can be detrimental to long-term memory and learning (Kirschner et al., 2006). Because students often lack the background knowledge and skills needed to tackle new tasks, teachers using minimally guided approaches end up having to provide considerable help anyway. Without frequent feedback and structured guidance, students can become lost or frustrated or develop misconceptions, making learning less effective (Kirschner et al., 2006).

Defining Explicit Instruction

Explicit instruction is sometimes unfairly linked to negative, lecture-based approaches—what many people think of as traditional direct instruction. Rosenshine (2008) notes that the term "direct instruction" can mean many things, both positive and negative.

For constructivist or progressive educators, it often brings to mind low-quality, rote lecturing where students are passive recipients of knowledge. The confusion arises because "direct instruction" and "explicit instruction" can have both general and specific meanings. When authors don't clarify how they're using the terms, readers can be left with a skewed understanding. Rosenshine (2008) identifies five overlapping uses of direct instruction:

1. Academic instruction that is teacher-led, regardless of quality
2. Procedures used by effective teachers in teacher-effect research
3. Procedures that teachers use to teach cognitive strategies
4. Methods used in the DISTAR (Direct Instruction Systems in Arithmetic and Reading) programs
5. Instruction portrayed negatively, such as lecturing while students sit passively

Because the term covers such a wide range—from effective, research-based practices to poor lecturing—many discussions of direct or explicit instruction can misrepresent what high-quality, explicit teaching actually looks like.

High-quality explicit instruction, supported by cognitive-science research, does more than guide students through tasks: it helps learners build structured knowledge within a discipline. Teachers break down tasks, provide scaffolds and guidance, give supportive feedback, and actively involve students in answering questions (Rosenshine, 2008). Instruction is primarily teacher-led, whole-group, and teacher-designed. Collaborative learning may be part of explicit instruction, but it is structured and purposeful. Students usually have assigned roles or tasks, and they rarely create their own understandings from scratch. Collaborative activities generally follow explicit modeling and guided practice and are used to reinforce, extend, and help students integrate disciplinary knowledge, ensuring that students don't just memorize facts but develop coherent, transferable mental frameworks for the content they are studying (Clark et al., 2012).

A Word on Multi-Tiered System of Supports and Interventions

Even the most well-intentioned intervention systems can do only so much if the core instruction—the Tier 1 instruction all students receive—is weak. Without strong, explicit, and systematic teaching, many students fail to master foundational skills and build the disciplinary knowledge they need to make sense of new material. This is particularly problematic because many students, even in secondary school, remain novices in complex domains like algebra, chemistry, or history; without robust Tier 1 instruction, they cannot develop the schemas necessary to efficiently process and retain new information. As a result, schools spend enormous amounts of time and resources trying to "fill gaps" through Multi-Tiered System of Supports (MTSS) or other intervention programs. Ineffective core instruction fails *most* at-risk learners, but ultimately it fails every student. In many schools, core instruction is insufficiently explicit, systematic, or aligned with research—especially in foundational areas like reading, math, and content-rich disciplinary subjects. Formative assessments may not align with curriculum, and screeners may be used in isolation without examining instructional quality. When students are flagged for intervention without first receiving high-quality core instruction, schools end up with overcrowded intervention systems where students rarely access grade-level content or develop the deep knowledge needed to progress independently, even when capable (TNTP, 2018).

When students don't get clear, explicit teaching initially, it's no surprise that many fail to master skills or develop shaky understandings. In reading, for instance, an over-reliance on leveled texts often limits exposure to the kind of rich vocabulary and content knowledge that kids really need. As a result, students may look like they have reading problems, when in reality they just haven't had access to enough background knowledge or appropriately complex texts. Fuchs and Fuchs (2011) point out that intervention systems won't work if Tier 1 instruction isn't strong. The National Early Literacy Panel (2008) echoes this, showing that high-quality, explicit teaching of foundational skills can prevent the vast majority of reading difficulties before interventions are even needed.

This challenge becomes even more pronounced in middle and high school. Here, a major barrier to MTSS success is the lack of disciplinary knowledge students bring to the table. In a study of over 3,500 high school students, O'Reilly and colleagues (2019) found that students with insufficient background knowledge in scientific or disciplinary topics scored significantly lower in reading comprehension, indicating that comprehension difficulties often arise because of knowledge gaps rather than basic reading skills alone. A student who hasn't built a strong base in science, history, or literature will inevitably struggle to make sense of complex texts in those subjects. Their difficulties often get framed as "reading problems," but more often they're really *knowledge problems*. This distinction matters, because while content expertise allows teachers to cover complex material, filling knowledge gaps requires explicit scaffolding and diagnostic skills—areas where many teachers, trained primarily as content specialists rather than interventionists, may struggle (National Academies of Education, 2024). While elementary teachers are usually generalists and tend to receive more training in pedagogical methods, middle and high school teachers are rarely given systematic preparation for addressing skill gaps. This makes it difficult to integrate MTSS effectively at the secondary level. Many secondary teachers feel unprepared to provide intensive, skill-based supports within their subject areas, especially when interventions require explicit literacy instruction or targeted scaffolding (Donegan et al., 2025). Without ongoing professional development and collaboration structures, MTSS risks becoming siloed—something only interventionists or specialists do—rather than a shared responsibility across all classrooms.

Another challenge to effective MTSS at the secondary level lies in assessment and progress monitoring. Unlike in elementary settings, secondary assessments are often summative rather than diagnostic, making it difficult to identify the specific sources of a student's struggles. This problem is compounded by the increasing complexity of disciplinary texts (Fukaya et al., 2024). In addition, older students may resist being pulled from class for remedial help, and when interventions are not age-appropriate or relevant, they often fail to produce meaningful gains (Hayes, 2021). By middle and high school, reading gaps are frequently deep and long-standing, which means that short, Tier 2 or Tier 3 interventions a few times per week are rarely sufficient to close them (National Research Council, 2012). These realities underscore the importance of strengthening Tier 1 instruction through explicit, knowledge-rich teaching practices; without this foundation, MTSS becomes less about targeted support and more about compensating for missed opportunities in core instruction. Research suggests that, even in secondary schools, only about 10% to 15% of students should require intensive Tier 3 interventions if Tier 1 and Tier 2 are working effectively (Schiller et al., 2020). In reality, many more are flagged, largely because insufficient core instruction leaves them without the knowledge and skills they need to succeed independently.

Final challenges of MTSS at the secondary level are scheduling and structural constraints. Secondary schedules—block or semester-long classes—make it difficult to deliver consistent interventions. Students may get support for only a semester and then lose it the next. Pulling students from electives or core content for intervention time creates trade-offs, as they miss exposure to the very disciplinary knowledge that could help them succeed. Large student loads—middle or high school teachers may see 100 to 150 students a day—further limit opportunities for ongoing progress monitoring compared with elementary. Even when MTSS provides targeted, explicit interventions, it cannot fully make up for years of missed opportunities to build deep, connected knowledge. The Institute for Education Sciences (IES, 2017) found that MTSS-based reading interventions can help in middle school but only when they are explicit, targeted, and supported by strong Tier 1 teaching. Similarly, Fuchs and colleagues (2010) argue that MTSS is still possible at the secondary level, but it must look different—integrating content-area instruction, using better progress monitoring, and addressing specific skill gaps rather than assuming grade-level standards alone are the problem. Without deliberately weaving disciplinary knowledge into both core instruction and interventions, students will continue to hit a wall with complex, knowledge-rich texts across every subject area.

Having a Plan and Working a Plan

While MTSS can identify gaps caused by weak core instruction, preventing those gaps in the first place requires a strong, well-sequenced curriculum. Explicit instruction without a strong curriculum is like great teaching with no map. You might have great techniques, but students won't reach deep understanding unless content is purposefully sequenced and built over time. Curricula choices play a fundamental role in strong explicit teaching—as it's the roadmap that ensures that instruction is coherent, sequenced, and aligned with how students learn best. Well-designed curriculum chunks content into manageable parts and builds knowledge progressively, aligning with how working memory processes new information and how schemas are formed. Explicit teaching depends on knowing what to teach next, how to scaffold it, and when to practice. A strong curriculum ensures that teachers can anticipate difficulties, pre-plan models and examples, and guide students through content that builds progressively. This is particularly true across disciplines, where students without sufficient background knowledge in science, history, or math struggle to integrate new concepts, even with explicit instruction. When curriculum is clear and aligned with evidence-based practices, all teachers have a shared foundation for delivering high-quality instruction and it prevents reliance on teacher-created materials that may vary in quality or miss essential content. A well-designed curriculum, delivered explicitly and with clarity, is foundational to maximizing student learning.

It is staggering that many teachers, knowing that a well-developed curriculum is essential for student success, begin the school year without a coherently sequenced, knowledge-rich plan. As a result, key elements of effective instruction—such as scaffolding, guided practice, and explicit teaching—may be missing, particularly in districts that emphasize student-centered or discovery-based learning models without sufficient instructional supports (TNTP, 2018). Systemic barriers—such as limited access to high-quality curricula, pacing schedules that assume a teacher can cover an entire curriculum in a single year, or insufficient support for implementation—often leave teachers starting the year already behind (Nevenglosky et al., 2019). Many districts, particularly at the secondary level, provide only standards rather than fully developed curricula, forcing teachers to create or adapt materials on their own. Teachers may also prioritize content that they personally enjoy or feel most confident teaching, which can lower rigor and leave critical disciplinary knowledge gaps for students (Ball et al., 2008; Darling-Hammond et al., 2017). Given the shortage of highly trained educators entering the profession, many teachers lack the preparation to curate curriculum materials that systematically build disciplinary knowledge and rigor, which students need to form strong schemas and succeed across subjects (Hirsch, 2006; Willingham, 2009). The uneven quality of curricula and instruction across classrooms and schools and even within the same building contributes to widening achievement gaps (Darling-Hammond et al., 2017). In many states,

Common Core or state standards outline what students should learn but not how, when, or in what sequence. Teachers are often left to interpret and sequence standards themselves, a process that demands deep pedagogical content knowledge and results in wide variation in instructional quality (Ball et al., 2008; Hirsch, 2014). Of course, having a commercial curriculum doesn't always prevent achievement gaps either; it is how teacher teams adapt, collaborate, and implement the curriculum with instructional approaches that are supported by empirical evidence, that makes the greatest impact (Levine & Marcus, 2007).

When students experience weak or unstructured instruction, the consequences extend beyond academics. Poor instructional practices can undermine motivation, reduce students' sense of competence, and, over time, lead to frustration, anxiety, and disruptive behavior. Research shows that instructional quality and classroom management are among the primary factors influencing both student behavior and academic achievement (Sugai & Horner, 2006; Wang et al., 1993). If teachers' instructional practices are unstructured or unpredictable, students don't know what is expected (academically or behaviorally) or when to listen, talk, or participate. They struggle to understand what success looks like, creating anxiety, power struggles, and misbehavior, especially for students who rely on clear cues. Additionally, because success directly contributes to student motivation and builds perceived competence (Ryan & Deci, 2000), a lack of success or a perceived lack of success can lead to misbehaviors as a defensive reaction to protect self-esteem. Unsurprisingly, students sense when instruction is disorganized—and they're more likely to challenge or ignore teacher authority.

How Teacher Teams Can Approach Curriculum Pacing and Planning

Teacher teams should develop a year-long curriculum map before the school year begins—or at the end of the previous year—identifying the sequence of units, pacing, and key assessments to monitor student progress toward learning goals. Even if the district provides a commercial curriculum, teams must invest the time to plan with it intentionally (Voogt, 2016). There is no such thing as a "turn-the-page" curriculum. Even the strongest programs require teachers to adapt lessons to their local pacing and standards and ensure the integration of impactful, evidence-based instructional strategies, which often are lacking in curricular materials. Teachers must plan with the end in mind—designing instruction around clear learning goals and formative assessments—to ensure that instruction is sequential, explicit, and aligned to assessments (Jensen, 2017), while making space for scaffolds and plenty of guided and independent practice. For example, a math team might align a unit assessment on multi-step equations with daily exit tickets that gradually build toward that complexity, while a science team might plan scaffolds for vocabulary and lab procedures weeks before a culminating lab report. Without this intentional work, even the best curriculum will fall flat, because materials alone cannot replace professional judgment or targeted planning.

Units should be planned with the end in mind, ensuring that assessments are intentional and aligned to overall learning objectives. As Wiggins and McTighe (2005) emphasize in their Understanding by Design framework, backward planning ensures that daily lessons and assessments build coherently toward clearly defined outcomes rather than becoming a series of disconnected activities. Teams should identify the essential background knowledge that students will need to tackle complex texts or problems in each discipline, and explicitly teach this knowledge rather than assuming that students will pick it up along the way (Carrell & Eisterhold, 1983). Research consistently shows that background knowledge is one of the strongest predictors of reading comprehension (Recht & Leslie, 1988; Willingham, 2006), which means that knowledge gaps—not just "skills"—are often what hold students back.

Regardless of discipline, anchoring units around a key written task helps students make connections across concepts, reflect on evidence, and demonstrate deep understanding, while making learning visible. For instance, in a history unit, the anchor task might be a document-based essay using multiple primary sources; in science, it might be an explanation of a lab investigation written in formal report style. When these tasks are embedded within the discipline—whether analyzing sources in history, explaining processes in science, or interpreting themes in literature—they reflect the unique "ways of thinking" in each subject and support the development of disciplinary literacy (Shanahan & Shanahan, 2008). Writing tasks should be embedded in the discipline, with built-in scaffolds, modeled examples, and guided practice (Spycher, 2017). Start the year with short, scaffolded writing tasks—such as summaries, explanations, or reflections—and gradually move toward more complex tasks (Xiao, 2022). This approach provides repeated practice and supports the development of strong schemas around core content.

In addition to being intentional in planning, teachers must be clear and deliberate about how students will be assessed, providing guidance on major assignments and expectations. Using rubrics aligned to learning goals clarifies expectations for students and ensures that assessment criteria remain consistent across classrooms, which strengthens reliability and fairness (Brookhart, 2013). Sharing rubrics with students before assignments also makes success criteria transparent, helping them self-assess and take greater ownership of their learning. Reviewing student work collectively allows teams to identify common misconceptions and adjust instruction responsively throughout the year. This process of collaborative inquiry—sometimes called looking at student work (LASW)—has been shown to improve instructional coherence and deepen teachers' understanding of expectations (Allen & Blythe, 2004). A practical routine might include devoting part of each Professional Learning Community meeting to reviewing a small sample of recent student work, asking: "What patterns do we see? What scaffolds need to be added? How should we adjust pacing?"

Equally important is ensuring that units include repeated practice and retrieval opportunities to support schema-building, with spaced practice and gradual release serving as key instructional strategies. Because many commercial curricula do not provide sufficient opportunities for retrieval, teaching teams must collaborate to intentionally embed these practices into their instruction. Research in cognitive psychology demonstrates that spacing and retrieval practice significantly enhances retention and transfer (Roediger & Butler, 2011; Pashler et al., 2007). Gradual release models, when paired with these strategies, help ensure that students move from guided practice to independent mastery with support at each stage (Pearson & Gallagher, 1983). It is also imperative that teams recognize the constraints of semester or block schedules and prioritize depth over breadth where possible. A focus on depth allows students to grapple with fewer concepts at a richer level of understanding, which supports disciplinary literacy and reduces cognitive overload (Schmidt et al., 2005). Building in review and spiral practice across units so that students encounter core concepts multiple times helps them move knowledge from working memory into long-term memory. Such spiral designs have long been advocated in curriculum theory (Bruner, 1960), and modern evidence confirms that revisiting key concepts across time supports durable schema development and transfer of learning.

Ultimately, a clear, coherent curriculum is one of the most powerful tools that schools have to address academic failure, behavioral problems, and low motivation, while being an imperative feature of explicit instruction—it provides the structure to students and teachers for success. Clear curriculum reduces cognitive overload for teachers *and* students and makes content manageable, builds prior knowledge systematically, and makes instruction more focused and intentional. When students know what to expect and can follow a logical sequence, they experience more success and more motivation to learn. When teachers and teacher teams take the time to develop a clear curriculum map for the school year, they are investing in equity, effective teaching, and student success. Teams collaborating on lesson plans work toward a shared mission rather than isolated decisions, sharing resources, lesson ideas, assessments, and instructional strategies. This builds collective efficacy—a top driver of student achievement (Hattie, 2018). In this way, strong curriculum design and collaborative planning become the foundation of MTSS itself, ensuring that Tier 1 instruction is so robust that fewer students need to be remediated later.

A Word on Standards

While a strong, coherent curriculum is essential for effective teaching, many schools rely on standards documents, such as the Common Core State Standards (CCSS) as a guide for what to teach. The CCSS have had a complex, double-edged impact on US education. While they were created to bring clarity, consistency, and rigor to instruction across states, their implementation has led to both notable benefits and significant drawbacks, depending on how well schools, districts, and educators have applied them. Common Core provided a national benchmark for what students should know and be able to do and helped in some cases to reduce inequities. With an emphasis on college and career readiness, the standards aimed to ensure that high school graduates were prepared for postsecondary demands. However, the CCSS were not all-encompassing and were developed largely in isolation from disciplinary knowledge, which is critical for comprehension and problem-solving, particularly in secondary education (Hirsch, 2014; Shanahan & Shanahan, 2014; Willingham & Lovette, 2014).

The CCSS has perhaps had the most noticeable impact in literacy, but its focus on abstract reading skills—like analyzing themes, identifying main ideas, and citing evidence—can overlook the content knowledge that students need to truly comprehend complex texts. David Coleman, the lead architect of the Common Core English Language Arts (ELA) standards, has acknowledged key limitations in how the standards have been implemented and interpreted in schools. While he stands by their rigor and intent, he has emphasized that background knowledge, curriculum, and instructional practice are critical to student success (Hess, 2012). This underscores a recurring theme: standards set the destination, but the roadmap—the curriculum, scaffolds, and explicit teaching—determines whether students arrive successfully. Cognitive science supports this perspective: reading comprehension is not simply a set of transferable skills. Teaching reading strategies can help students access complex text, but comprehension cannot be reduced to discrete, isolated skills (Shanahan, 2018b). For example, students are unlikely to analyze a theme or draw inferences from a text about the Civil War, climate change, or Shakespeare without understanding the topic or language, even if they have practiced general reading strategies (Shanahan, 2018a; Willingham & Lovette, 2014). Even when standards are clear and rigorous, students will meet them only if instruction is explicit, well sequenced, and supported by sufficient background knowledge.

Because the Common Core ELA standards are skills-based and recursive, many districts have designed instruction around repeated practice of abstract skills rather than building coherent, content-rich understanding. As a result, students often read disconnected passages instead of engaging with content that builds knowledge systematically. This practice limits opportunities to build deep background knowledge, follow complex arguments, or see concepts develop across a full work—whether a novel, historical document, or scientific report. Reading extended works, anchored in a well-sequenced curriculum, allows students to practice sustained comprehension, notice patterns, develop rich schemas, and strengthen inferential reasoning. For instance, Yoo (2024) highlights the importance of inference-making in reading comprehension when students engage in activities requiring analysis of longer texts, demonstrating improved comprehension skills over time. When paired with writing tasks that ask students to summarize, analyze, or reflect on these texts, students can consolidate understanding and transfer it to new contexts. The standards themselves are expectations, not a curriculum, and do not explicitly prescribe the need for shifts toward knowledge-rich, coherent curricula—but what we know from cognitive science certainly does.

This becomes even more critical in secondary education, where disciplinary texts demand specialized forms of reading and writing. The CCSS literacy standards for history and science highlight the importance of explicit instruction in disciplinary literacy, yet many content-area teachers do not see modeling disciplinary reading and writing as part of their role. Students need support not only in general strategies but also in learning how historians weigh sources, how scientists interpret data, and how mathematicians explain reasoning (Shanahan & Shanahan, 2008). Without this awareness, students risk approaching all texts as if they were the same, undermining their ability to engage with complex disciplinary content. In disciplinary literacy, the power lies in recognizing how authors of these texts anticipate their readers' interactions with their works. For instance, historians expect readers to corroborate sources and contextualize information, while scientists anticipate readers to hypothesize and analyze data. This understanding enables students to approach texts with the appropriate strategies and mindset for each discipline (Shanahan & Shanahan, 2012). Ultimately, standards can point to what students should be able to do, but without curriculum and pedagogy that deliberately cultivate disciplinary knowledge, students' comprehension will remain shallow and fragmented.

Standards alone cannot drive meaningful learning; what matters most is how content is taught. High-quality outcomes depend on the combination of a well-sequenced, knowledge-rich curriculum and instruction that is explicit, scaffolded, and guided. For instance, in a science class, this might include explicit modeling how to interpret a data table before asking students to draw conclusions from it. This means that teachers need professional development not just on curriculum content but also on how to deliver it explicitly, plan lessons collaboratively, integrate writing and other synthesizing tasks, and adjust instruction responsively based on student needs. When schools foster a culture that values evidence-based practices, including explicit instruction grounded in cognitive science, students are far more likely to master foundational knowledge, build new skills efficiently, and engage meaningfully with complex texts. In short, standards set the destination, a coherent curriculum maps the route, and explicit instruction is the vehicle that ensures that students arrive successfully.

These challenges are not confined in literacy. Standards in math, science, and social studies also define what students should learn, but they often do not prescribe how content should be sequenced, scaffolded, or taught explicitly. As a result, students may encounter fragmented or shallow instruction in these subjects as well, limiting their development of deep disciplinary knowledge. Worse still, in subjects like math, science, and social studies, instructional approaches such as flipped classrooms or discovery-first models are frequently emphasized, but these formats often provide insufficient direct, explicit guidance—guidance that research shows is essential for students to successfully engage with complex texts and tasks (Alfieri et al., 2011). Just as literacy comprehension depends on background knowledge and vocabulary, problem-solving in math or understanding complex scientific or historical concepts requires coherent, scaffolded instruction grounded in domain-specific knowledge. Across subjects, students not only are completing tasks but are learning to write, justify, and analyze—disciplinary habits of mind that deepen their understanding and make their learning transferable (Finley, 2015; Hughes et al., 2017). In all subjects, explicit teaching combined with a well-sequenced, knowledge-rich curriculum helps students build robust schemas, transfer learning, and engage meaningfully with increasingly complex tasks.

States that Prioritize Knowledge-Rich Curriculum

States that prioritize coherent, knowledge-rich curricula and invest in teacher preparation create the conditions for explicit instruction to succeed—and Louisiana is one of the few states recognized nationally for moving in this direction systematically. Having leveraged the power and potential of curriculum to bolster student learning and build disciplinary knowledge, the state provides state-vetted and recommended curriculum options, as opposed to leaving materials entirely to district choice (Baird et al., 2019). Curriculum is the central lever for improving equity and closing achievement gaps, as demonstrated by Louisiana's gains in reading proficiency among economically disadvantaged fourth graders, who scored 209 on the 2024 National Assessment of Educational Progress (NAEP) reading assessment, significantly narrowing the gap with their peers (National Center for Education Statistics, 2024). The state provides curriculum-aligned tools for intervention, English learners, and students with disabilities. Louisiana has made significant in-roads in creating a knowledge-rich curriculum, especially in ELA, centering units on complex anchor texts and thematic study to systematically build vocabulary, background knowledge, and critical thinking over time. This approach allows students to engage deeply with disciplinary content, develop robust schemas, and practice inference, analysis, and synthesis across extended texts—skills essential for success in both reading and writing. Assessments are increasingly aligned to the texts and tasks in the curriculum, moving away from reliance on unrelated 'cold-read' passages. Much of the strongest evidence comes from elementary grades, though secondary efforts are expanding.

Teacher preparation is a critical component of this success. The Louisiana Teacher Leader program trains thousands of educators to lead curriculum implementation at the school level, emphasizing content knowledge, instructional delivery, and unit internalization—how skills and knowledge build sequentially across a unit (Louisiana Department of Education). This high-fidelity, teacher-centered model ensures that explicit instruction is delivered consistently, reducing reliance on remediation. In a 2019 RAND study, researchers found that Louisiana teachers were more likely to use high-quality, standards-aligned curricula and report confidence in their instructional materials compared with teachers in other states (Kaufman et al., 2020). The Fordham Institute has also praised Louisiana's Guidebooks as a model of content-rich ELA curriculum design.

While other states, such as Wisconsin and Minnesota, have begun emphasizing knowledge-rich curricula, much of this work remains concentrated in early literacy, with limited implementation at the secondary level. In contrast, states like Mississippi and Tennessee have implemented comprehensive, knowledge-rich policies that span both early and secondary education, with promising results. Mississippi's Literacy-Based Promotion Act, originally focused on early reading skills, has been expanded over time, contributing to measurable gains in reading and math by middle and high school as well as improved NAEP outcomes (Mississippi First, 2024). Similarly, Tennessee's statewide adoption of high-quality, knowledge-rich curricula—supported through initiatives such as the Tennessee Literacy Networks—has enhanced student engagement, deepened content understanding, and strengthened writing and analytical skills in secondary classrooms, particularly in rural districts (NIET, 2023; The 74 Million, 2023). These examples illustrate that comprehensive, knowledge-rich curricula, when implemented systematically, can drive meaningful learning across grade levels (including secondary education), strengthen Tier 1 instruction, reduce gaps that MTSS would otherwise need to remediate, and provide students with the disciplinary knowledge and skills necessary for complex reading, writing, and reasoning tasks across subjects.

The Impact of a Good Teacher

While these states demonstrate how strong curriculum and aligned instruction can support learning, the quality of implementation ultimately depends on the teacher. It goes without saying that much of the reforms that many schools and students need come down to the quality of the teacher in the classroom. Even the most well-designed curriculum cannot compensate for weak instruction. Students will struggle if teachers do not provide explicit, evidence-based teaching, and low teacher quality exacerbates the problem. Research consistently shows the impact of value-added teachers on student outcomes, even well into adulthood (Chetty et al., 2014; Hanushek, 2011; Kane et al., 2008). This is particularly true when it comes to effective teachers in early grades as well as in Urban and high-poverty schools. Fidelity of implementation is critical: the effectiveness of any instructional strategy depends on how well teachers deliver it. Great teachers know when to slow down, reteach, or extend their instruction on the basis of formative assessments, which they often take several times throughout a class period. Highly effective teachers check for understanding between 5 and 15+ times per lesson—a process that Leahy and colleagues (2005) describe as happening "minute by minute, day by day" (Black & Wiliam, 1998; Fisher & Frey, 2016; Lemov, 2010; Rosenshine, 2012). For explicit instruction to achieve its potential, it must be delivered by skilled, reflective, and responsive teachers who can adapt instruction in real time. In this sense, explicit instruction and teacher expertise are interdependent: neither can succeed without the other, and strong teacher practice amplifies the benefits of a coherent, knowledge-rich curriculum.

Yet for teachers to implement explicit, research-backed practices effectively, they must first be trained to understand and apply them—a step where many programs fall short. In the United States, the dominant instructional theory presented to aspiring teachers has historically been constructivism, particularly in the form of progressive, student-centered learning theories. Aspiring teachers are often trained to prioritize engagement, student autonomy, and real-world problem solving over explicit instruction. Theories of social constructivism promote group-based learning, discussions, and teacher support as learning unfolds, while inquiry-based and discovery learning are strongly encouraged in math and science education courses. Multiple National Council on Teacher Quality (NCTQ) reports note that "most teacher education programs continue to emphasize constructivist methods, even when the scientific evidence supports more explicit methods instruction—especially for early reading" (Drake & Walsh, 2020). Even widely used education textbooks emphasize developmental stages, inquiry models, and constructivist theories, despite substantial evidence that explicit instruction and cognitive-science principles have more consistent support for improving student outcomes than constructivist approaches (Holden & Martinenghi, 2025; Mason & Otero, 2021; Pondiscio, 2021; Stockard et al., 2018; Wexler, 2021).

One of the most promising solutions to the challenges of improving student outcomes is providing teachers with preparation that aligns closely with evidence from cognitive science, especially around explicit instruction. Teacher preparation programs should include a deeper understanding of how memory works, the importance of retrieval practice, spacing (distributed practice), formative assessments, and working memory. It would seem only logical that teachers learn the fundamentals of children's cognition, emotion, and motivation because beliefs about what children are capable of inevitably influence teaching practice (Willingham, 2019). While not everything that is of concern to scientists is valuable to educators, understanding evidence-based instructional strategies that reliably improve learning certainly is. Implementing accountability measures for teacher preparation programs—ensuring alignment with research-backed teaching methods—could encourage schools of education to prioritize evidence-based practices grounded in cognitive science and what we know about how students learn.

Even after teachers graduate from preparation programs, they need ongoing professional development to stay current with best practices and to continuously refine their methods using evidence-based strategies. Schools that invest in workshops and training grounded in the latest research on retrieval practice, explicit instruction, and cognitive load theory—and that encourage critical reflection on existing pedagogy—create a culture of continuous improvement for the benefit of students. Without sustained investment in teacher learning, we cannot expect meaningful improvements in student outcomes.

Explicit Instruction vs. Passive Learning

Some might argue that explicit instruction encourages passive learning—students sit, listen, and imitate. They might argue that it is not how deep understanding is built. The fear that explicit instruction teaches students what to do but not *why* it works, that engagement will be low, or that opportunities will be missed for peer-to-peer learning demonstrates a misconception of what true, explicit instruction should look like as well as a misconception about what leads to meaningful engagement in learning. Explicit instruction does not involve students becoming empty vessels for learning to fill them. Rather, explicit instruction involves quite a lot of dialogue between teacher and students. There are frequent checks for understanding and opportunities for misconceptions to be addressed. And while discovery-based or inquiry-based classrooms often emphasize student-led exploration, explicit instruction emphasizes student cognitive engagement—meaning that students are actively thinking, responding, practicing, and receiving feedback throughout the lesson. Table 1.1 provides some examples of what engagement looks like in an explicit instructional model.

TABLE 1.1 What Engagement Looks Like in Explicit Instruction

Form of Interaction	Purpose
Frequent Responses	Choral responses, thumbs up/down, whiteboards, cold calling with guided supports (not as a "got you")—all ensure that all students, not just a few, are thinking.
Questioning and Checks for Understanding	Teachers frequently ask "Why?", and "How do you know?", or "What's the next step?" to promote active reasoning
Guided Practice	Students solve problems with immediate feedback from the teacher, often in pairs or small groups
Turn-and-Talks	Students explain ideas to partners or compare strategies briefly during transitions; these should be highly structured and modeled for students, so that conversations are meaningful
Independent Work with Accountability	Students engage in focused practice—but with tasks that are aligned, scaffolded and reviewed
Cumulative Review & Retrieval	Students pull prior knowledge into new contexts—forcing active memory engagement

Forms of student engagement in explicit instruction, including the purpose of each interaction and how it promotes active learning and reasoning.

What about Advanced Students?

The assumption tends to be that advanced learners do not need the same explicit instruction because they are able to master material faster. This assumption tends to be based more in perceptions on myths of "natural learners"—or the idea that they are best served by open-ended, unstructured environments. But no student—advanced or otherwise—bypasses the need to encode knowledge, build schemas, or receive structured input (Kirschner et al., 2006; Sweller, 2011; Willingham, 2009). Progressive education models often suggest that student discovery is inherently superior to teacher-led models—especially for advanced students who are seen as independent thinkers, and while advanced learners may grasp surface-level content quickly, the complexity of deep transfer, abstraction, or high-level application still requires direct instruction, worked examples, and scaffolding of cognitive processes, particularly when it comes to disciplinary learning that is more complex (i.e., writing, math proofs, scientific reasoning). Oftentimes, "gifted" instruction becomes busywork or overly self-directed activities that lower engagement and undercut achievement.

The need to provide advanced students with deeper, faster-paced, rigorous, and explicit teaching complements a cognitive-science approach, where teachers recognize that all students need schema-building, benefit from modeling, are subject to working memory limits, and deserve rigorous instruction. Cognitive science suggests that even advanced students learn best when instruction starts with clarity, modeling, and scaffolding, then moves toward independent or inquiry-based tasks (Sweller et al., 2011). Experimental evidence from studies of advanced students suggests that fully guided inquiry leads to greater learning, flow, and positive mood compared with unguided approaches (Eysink et al., 2015; Horak & Galluzzo, 2017). Advanced learners often do benefit from open, complex tasks—but empirical research shows that this benefit is contingent on strong external regulation (scaffolding, sequencing, or explicit guidance). High-quality, meta-analytic evidence focused solely on gifted learners and purely constructivist (unguided) approaches is limited; existing empirical studies tend to show that even gifted students gain from careful instructional design that incorporates explicit guidance and support (Lim, 2023) and that outcomes depend heavily on context and implementation (Shore, 2021).

Building Self-Regulated Learners

Many people mistakenly assume that explicit teaching practices (like explicit instruction, retrieval practice, and worked examples) don't promote self-regulated learning because they confuse "structure" with "control" or see teacher-led practices as inherently disempowering to students, because of the assumption that explicit instruction means lecturing, and only student-centered methods promote agency. Constructivist approaches often equate discovery or inquiry with ownership, but ownership doesn't require *unstructured* learning; this misses the motivational components embedded in self-regulation, like goal-setting, metacognition, and feedback.

In truth, cognitive science supports structured, scaffolded environments where self-regulation is explicitly taught and gradually released to students. Self-regulated learning requires cognitive tools—strategies like retrieval practice, elaboration, and spacing aren't just about memory, but they're tools that students can use independently (Dunlosky et al., 2013). Structure precedes autonomy; novices need explicit modeling and clear goals to internalize strategies (Sweller et al., 2007; Zimmerman, 2002). Teachers who model planning, checking for understanding, and revising responses help students internalize those habits (Rosenshine, 2012; Veenman, 2013). Once students have practiced self-regulatory strategies with guidance, they're more likely to use them independently (Schunk & Zimmerman, 2008). The goal of a well-designed and implemented explicit teaching lesson is that every student is thinking, retrieving, and applying—not just watching or copying. Inquiry or discovery-based approaches often equate student interaction with student-led exploration or group projects. In contrast, explicit instruction is teacher-led but student-engaged. Students are interacting with ideas, not just with peers. The interaction is structured, not open-ended—which is key to avoiding cognitive overload. A lesson is teacher-centered only if the teacher is the only one thinking (Rosenshine, 2012). Interaction for its own sake doesn't improve learning. Cognitively productive interaction—where students retrieve, reason, and apply with feedback—is what leads to durable learning. And that's exactly what explicit instruction, properly done, achieves.

SCENARIO: EXPLICIT INSTRUCTION VS. INQUIRY INSTRUCTION IN A TENTH-GRADE ENGLISH CLASSROOM

In his tenth-grade English classroom, Mr. Adams is preparing to have students analyze Martin Luther King Jr.'s "Letter from Birmingham Jail." His lesson focus is to analyze rhetorical strategies found in the letter (i.e., ethos, pathos, and logos). Mr. Adams begins the lesson by stating the objective and reviewing success criteria for the learning which includes: "I can define ethos, pathos, and logos, and identify examples in the text." Students copy the success criteria into their notebooks, and Mr. Adams reviews each criterion and gives a model response.

Using a short slide deck, Mr. Adams defines rhetorical appeals, providing examples from ads and political speeches—and models text annotation with the first two paragraphs of King's letter. He thinks aloud while marking the text, asking himself: "notice here how King uses emotional language—*pathos*—to appeal to the reader's sense of justice." After a few additional examples, students begin working in pairs to annotate the next paragraph. Mr. Adams circulates, using a roaming clipboard to collect formative data. He pauses at groups to address common misconceptions as he rotates the room, providing frequent checks for understanding and additional examples, explanations, and questioning techniques, to guide student thinking.

Before students leave, Mr. Adams directs students' attention back to the learning target and has students provide a confidence check (quick thumbs up if they feel confident, sideways if they're still figuring it out, and down if they're still unsure) about the day's learning. Then he has individual students complete a quick short-answer response, analyzing one rhetorical appeal in a new excerpt. They must provide textual evidence to explain its effect. Mr. Adams takes responses and, before students even leave for the day, quickly sorts them using a simple coding system (check mark = correct, square = needs development, and a circle = revise) which he will use to have students retrieve prior-day learning tomorrow.

He assures the students that they engaged in a lot of "thinking today" on *pathos* and that tomorrow they will focus on *ethos* to see how King adds credibility to his argument. He also tells students that they will have a chance to revise their short responses with feedback.

Across the hall, Ms. Ramirez's goal is to teach the same lesson as Mr. Adams. Her objective says that "students will work collaboratively to analyze how King uses rhetorical appeals (ethos, pathos and logos) in his writing." Ms. Ramirez begins the class by asking students: "When have you seen persuasive writing used in your own life—on TikTok, ads or debates?" Students give varying responses, some more robust than others. Ms. Ramirez then breaks students into three groups, providing each with excerpts from King's letter that demonstrate ethos, pathos, and logos, respectively. Each group analyzes selected sections of the letter where their assigned appeal is strongest. They collaboratively annotate the text and begin to prepare a mini-presentation for their classmates. Groups are meant to then re-form into "expert groups" to teach their rhetorical appeal to peers, yet students are struggling to infer what type of device their portion of text highlights. As students debate their passages, Ms. Ramirez is circulating the room slowly, pausing to listen in with one group. She listens for student talk that reflects emergent understanding—but does not directly correct or explain when students are not entirely sure whether the example is one of ethos or pathos. When a student asks her, "Is this quote ethos or logos?" she responds, "Interesting—what makes you lean one way or the other?" Throughout the class, Ms. Ramirez keeps prompting students: "I heard someone say King was 'making us trust him'—what might we call that kind of strategy?" Still, she never directly names the device. Students only manage to get through annotating the excerpts—they never reach the presentation or expert group jigsaw—though one group seems to be making fair progress. When students leave, Ms. Ramirez feels good. She reflects that students were actively engaged in discovering how language worked, and she enjoyed the productive struggle she saw as students attempted to infer the strategy.

Additionally, she felt she gathered a lot of powerful formative data, because she was able to listen in on all of the groups as they debated about their passages. It is clear they just need more time with the excerpt tomorrow. She had originally planned on having expert groups share their thinking, and holding a Socratic seminar, but she will move those plans to the end of the week. By the end of the week, Mr. Adam's students have had opportunities to work collaboratively applying their knowledge to new texts, while Ms. Ramriez's class engage in their expert groups and a jigsaw.

Ms. Ramirez is a popular teacher; students feel that she is "fun." Teachers comment on how there is a buzz around her classroom of activity and engagement, and she often is a mentor teacher to those new to the school. And while she does promote student agency and engagement, she struggles to balance her strategies with building clear foundational knowledge and understanding in her students. Her discovery approaches assume that students automatically pick up concepts through exploration and collaborative activities or that they come to her already possessing a deep knowledge about concepts and ideas that are particularly complex, discipline-specific conceptions (like rhetorical appeals).

When her class analyzed the letter, students spent most of their cognitive energy attempting the task without first understanding the rhetorical strategies involved. Without explicit instruction and scaffolding, their working memory was overloaded with inference-making, leaving little capacity for deeper processing and schema development. In fact, on a comprehension check administered at the end of the week, it was Mr. Adams's students—who received explicit instruction with modeling, guided practice with feedback, and independent practice—who outperformed Ms. Ramirez's. Had she begun with clear explanations, definitions, and modeled examples of rhetorical appeals, her students would have had the tools to engage more meaningfully in discovery and the mental space to comprehend the complex text. This sends a conflicting message to Ms. Ramirez: she is praised as a distinguished teacher and recognized for using the "high-yield" practices promoted by her district. Yet her students are not making the expected gains. The disconnect underscores a larger problem in education—when engagement is valued over explicit learning, students may leave classrooms energized but underprepared.

References

Alfieri, L., Brooks, P. J., Aldrich, N. J., & Tenenbaum, H. R. (2011). Does discovery-based instruction enhance learning? *Journal of Educational Psychology, 103*(1), 1–18. https://doi.org/10.1037/a0021017

Allen, D., & Blythe, T. (2004). *The facilitator's book of questions: Tools for looking together at student and teacher work.* Teachers College Press.

Altindis, N., Bowe, K. A., Couch, B., Bauer, C. F., & Aikens, M. L. (2024). Exploring the role of disciplinary knowledge in students' covariational reasoning during graphical interpretation. *International Journal of STEM Education, 11,* 32. https://doi.org/10.1186/s40594-024-00492-5

Anderson, R. C. (1977). The notion of schemata and the educational enterprise: General discussion of the conference. In R. C. Anderson, R. J. Spiro, & W. E. Montague (Eds.), *Schooling and the acquisition of knowledge* (pp. 415–431). Routledge. https://doi.org/10.4324/9781315271644-33

Baddeley, A. D. (1992). Working memory. *Science, 255*(5044), 556–559. https://doi.org/10.1126/science.1736359

Baird, M. D., Cannon, J. S., Culbertson, S., Hamilton, L. S., Hannan, M. Q., Kaufman, J. H., Meyers, S., & Steiner, E. D. (2019, June 11). *What other states can learn from Louisiana's ambitious efforts to reshape its education system* (RAND Research Brief RB-10072). RAND Corporation. https://www.rand.org/pubs/research_briefs/RB10072.html

Ball, D. L., Thames, M. H., & Phelps, G. (2008). Content knowledge for teaching: What makes it special? *Journal of Teacher Education, 59*(5), 389–407.

Black, P., & Wiliam, D. (1998). Assessment and classroom learning. *Assessment in Education: Principles, Policy & Practice, 5*(1), 7–74. https://doi.org/10.1080/0969595980050102

Brookhart, S. M. (2013). The use of teacher judgment for summative assessment in the USA. *Assessment in Education: Principles, Policy & Practice, 20*, 69–90.

Bruner, J. S. (1960). *The process of education.* Harvard University Press. https://doi.org/10.1080/0969594X.2012.703170

Carrell, P. L., & Eisterhold, J. C. (1983). Schema theory and ESL Reading pedagogy. *TESOL Quarterly, 17*(4), 553–573. https://doi.org/10.2307/3586613

Casey, B. J., Tottenham, N., Liston, C., & Durston, S. (2005). Imaging the developing brain: What have we learned about cognitive development? *Trends in Cognitive Sciences, 9*(3), 104–110. https://doi.org/10.1016/j.tics.2005.01.011

Cepeda, N. J., Pashler, H., Vul, E., Wixted, J. T., & Rohrer, D. (2006). Distributed practice in verbal recall tasks: A review and quantitative synthesis. *Psychological Bulletin, 132*(3), 354–380. https://doi.org/10.1037/0033-2909.132.3.354

Chetty, R., Friedman, J. N., & Rockoff, J. E. (2014). Measuring the impacts of teachers II: Teacher value-added and student outcomes in adulthood. *American Economic Review, 104*(9), 2633–2679. https://doi.org/10.1257/aer.104.9.2633

Chi, M. T. H., Glaser, R., & Farr, M. J. (1988). *The nature of expertise.* Erlbaum.

Clark, R., Kirschner, P.A., Sweller, J. (2012). Putting students on the path to learning: The case for fully guided instruction. *American Educator, 36*(1), 6–11. https://eric.ed.gov/?id=EJ971752

Darling-Hammond, L., Hyler, M. E., & Gardner, M. (2017). *Effective teacher professional development.* Learning Policy Institute. https://doi.org/10.54300/122.311

Donegan, R. E., Casale, E. G., & Torelli, J. (2025). Teachers' self-reported knowledge and perceptions of intensive interventions: An initial investigation. *Reading and Writing.* https://doi.org/10.1007/s11145-025-10650-y

Drake, G., & Walsh, K. (2020). *2020 Teacher Prep Review: Program performance in early reading instruction.* National Council on Teacher Quality. https://www.nctq.org/publications/2020-Teacher-Prep-Review:-Program-Performance-in-Early-Reading-Instruction

Dunlosky, J., Rawson, K. A., Marsh, E. J., Nathan, M. J., & Willingham, D. T. (2013). Improving students' learning with effective learning techniques: Promising directions from cognitive and educational psychology. *Psychological Science in the Public Interest, 14*(1), 4–58. https://doi.org/10.1177/1529100612453266

Eysink, T. H. S., Gersen, L., & Gijlers, H. (2015). Inquiry learning for gifted children. *High Ability Studies, 26*(1), 63–74. https://doi.org/10.1080/13598139.2015.1038379

Finley, T. (2015, October 6). The nuts and bolts of explicit modeling. *Edutopia.* https://www.edutopia.org/blog/nuts-and-bolts-explicit-modeling-todd-finley

Fisher, D., & Frey, N. (2016). *The formative assessment action plan: Practical steps to more successful teaching and learning.* ASCD.

Fuchs, D., Fuchs, L. S., & Compton, D. L. (2010). The contribution of reading interventions to the prevention of reading disabilities in the early grades. *Learning Disabilities Research & Practice, 25*(1), 11–19. https://doi.org/10.1111/j.1540-5826.2009.00285.x

Fuchs, D. & Fuchs, L.S. (2011). Introduction to response to intervention: What, why, and how valid is it? *Reading Research Quarterly, 41*(1), 93–99. https://doi.org/10.1598/RRQ.41.1.4

Fukaya, T., Nakamura, D., & Kitayama, Y. (2024). A systematic review and meta-analysis of intervention studies on mathematics and science pedagogical content knowledge. *Frontiers in Education, 9,* 1435758. https://doi.org/10.3389/feduc.2024.1435758

Hanushek, E. A. (2011). The economic value of higher teacher quality. *Economics of Education Review, 30*(3), 466–479. https://doi.org/10.1016/j.econedurev.2010.12.006

Hattie, J. (2018, March 27). Collective teacher efficacy. *Visible Learning*. https://visible-learning.org/2018/03/collective-teacher-efficacy-hattie/

Hattie, J. (2023). *Visible learning: The sequel: A synthesis of over 2,100 meta-analyses relating to achievement*. Routledge.

Hayes, L. (2021). *Strengthening intensive intervention preparation: A guide for teacher preparation faculty (ED615581)*. National Center on Intensive Intervention. https://files.eric.ed.gov/fulltext/ED615581.pdf

Hess, R. (2012, June 11). Straight up conversation: Common core architect and new college board President David Coleman. *Education Week*. https://www.edweek.org/education/opinion-straight-up-conversation-common-core-architect-and-new-college-board-president-david-coleman/2012/06

Hirsch, E. D. (2006). *The knowledge deficit: Closing the shocking education gap for American children*. Houghton Mifflin.

Hirsch, E. D. (2014). *Why knowledge matters: Reshaping the American curriculum*. Harvard Education Press.

Holden, R., & Martinenghi, F. I. (2025). Getting explicit instruction right. *arXiv*. https://doi.org/10.48550/arXiv.2506.10480

Horak, A. K., & Galluzzo, G. R. (2017). Gifted middle school students' achievement and perceptions of science classroom quality during problem-based learning. *Journal of Advanced Academics, 28*(1), 3–28. https://doi.org/10.1177/1932202X16683424

Hughes, C. A., Morris, J. R., Therrien, W. J., & Benson, S. K. (2017). Explicit instruction: Historical and contemporary contexts. *Learning Disabilities Research & Practice, 32*(3), 140–148. https://doi.org/10.1111/ldrp.12142

Institute of Education Sciences (IES). (2017). *What works clearinghouse: Academic achievement outcomes for students with disabilities in middle school and high school: A review of the evidence*. U.S. Department of Education.

Jensen, J. L. (2017). Using backward design in education research. *Frontiers in Education, 2*, 1–7. https://doi.org/10.3389/feduc.2017.00056

Kane, T. J., Rockoff, J. E., & Staiger, D. O. (2008). *Estimating teacher impacts on student achievement: An experimental evaluation*. National Bureau of Economic Research.

Kaufman, J. H., Steiner, E. D., & Baird, M. D. (2020). *How instructional materials are used and supported in U.S. K-12 classrooms* (Research Report).

RAND Corporation. https://www.rand.org/pubs/research_reports/RRA134-1.html

Kirschner, P. A., Sweller, J., & Clark, R. E. (2006). Why minimal guidance during instruction does not work: An analysis of the failure of constructivist, discovery, problem-based, experiential, and inquiry-based teaching. *Educational Psychologist, 41*(2), 75–86. https://doi.org/10.1207/s15326985ep4102_1

Lazonder, A. W., & Harmsen, R. (2016). Meta-analysis of inquiry-based learning: Effects of guidance. *Review of Educational Research, 86*(3), 681–718. https://doi.org/10.3102/0034654315627366

Leahy, S., Lyon, C., Thompson, M., & Wiliam, D. (2005). Classroom assessment: Minute by minute, day by day. *Educational Leadership, 63*(3), 18–24.

Lemov, D. (2010). *Teach like a champion: 49 techniques that put students on the path to college.* Jossey-Bass.

Levine, T. H., & Marcus, A. S. (2007). Closing the achievement gap through teacher collaboration: Facilitating multiple trajectories of teacher learning. *Journal of Advanced Academics, 19*(1), 116–138.

Lim, Y. (2023). Invention versus example instruction for gifted and non-gifted adolescents: Effects on transfer in problem solving. *Instructional Science, 51*(3), 413–437. https://doi.org/10.1007/s11251-023-09616-w.

Louisiana Department of Education. (n.d.). *Louisiana Content Leaders.* https://doe.louisiana.gov/educators/professional-development/louisiana-content-leaders

Mason, L., & Otero, M. (2021). Just how effective is direct instruction? *Perspectives on Behavior Science, 44*(2–3), 225–244. https://doi.org/10.1007/s40614-021-00295-x.

Mississippi First. (2024). *Contextualizing Mississippi's 2024 NAEP scores.* https://www.mississippifirst.org/contextualizing-mississippis-2024-naep-scores/

National Academy of Education (2024). *Evaluating and improving teacher preparation programs.* K. M. Zeichner, L. Darling-Hammond, A. I. Berman, D. Dong, & G. Sykes (Eds.). National Academy of Education.

National Center for Education Statistics. (2024). *Louisiana, grade 4 reading: 2024 state snapshot report* (NAEP 2024-220). https://nces.ed.gov/nationsreportcard/subject/publications/stt2024/pdf/2024220LA4.pdf

National Early Literacy Panel. (2008). *Developing early literacy: Report of the National Early Literacy Panel*. National Institute for Literacy. https://lincs.ed.gov/publications/pdf/NELPReport09.pdf

National Institute for Excellence in Teaching (NIET). (2023). *Reading takes off in Tennessee classrooms with high-quality curriculum*.

National Research Council. (2001). *Early childhood development and learning: New knowledge for policy*. The National Academies Press. https://doi.org/10.17226/10067

National Research Council. (2012). *Improving adult literacy instruction: Options for practice and research*. National Academies Press. https://doi.org/10.17226/13242

Nevenglosky, E. A., Cale, C., & Aguilar, S. P. (2019). Barriers to effective curriculum implementation. *Research in Higher Education Journal*, *36*, 1–12.

O'Reilly, T., Wang, Z., & Sabatini, J. P. (2019). How much knowledge is too little? When a lack of knowledge becomes a barrier to comprehension. *Psychological Science*, *30*(9), 1344–1351. https://doi.org/10.1177/0956797619862276

Pashler, H., Rohrer, D., Cepeda, N.J., Carpenter, S.K. (2007). Enhancing learning and retarding forgetting: Choices and consequences. *Psychonomic Bulletin & Review*, *14*, 187–193. https://doi.org/10.3758/BF03194050

Pearson, P. D., & Gallagher, M. C. (1983). The instruction of reading comprehension. *Contemporary Educational Psychology*, *8*(3), 317–344. https://doi.org/10.1016/0361-476X(83)90019-X

Petersen, C. L., Baepler, P., Beitz, A., Ching, P., Gorman, K. S., Neudauer, C. L., Rozaitis, W., Walker, J. D., & Winger, D. (2020). The tyranny of content: "Content coverage" as a barrier to evidence-based teaching approaches and ways to overcome it. *CBE—Life Sciences Education*, *19*(2). https://doi.org/10.1187/cbe.19-04-0079

Pondiscio, R. (2021, January 7). Explicit teaching vs. constructivism: The misadventures of Bean Dad. *Thomas B. Fordham Institute*. https://fordhaminstitute.org/national/commentary/explicit-teaching-vs-constructivism-misadventures-bean-dad

Recht, D. R., & Leslie, L. (1988). Effect of prior knowledge on reading comprehension. *Journal of Educational Psychology*, *80*(4), 468–474. https://doi.org/10.1037/0022-0663.80.1.16

Roediger, H. L., & Butler, A. C. (2011). The critical role of retrieval practice in long-term retention. *Trends in Cognitive Sciences*, *15*(1), 20–27. https://doi.org/10.1016/j.tics.2010.09.003

Rosenshine, B. (2008). *Five meanings of direct instruction*. Center on Innovation & Improvement.

Rosenshine, B. (2012). Principles of instruction: Research-based strategies that all teachers should know. *American Educator*, *36*(1), 12–19.

Ryan, R. M., & Deci, E. L. (2000). Self-determination theory and the facilitation of intrinsic motivation, social development, and well-being. *American Psychologist*, *55*(1), 68–78. https://doi.org/10.1037/0003-066X.55.1.68

Schiller, E., Chow, K., Thayer, S., Nakamura, J., Wilkerson, S. B., & Puma, M. (2020). *What tools have states developed or adapted to assess schools' implementation of a multi-tiered system of supports/response to intervention framework? (REL 2020-017)*. U.S. Department of Education, Institute of Education Sciences, National Center for Education Evaluation and Regional Assistance.

Schmidt, W. H., Wang, H. C., & McKnight, C. C. (2005). Curriculum coherence: An examination of U.S. mathematics and science content standards from an international. *Journal of Curriculum Studies*, *37*(5), 525–559. https://doi.org/10.1080/0022027042000294682

Schunk, D. H., & Zimmerman, B. J. (Eds.) (2008). *Motivation and self-regulated learning: Theory, research, and applications*. Routledge.

Shanahan, T. (2018a, April 15). Knowing and reading — What can we do to make sure kids know enough to comprehend. *Shanahan on Literacy*. https://www.shanahanonliteracy.com/blog/knowing-and-reading-what-can-we-do-to-make-sure-kids-know-enough-to-comprehend\

Shanahan, T. (2018b, May 19). Comprehension skills or strategies: Is there a difference and does it matter? *Shanahan on Literacy*. https://www.shanahanonliteracy.com/blog/comprehension-skills-or-strategies-is-there-a-difference-and-does-it-matter

Shanahan, T., & Shanahan, C. (2008). Teaching disciplinary literacy to adolescents: Rethinking content-area literacy. *Harvard Educational Review*, *78*(1), 40–59.

Shanahan, T., & Shanahan, C. (2012). What is disciplinary literacy and why does it matter? *Topics in Language Disorders*, *32*(1), 7–18. https://doi.org/10.1097/TLD.0b013e318244557a

Shanahan, C., & Shanahan, T. (2014). Does disciplinary literacy have a place in elementary school? *The Reading Teacher, 67*(8), 636–639. https://doi.org/10.1002/trtr.1257

Shore, B. M. (2021). Applying social-constructivist theory in gifted education. *Gifted Education International, 37*(2), 121–137.

Spycher, P. (2017). *Scaffolding writing through the "Teaching and Learning Cycle"*. WestEd.

Stockard, J., Wood, T. W., Coughlin, C., & Rasplica Khoury, C. (2018). The effectiveness of direct instruction curricula: A meta-analysis of a half century of research. *Review of Educational Research, 88*(4), 479–507. https://doi.org/10.3102/0034654317751919

Sugai, G., & Horner, R. R. (2006). A promising approach for expanding and sustaining school-wide positive behavior support. *School Psychology Review, 35*(2), 245–259.

Sweller, J. (1988). Cognitive load during problem solving: Effects on learning. *Cognitive Science, 12*(2), 257–285. https://doi.org/10.1207/s15516709cog1202_4

Sweller, J. (2011). Cognitive load theory. In J. P. Mestre & B. H. Ross (Eds.), *The psychology of learning and motivation: Cognition in education* (pp. 37–76). Elsevier Academic Press. https://doi.org/10.1016/B978-0-12-387691-1.00002-8

Sweller, J., Ayres, P., & Kalyuga, S. (2011). *Cognitive load theory*. Springer. https://doi.org/10.1007/978-1-4419-8126-4

Sweller, J., Kirschner, P. A., & Clark, R. E. (2007). Why minimally guided learning does not work: A reply to critics. *Educational Psychologist, 42*(2), 115–121. https://doi.org/10.1080/00461520701263426

The 74 Million. (2023, September 21). *Curriculum case study: How one rural Tennessee school district is turning the tide*. https://www.the74million.org/article/curriculum-case-study-how-one-rural-tennessee-school-district-with-25-percent-student-literacy-and-nearly-a-quarter-of-kids-living-in-poverty-is-turning-the-tide/

The New Teacher Project (TNTP). (2018). *The opportunity myth: What students can show us about how school is letting them down and how to fix it*. https://tntp.org/our-work

Veenman, M. V. J. (2013). Training metacognitive skills in students with availability and production deficiencies. In H. Bembenutty, T. Cleary, & A. Kitsantas (Eds.), *Applications of self-regulated learning across diverse disciplines: A tribute to Barry J. Zimmerman* (pp. 299–324). Information Age Publishing.

Voogt, J. M. (2016). Teacher collaboration in curriculum design teams. *Learning and Instruction, 41*, 1–12. https://doi.org/10.1080/13803611.2016.1247725

Wang, M. C., Haertel, G. D., & Walberg, H. J. (1993). Fostering educational resilience in inner-city schools. *Educational Psychologist, 28*(1), 53–72. https://doi.org/10.1207/s15326985ep2801_5

Wexler, N. (2021, December 14). Why so many kids struggle to learn. *The American Scholar.* https://theamericanscholar.org/why-so-many-kids-struggle-to-learn/

Wiggins, G., & McTighe, J. (2005). *Understanding by design* (Expanded 2nd ed.). Alexandria, VA: ASCD.

Willingham, D. T. (2006). How knowledge helps: It speeds and strengthens reading comprehension, learning—And thinking. *American Educator, 30*(1), 30–37.

Willingham, D. T. (2009). *Why don't students like school? A cognitive scientist answers questions about how the mind works and what it means for the classroom.* Jossey-Bass.

Willingham, D. T. (2019). Ask the cognitive scientist: Should teachers know the basic science of how children learn? *American Educator, 43*(2), 4–9.

Willingham, D. T., & Lovette, G. (2014, September 26). *Can reading comprehension be taught? Teachers College Record.* http://www.danielwillingham.com/uploads/5/0/0/7/5007325/willingham&lovette_2014_can_reading_comprehension_be_taught_.pdf

Xiao, L. (2022). A scaffolding teaching design: Reading for writing. *International Journal of Education and Humanities.* https://doi.org/10.54097/jc4np221

Yoo, Y. (2024). On the dynamics of inferential behavior while reading expository and narrative texts. *Brain Sciences, 14*(5), 428. https://doi.org/10.3390/brainsci14050428

Zimmerman, B. J. (2002). Becoming a self-regulated learner: An overview. *Theory Into Practice, 41*(2), 64–70. https://doi.org/10.1207/s15430421tip4102_2

2

Building Knowledge

With the advent of the "reading wars," knowledge-building has re-emerged as a central theme in education, but the importance of background knowledge in reading and learning has been a well-established principle in cognitive science for decades. What's changed is that a growing body of research—and the failures of certain instructional models—has pushed it back to the forefront. As early as the 1930s and continuing through the 1970s and 1980s, psychologists such as Frederic Bartlett (1932), David Rumelhart (1980), and Richard Anderson (Anderson & Pearson, 1984) developed schema theory—the idea that new information is understood more easily when it connects to existing knowledge structures. Research by Mandler and Anderson (1971) demonstrated that students with more relevant background knowledge comprehend and recall more effectively—even when their general reading ability is weaker (Anderson & Pearson, 1984; Mandler & Anderson, 1971). In the landmark "Baseball Study" (1987), Recht and Leslie found that students with high baseball knowledge, even if they were poor readers, comprehended a baseball text better than strong readers with low knowledge. This study is a keystone in the argument that knowledge is more important than generalized reading "skills."

The rise of whole language and the de-prioritization of knowledge occurred in the US during the late 1980s and 1990s. It wasn't that whole-language proponents didn't believe in the importance of knowledge per se, but the *type* of knowledge they valued and the *mechanism* for acquiring it shifted dramatically. Whole-language proponents, influenced by constructivist theories such as those forwarded by Goodman (1967), Smith (1971), and Cambourne (1988), argued that reading and writing are natural, meaning-making processes—not a set of discrete skills to be explicitly taught. They emphasized contextual and experiential knowledge, meaning that students learn best when they are *immersed* in rich, authentic texts that connect to their lives and interests (Cambourne, 1988; Goodman, 1967; Smith, 1971). In this view, personal meaning and comprehension became the focus of reading skills and outweighed explicit instruction in decoding patterns or mastery of discrete skills. By assuming that literacy would emerge naturally through exposure to meaningful text, the movement downplayed the need for systematic instruction in phonemic awareness and decoding, vocabulary, and background knowledge about the world. The general feeling was that children would pick these things up through reading and experience—and many whole-language proponents would eventually come to the belief that anything focused on explicit knowledge-based teaching was rigid, rote, and anti-child (Cambourne, 1988; Goodman, 1967; Smith, 1971).

The whole-language approach, with its focus on immersive literacy, and the devaluing of teachers as experts, privileged meaning-making and engagement over explicit skill development (Bowers, 2020). The lasting impacts of this approach to reading instruction are profound. Even though many states are now making significant progress in aligning early literacy instruction with the Science of Reading, the legacy of whole language continues to shape teachers' perceptions of what "effective" reading and writing instruction looks like. Yet if the whole-language movement has taught us anything, it is that an instructional philosophy misaligned with how learning actually occurs can impede an entire nation's literacy development—and that same philosophical tension extends far beyond literacy to education as a whole.

By secondary school, many teachers assume that students already know how to read and write—that literacy is a finished skill. This assumption reflects, in part, the legacy of whole-language approaches, which treated literacy as a natural process: children were expected to acquire reading skills largely through immersion in meaningful texts rather than through continual, structured, explicit teaching. However, research critiques these assumptions, showing that explicit instruction remains essential for comprehension, decoding, and long-term literacy growth (Moje, 2008; National Research Council, 2012; Shanahan & Shanahan, 2008). Secondary teachers often still view reading as a set of transferable comprehension *skills* rather than as a knowledge-rich process (Shanahan, 2019). The education field as a whole has long equated engagement and autonomy with learning—which is why secondary teachers are often pushed to engage students in project-based learning, discovery, and inquiry—despite the fact that these methods often assume students already have the background knowledge and literacy skills they need to engage productively—something many do not (Boardman, 2024; Duke et al., 2020; Meng, 2023; Mutanga, 2024; Syahdia et al., 2024).

This approach has shaped instruction in other content areas, particularly in math. Beginning in the 1980s and 1990s, with the NCTM (National Council of Teachers of Mathematics) Standards, math education moved away from teacher-led, practice-rich instruction toward constructivist, discovery-based approaches. Students were encouraged to invent strategies, discover patterns, and explain reasoning prior to mastering algorithms (NCTM, 1989). The assumption was that deep conceptual understanding must come before procedural skill, and this is a practice we still see in many mathematical pedagogies today (NCTM, 1989, 2000). Math, however, has not received the same national attention that literacy has in recent years, and many classrooms still operate under discovery-based models (Kappassova et al., 2025). Despite research showing that ignoring memorization and practice leaves students without sufficient automaticity to handle complex problem-solving, instructional programs continue to emphasize multiple strategies and "productive struggle" as ends in themselves (Boaler, 2016). Yet a robust body of evidence demonstrates that automatic recall of basic facts frees up working memory and enables deeper reasoning (Baroody, 2006; Geary, 2011). Procedural fluency and conceptual understanding develop reciprocally, but fluent skill practice actually *supports* conceptual insight by freeing working memory for reasoning (Gilmore, 2017).

These methods have had significant impact on math learning outcomes for students. A shift away from explicit teaching has led to reduced automaticity in basic facts and algorithms, greater inequity, and lower national performance (OECD, 2023). When students are held in extended "conceptual only" phases without access to efficient methods, learning often stalls and frustration grows, as students expend cognitive resources deciding which strategy to use rather than mastering mathematics (Kirschner et al., 2006; Sweller, 1988). Similarly, approaches that insist that students must first achieve conceptual understanding before learning algorithms run counter to cognitive-science findings: guided instruction paired with timely feedback accelerates learning and reduces cognitive overload (Kirschner et al., 2006; Sweller, 1988). Without a balance of guided procedural practice and conceptual understanding, many students are left underprepared to tackle multi-step, complex problems, as their working memory is consumed by strategy selection rather than mastering the mathematics itself (Siegler et al., 2012). Similarly, the same complex schema-building process that we see in literacy exists in other disciplines as well. In both cases, comprehension (of text or math problems) is *not* about applying a general strategy but about having a well-organized network of knowledge that allows the learner to interpret meaning efficiently (Fuchs et al., 2019). All disciplines require explicit teaching to ensure that students connect ideas to existing schemas and recognize deep structures rather than surface features.

Much like reading, the ideals of philosophical approaches like constructivism, discovery-based learning, and inquiry remain entrenched in teacher preparation programs, curriculum design, and policy language (Allen, 2022). Yet the reality that knowledge is the foundation of comprehension and thinking illustrates how critical a knowledge-based approach is to our instructional practices. In every discipline—literacy, science, math, history, or the arts—new learning *depends* on what learners already know. Background knowledge provides the mental scaffolding that allows students to interpret, infer, and connect new ideas. Without it, working memory becomes overloaded by basic processing demands (Sweller, 1988; Willingham, 2009). When essential facts, vocabulary, and concepts are stored in long-term memory, they no longer consume working memory space. That frees up cognitive capacity for higher-order reasoning, analysis, and problem-solving (Sweller et al., 2011a). In math, automatic recall of facts and procedures enables conceptual problem-solving; in science, prior conceptual frameworks help students interpret experiments or phenomena.

Explicit instruction sees knowledge as the fuel for thinking, where inquiry- or discovery-based approaches often see it as a secondary process—and that's where much of the reading and learning gap emerges (Hirsch, 2006; Kirschner et al., 2006; Willingham, 2009). To systematically and consistently build knowledge in literacy and math, teachers need to move beyond isolated skills and toward structured, cumulative instruction that prioritizes content depth, vocabulary development, and conceptual coherence. Decades of research show that background knowledge is a critical driver of comprehension and reasoning: students with stronger prior knowledge consistently outperform peers with weaker knowledge, even when reading ability is controlled (Anderson & Pearson, 1984; Cabell & Hwang, 2020; Recht & Leslie, 1988). A knowledge-building focus not only strengthens long-term learning but also improves performance on standards-based assessments by directly supporting the cognitive processes required for higher-order thinking. This approach further requires that we embrace explicit, teacher-directed instruction—including structured, scaffolded practice in both literacy and math—where corrective and encouraging feedback guides students toward accuracy—rather than leaving them to "struggle productively" without sufficient support (Hattie & Timperley, 2007).

The core principles of cognitive science tell us that knowledge builds on knowledge: the more students know, the easier it is for them to learn more. Students learn best when new information connects to existing mental models, or schemas, which supports comprehension and long-term retention (Anderson & Pearson, 1984; Willingham, 2009). A major challenge to realizing this in practice lies in curriculum design. In response to teacher shortages and shifts in literacy instruction, many states have adopted comprehensive, ready-to-implement "boxed" curriculum programs—but these often fall short of delivering effective, evidence-based instruction. Curriculum programs frequently neglect background knowledge and fail to intentionally scaffold text complexity throughout instructional units (Reynolds & Fisher, 2022). Even curricula marketed as "knowledge-based" often revert to assessing isolated comprehension skills—or standards—while many elementary programs move rapidly from one disconnected topic to another, limiting vocabulary growth and schema development (Cabell & Hwang, 2020). This oversight represents a lost opportunity to cultivate the world knowledge that underpins reading comprehension and later academic success (Buck, 2017; Neuman et al., 2014). Without consistent, cumulative content instruction, students—particularly those without access to rich home literacy experiences—face a profound disadvantage.

By secondary school, many assume that students naturally accumulate background knowledge through exposure to multiple classes across content areas. Yet research shows that secondary students rarely receive coherent, cumulative knowledge across disciplines (Sikorski & Straus, 2025). Courses are often siloed, and teachers frequently assume—or hope—that students are already literate enough to read complex content independently (Keogh & McGillicuddy, 2025). Few teachers are explicitly taught how to frontload background knowledge, model disciplinary reasoning, provide domain-specific vocabulary instruction, or select and sequence texts (within their discipline) to build coherent understanding over time. When these strategies are absent, students experience a patchwork of disconnected lessons that hinder not only comprehension but also the development of critical disciplinary thinking skills. In reality, even strong content requires explicit modeling and scaffolding; gradual release of responsibility ensures that students develop independent analytical skills while managing cognitive load (Kirschner et al., 2006; Sweller, 1988).

As students advance, disciplinary literacy becomes central to meaningful knowledge-building. Unlike generic reading strategies, disciplinary literacy teaches students to read, think, and communicate like historians, scientists, and literary critics (Shanahan & Shanahan, 2008). It intentionally builds domain-specific vocabulary alongside conceptual knowledge, recognizing that comprehension of complex texts depends on both language and background knowledge (Beck et al., 2013). This approach not only deepens content understanding and epistemic knowledge but also strengthens long-term retention. By fostering transfer of disciplinary thinking across domains, students learn strategies for analyzing evidence and constructing arguments that apply in multiple subjects.

This need for coherent, knowledge-driven instruction becomes even more critical in secondary math, where connections across domains—such as algebra to geometry or linear functions to real-world modeling—are essential for deep understanding. When conceptual connections are built alongside, rather than instead of, procedural fluency, students can apply mathematics both accurately and flexibly. Students benefit from worked examples, error analysis, and guided discussion of reasoning, which reduces cognitive load while reinforcing understanding (Kirschner et al., 2006; Sweller, 1988). Additionally, multiple representations—visual, symbolic, and verbal—help students see the procedures operate within conceptual frameworks, enabling flexible problem-solving across contexts.

Core Teacher Actions for Building a Knowledge-Rich, Explicitly Scaffolded Curriculum

Regardless of discipline, teachers can build a knowledge-rich curriculum through intentional planning. While commercial curricula can offer valuable structure and resources, they should be viewed as tools—most effective when paired with evidence-based instructional practices that promote deep understanding and long-term retention. This requires that both building- and district-level leaders recognize that boxed curricula rarely provide all the elements needed to create optimal conditions for student learning—a finding consistently supported by evidence-based research on the limitations of commercial programs (Cabell & Hwang, 2020; Polikoff & Dean, 2019; Hirsch, 2016; Neuman et al., 2014; Willingham, 2017).

Begin with Intentional Knowledge Design
A knowledge-rich curriculum begins with clarity about what students should know—not just what they should do. Regardless of discipline, teachers must identify the essential

concepts, principles, and facts that form the foundation for the discipline. Since we know that new learning builds on existing schema, knowledge must be intentionally sequenced so that it accumulates and connects over time (Anderson & Pearson, 1984; Willingham, 2009). Rather than covering disconnected topics, teachers should prioritize coherence and revisit key ideas across units and grade levels to strengthen long-term retention. In doing so, educators move away from a "coverage" mindset toward a "coherence" mindset—one where each instructional choice contributes to an expanding web of understanding. Effective knowledge design ensures that every lesson serves a larger conceptual narrative, helping students recognize patterns and relationships that make future learning easier to grasp. This should be through intentional, explicit design.

Making Thinking Visible through Explicit Instruction and Scaffolding
Once the essential knowledge is established, teachers must make expert thinking visible through explicit instruction. This process involves deliberately modeling cognitive steps, providing guided practice, and gradually releasing responsibility as students gain mastery (Archer & Hughes, 2011; Rosenshine, 2012). Across disciplines and grade levels, explicit instruction honors the limits of working memory and prevents cognitive overload by breaking complex processes into manageable components (Kirschner et al., 2006; Sweller, 1988). Scaffolded learning experiences—through guided questioning, worked examples, and structured practice—allows students to internalize the habits of disciplinary thinking (Ge & Land, 2003). Over time, this scaffolding builds not only procedural fluency but conceptual understanding. Retrieval practice and cumulative review further strengthen schema, ensuring that prior knowledge remains accessible as students encounter new, more challenging content. In short, explicit instruction and intentional scaffolding create the bridge between knowing *about* a discipline and thinking *within* it.

Reinforce Learning through Assessment, Language, and Cross-Disciplinary Coherence

Finally, a knowledge-rich, scaffolded curriculum requires that teachers assess what students *understand*—not merely what they can recall. Assessments should align with the disciplinary ways of reasoning that instruction aims to develop, reinforcing the application of knowledge to novel contexts. In this sense, well-designed formative assessments serve as tools for feedback, guiding both teaching and learning in real time (Hattie & Timperley, 2007). Equally important is the integration of language and content: academic vocabulary should be explicitly taught in context so that students develop both linguistic precision and conceptual depth (Beck et al., 2013). When teachers across subjects coordinate around shared knowledge goals and academic language, they transform fragmented experiences into coherent learning. Collaboration across disciplines ensures that knowledge builds cumulatively rather than in silos, promoting transfer and equity. Students who may lack background knowledge outside of school gain structured opportunities to build it systematically, enabling them to access—and eventually create—complex ideas within and beyond their disciplines (Hirsch, 2016).

Does Strategy Instruction Ever Work in Literacy?

Strategy instruction in reading refers to the explicit teaching of cognitive and metacognitive techniques that help students understand, monitor, and make meaning from text. Rather than focusing on decoding or content knowledge, strategy instruction teaches students how to think while reading. According to the National Reading Panel (2000), teaching a small set of comprehension strategies—such as summarizing, questioning, and clarifying—can improve understanding, particularly when these strategies are explicitly taught and practiced. Willingham (2006) and Shanahan (2015) emphasize that while strategy instruction has value, it should be (1) limited in duration, (2) explicitly modeled, (3) integrated quickly into content-rich instruction, and (4) not mistaken as a substitute for knowledge-building or fluency development. This kind of instruction is most effective when paired with authentic texts and meaningful applications. Rather than oversaturating students with strategies, teachers should focus on a few high-leverage ones and ensure that students have the background knowledge necessary to apply them meaningfully. Table 2.1 outlines commonly taught reading comprehension strategies and research supporting their effectiveness.

Many of the strategies are supported by empirical research and are most effective when they are taught explicitly, used flexibly and in authentic reading, embedded in knowledge-building curricula, and paired with rich, complex texts. While most strategies have evidence at both elementary and secondary levels, secondary students often require stronger scaffolding when texts become more complex—ironically, the opposite of how they are frequently

TABLE 2.1 Reading Strategies and Research Support

Strategy Type	Specific Strategy	Research Support	Effectiveness/Caveats
Before reading	Previewing text	Moderate support (NRP, 2000)	Secondary vs. Elementary: Supported at both levels but more critical in secondary due to text complexity (Afflerbach, 1990; NRP, 2000). Works for narrative and informational texts.
	Activating prior knowledge	Strong support (Anderson & Pearson, 1984; Willingham, 2006)	One of the **most effective** ways to enhance comprehension when prior knowledge is relevant. Strong evidence at both secondary and elementary levels (Anderson & Pearson, 1984; Willingham, 2006). Particularly effective for secondary students accessing complex content; applies across text types
	Setting a purpose	Moderate (NRP, 2000)	Moderate support at both secondary and elementary levels; slightly stronger for struggling readers (Duke & Pearson, 2002).

(Continued)

TABLE 2.1 (Continued)

Strategy Type	Specific Strategy	Research Support	Effectiveness/Caveats
During reading	Monitoring comprehension	Strong (NRP, 2000; Pressley & Afflerbach, 1995)	Linked to metacognition; improves self-correction and awareness. Strong support at elementary and secondary levels (Pressley & Afflerbach, 1995).
	Asking questions	Strong (NRP, 2000; Rosenshine et al., 1996)	Strong evidence for both elementary and secondary (Rosenshine et al., 1996). When students ask their own questions, it deepens engagement and comprehension.
	Making predictions	Moderate (Duke & Pearson, 2002; NRP, 2000)	Moderate support for elementary and secondary. Useful in narrative texts; must be connected to evidence in text.
	Visualizing	Moderate (NRP, 2000)	Moderate support in elementary and secondary; more effective for concrete content or narratives.
	Summarizing	**Very strong** (Dole et al., 1991; NRP, 2000)	One of the **most powerful** strategies when explicitly taught and practiced in secondary and elementary.
After reading	Rereading	Strong (Willingham, 2006; NRP)	Strong support in elementary and secondary. Improves fluency and comprehension—especially when done with purpose.
	Synthesizing	Moderate (NRP, 2000)	Moderate support in secondary and elementary. More challenging at secondary due to cognitive demand. Requires strong content understanding; often conflated with summarizing.
	Evaluating	Emerging evidence	Depends on text complexity and cognitive maturity; important in disciplinary literacy.
	Drawing inferences	**Strong** (Cain & Oakhill, 2007; Oakhill et al., 2003)	Strong evidence in elementary and secondary. Crucial to comprehension; strongly linked to vocabulary and background knowledge.
	Answering comprehension questions	**Strong** (NRP, 2000; Rosenshine, 2012)	Works best when combined with **explicit instruction and discussion**, not as isolated test prep. Strong support in secondary and elementary.

Evidence-based reading strategies organized by stage of reading, with research support, effectiveness, and caveats for implementation across elementary and secondary levels.

instructed. Importantly, strategy instruction alone is insufficient without content knowledge; strategies enhance learning only when students have the necessary background knowledge.

Does Strategy-Based Instruction Ever Work in Math?

In many math classrooms, students are asked to experiment with strategies (e.g., guess-and-check, draw a picture, make a table) *before* they have had adequate instruction in efficient algorithms or core procedures. Research suggests this can be problematic—students may generate inefficient strategies and struggle with deeper learning unless later supported by explicit instruction and structured practice (Paas & Van Merriënboer, 1994; Rittle-Johnson et al., 2001). From a cognitive-science perspective, algorithms are stored procedures—mental frameworks that automate lower-level steps. A student who is fluent in long division or solving linear equations can focus on the structure of the problem—rations, proportionality, or reasoning about rate of change—rather than getting bogged down in basic calculations. There is a persistent myth that teaching algorithms impedes understanding—that "drill" replaces "thinking." But the evidence shows the opposite: procedural knowledge actually supports conceptual insights (Geary, 2011; Rittle-Johnson & Schneider, 2015; Willingham, 2009). Algorithms also serve as building blocks for future learning. Once students internalize a process, they can generalize it to novel situations. In cognitive-science terms, algorithms act as transfer tools. They allow students to recognize deep structural similarities between problems that look different on the surface (Chi et al., 1981; Gentner, 1983).

Strategy-based instruction can work in math—but only when it's used at the right time, with the right foundation. Timing and context are crucial. Strategy instruction without procedural fluency often fails. If students are asked to experiment with strategies before they have learned efficient algorithms or core

TABLE 2.2 High-Value Math Strategies with Empirical Support

Strategy	Why It Works	Research Support
Decomposing & recomposing	Builds mental math fluency and place value understanding	National Mathematics Advisory Panel (2008) – Strong evidence, meta-analyses support improved computation and conceptual understanding
Visual representations	Links symbolic math to concrete or visual understanding; aids abstract reasoning	NCTM (2000), Arcavi (2003) – Strong; particularly effective in algebra and problem-solving
Worked examples	Step-by-step modeling reduces cognitive load, builds schema	Sweller (1988), Clark et al. (2011) – Strong support, especially for novices
Equation reasoning	Develops algebraic thinking and structure sense	Carpenter et al. (1999), Star (2005) – Strong; improves transfer to novel problems
Spaced & interleaved practice	Enhances long-term retention and transfer	Rohrer and Taylor (2007), Cepeda et al. (2006) – Strong cognitive psychology evidence

High-value math strategies supported by empirical research, including explanations of why they are effective and key references demonstrating their impact.

procedures, working memory is overloaded. Yet when students have mastered algorithms and foundational procedures, strategy instruction can enhance conceptual understanding and problem-solving flexibility. This helps students see multiple approaches to the same problem and recognize underlying structures, which supports transfer to new contexts (Rittle-Johnson & Schneider, 2015). With that in mind, timing matters and explicit instruction is essential: even the evidence-backed strategies listed in Table 2.2 fail if students are left to discover them unguided.

What about Learner Variability?

Learner variability refers to the idea that students differ in prior knowledge, interests, motivation, cognitive strengths, working memory capacity, attention span, language proficiency, and processing speed. These differences influence how students engage with and learn content. Proponents of inquiry, discovery-based, and constructivist methods often respond by advocating differentiated tasks, open-ended inquiry, student-paced learning, and Universal Design for Learning (UDL) as a framework to support diverse learners (CAST, 2018). While cognitive science accepts that learner variability exists, it proposes a different response. Explicit instruction benefits *all* learners: novice, struggling, and even advanced students gain from well-structured, explicit, scaffolded teaching (Rosenshine, 2012). Learners with limited working memory struggle to process disorganized or unstructured information, so they benefit more from clear goals, step-by-step modeling, worked examples, and cumulative review (Sweller et al., 2011a). Willingham (2009) and others argue that differences in background knowledge are among the primary drivers of performance gaps—especially in reading comprehension.

Cognitive science addresses learner variability through systematic and cumulative knowledge-building. Rather than tailoring content to each individual—which can fragment learning—cognitive scientists emphasize instructional design that (1) gives all students access to the same rich content, (2) provides scaffolds and supports during learning, and (3) removes supports as students gain independence (Clark et al., 2012). While learners vary, this does not mean they need *different* content or learning paths. Instead, all students should be supported in reaching the same rigorous goals. In fact, evidence suggests that human learners are more similar than different in how they process and acquire information—countering claims made by constructivist or personalized learning paradigms. There is no credible evidence that tailoring instruction to "learning styles" improves outcomes (Pashler et al., 2007). The basic mechanisms of learning—such as retrieval, spacing, and feedback—work similarly across learners. In fact, the common ground in how we learn outweighs differences in style.

Reading acquisition also follows a relatively universal path (Seidenberg, 2017). Despite some variability, most learners benefit from systematic, explicit phonics instruction, and over-individualized or discovery-based approaches in early reading can lead to negative outcomes (Ehri et al., 2001; Institute of Education Sciences, 2014; National Reading Panel, 2000; Peak, 2022). Cognitive science has not found that each child learns in a fundamentally unique way; rather, children are more alike than different in how they think and learn (Willingham, 2009). While UDL is grounded in accommodating learner variability, much of what works in UDL aligns with universal cognitive principles: research indicates that providing learners with multiple representations of content (Clark & Paivio, 1991; Vogt et al., 2020) and chunked, scaffolded instruction (Paas & Van Merriënboer, 1994) reduces cognitive load, supports schema formation, and enhances learning outcomes. Cognitive science does not deny individual differences—such as background knowledge or motivation—but emphasizes that the mechanisms of learning are broadly consistent, and well-designed instruction tends to benefit all learners.

UDL, constructivist, and personalized learning models emphasize the importance of learner engagement and learner variability, often suggesting that lessons should maximize engagement by offering multiple pathways. However, cognitive science reveals that engagement alone does not drive learning—rather, learning drives engagement (Willingham, 2009). While learners do vary, not all differences are instructionally relevant, especially when it comes to how students process or comprehend content. Research also shows that when instruction overemphasizes variability at the expense of content coherence, it can create widening knowledge gaps between students. Stanovich (1986) describes this as the "Matthew Effect": students with more background knowledge learn more from instruction, while those with less knowledge fall further behind. This underscores the importance of shared knowledge-building as an equity issue—not just an instructional preference. Engagement is a mediator of learning, not its cause; students can be highly engaged and still learn very little. Furthermore, designing instruction solely around engagement or student-driven exploration risks overloading students' working memory—especially for novices (Sweller et al., 2011b).

Overemphasis on Engagement in Curriculum Design

While engagement is often treated as the primary goal in curriculum design, cognitive-science and empirical research indicates that it is at best a facilitator, not a substitute for structured learning. Studies consistently show that tasks designed solely to capture interest—through gamification, flashy technology, or novelty—rarely lead to measurable improvements in comprehension, retention, or problem-solving (Clark et al., 2012; Hattie, 2009; National Research Council, 2012). It is a fallacy to assume that student motivation and engagement can be reliably engineered simply by (1) identifying student interests, (2) reworking curriculum to align with those interests, or (3) ensuring that students "see themselves" reflected in the content; empirical research shows that while these strategies may increase short-term attention or relevance, they do not consistently improve learning outcomes, which depend primarily on coherent, knowledge-rich instruction paired with scaffolded practice and meaningful cognitive challenge (Clark et al., 2012; Hamari et al., 2016; Hattie, 2009; Ryan & Deci, 2000; Willingham, 2009). Research in cognitive science and educational psychology indicates that motivation is largely shaped by students' sense of competence, the meaningfulness of tasks, and the ability to succeed in challenging work—not by novelty or external rewards (Hattie, 2009; Ryan & Deci, 2000; Willingham, 2009). Empirical studies of gamification and engagement-focused interventions show minimal or inconsistent effects on learning outcomes when content, background knowledge, and structured practice are not prioritized (Clark et al., 2012; Hamari et al., 2016). Engagement is not a "switch" that can be flipped; it emerges naturally when students experience success in learning that is coherent, scaffolded, and connected to prior knowledge. Consequently, designing curriculum primarily to be engaging is insufficient and can even distract from the more fundamental task of building knowledge, skills, and transferable understanding.

Fredricks and colleagues (2004) point out that while engagement correlates with academic success, there is a lack of causal evidence showing that designing specifically for engagement leads to improved achievement. Likewise, Hattie's (2009) meta-analysis shows that direct instructional practices—such as teacher clarity, feedback, practice, and explicit instruction—are associated with substantially higher effect sizes than many other commonly promoted approaches, including those focused primarily on engagement and motivation. While differentiation is widely promoted, its average effect size in Hattie's research is moderate (0.46), far lower than high-impact practices like teacher clarity (0.84) or feedback (0.73). And despite its popularity, personalization lacks consistent empirical support showing that it improves academic outcomes across diverse learners (Pane et al., 2015). Very little causal or experimental evidence supports the idea that designing lessons solely for engagement improves academic outcomes for all students. Engagement matters—but only as part of a coherent, high-quality instructional approach.

While constructivists value knowledge, they often overemphasize the path to acquiring it. As a result, research consistently shows that minimally guided constructivist methods—such as pure inquiry, discovery, or open-ended exploration—do not reliably lead to transferable or durable learning for novice learners (Clark et al., 2012). When the method takes precedence over the outcome, instruction can become inefficient, ineffective, and even misleading. This often leads to poorer outcomes, particularly for novice learners. Hirsch (2016) argues that constructivist approaches often sacrifice cultural literacy and shared knowledge for individualized paths. This undermines equity and academic rigor. Instead, a core knowledge approach—grounded in systematically taught, content-rich curricula—better supports reading comprehension, critical thinking, and lifelong learning. The aims of constructivism—student agency and conceptual understanding—are worthwhile, but if the instructional methods fail to reliably produce those outcomes, it becomes necessary to rethink our pedagogical priorities.

References

Afflerbach, P. (1990). The influence of prior knowledge on expert readers' main idea construction strategies. *Reading Research Quarterly*, *25*(1), 31–46. https://doi.org/10.1080/10862969009547700

Allen, A. (2022). An introduction to constructivism: Its theoretical roots and impact on contemporary education. *Journal of Learning Design and Leadership*, *1*(1), 1–11.

Anderson, R. C., & Pearson, P. D. (1984). A schema-theoretic view of basic processes in reading comprehension. In P. D. Pearson (Ed.), *Handbook of reading research* (pp. 255–291). Longman.

Arcavi, A. (2003). The role of visual representations in the learning of mathematics. *Educational Studies in Mathematics*, *52*, 215–241. https://doi.org/10.1023/A:1024312321077

Archer, A. L., & Hughes, C. A. (2011). *Explicit instruction: Effective and efficient teaching*. Guilford Press.

Baroody, A. J. (2006). Why children have difficulties mastering the basic number combinations and how to help them. *Teaching Children Mathematics*, *13*(1), 22–31.

Bartlett, F. C. (1932). *Remembering: A study in experimental and social psychology*. Cambridge University Press.

Beck, I. L., McKeown, M. G., & Kucan, L. (2013). *Bringing words to life: Robust vocabulary instruction* (2nd ed.). The Guilford Press.

Boaler, J. (2016). *Mathematical mindsets*. Jossey-Bass.

Boardman, A. G. (2024). Examining enactments of project-based learning in secondary English language arts classrooms. *Journal of Educational Research and Practice*, *14*(1), 1–15. https://doi.org/10.1177/23328584241269829

Bowers, J. S. (2020). Reconsidering the evidence that systematic phonics is more effective than alternative methods of reading instruction. *Educational Psychology Review, 32*, 681–705. https://doi.org/10.1007/s10648-019-09515-y

Buck, D. (2017). *Think again: Should elementary schools teach reading comprehension?* Thomas B. Fordham Institute.

Cabell, S. Q., & Hwang, H. J. (2020). Building content knowledge to boost comprehension in the primary grades. *Reading Research Quarterly, 55*(1), 99–107. https://doi.org/10.1002/rrq.338

Cain, K., & Oakhill, J. (2007). Reading comprehension and vocabulary: What's the connection? *Senior Library, 17*, 315–361.

Cambourne, B. (1988). *The whole story: Natural learning and the acquisition of literacy in the classroom.* Scholastic.

Carpenter, T. P., Franke, M. L., & Levi, L. (1999). *Children's mathematics: Cognitively guided instruction.* Heinemann.

CAST. (2018). *Universal design for learning guidelines version 2.2.* https://udlguidelines.cast.org/

Cepeda, N. J., Pashler, H., Vul, E., Wixted, J. T., & Rohrer, D. (2006). Distributed practice in verbal recall tasks: A review and quantitative synthesis. *Psychological Bulletin, 132*(3), 354–380. https://doi.org/10.1037/0033-2909.132.3.354

Chi, M. T. H., Feltovich, P. J., & Glaser, R. (1981). Categorization and representation of physics problems by experts and novices. *Cognitive Science, 5*(2), 121–152. https://doi.org/10.1207/s15516709cog0502_2

Clark, R. E., Kirschner, P. A., & Sweller, J. (2012). Putting students on the path to learning: The case for fully guided instruction. *American Educator, 36*(1), 6–11.

Clark, R. C., Nguyen, F., & Sweller, J. (2011). *Efficiency in learning: Evidence-based guidelines to manage cognitive load.* Wiley.

Clark, J. M., & Paivio, A. (1991). Dual coding theory and education. *Educational Psychology Review, 3*(3), 149–210.

Dole, J. A., Duffy, G. G., Roehler, L. R., & Pearson, P. D. (1991). Moving from the old to the new: Research on reading comprehension instruction. *Review of Educational Research, 61*(2), 239–264. https://doi.org/10.3102/00346543061002239

Duke, N. K., Halvorsen, A. L., Strachan, S. L., Kim, J., & Konstantopoulos, S. (2020). *Putting PjBL to the test: The impact of project-based learning on second graders' social studies and literacy learning and motivation in low-SES school settings (research brief).* Lucas Education Research.

Duke, N. K., & Pearson, P. D. (2002). Effective practices for developing reading comprehension. In A. E. Farstrup & S. J. Samuels (Eds.), *What research has to say about reading instruction* (3rd ed., pp. 205–242). International Reading Association.

Ehri, L. C., Nunes, S. R., Stahl, S. A., & Willows, D. M. (2001). Systematic phonics instruction helps students learn to read: Evidence from the National Reading Panel's meta-analysis. *Reading Research Quarterly*, *36*(3), 250–287. https://doi.org/10.1598/RRQ.36.3.2

Fredricks, J. A., Blumenfeld, P. C., & Paris, A. H. (2004). School engagement: Potential of the concept, state of the evidence. *Review of Educational Research*, *74*(1), 59–109. https://doi.org/10.3102/00346543074001059

Fuchs, L. S., Fuchs, D., Seethaler, P. M., Cutting, L. E., & Mancilla-Martinez, J. (2019). Connections between reading comprehension and word-problem solving via oral language comprehension: Implications for comorbid learning disabilities. *New Directions for Child and Adolescent Development*, *2019*(165), 73–90. https://doi.org/10.1002/cad.20288

Ge, X., & Land, S. M. (2003). Scaffolding students' problem-solving processes in an ill-structured task using question prompts and peer interactions. *Educational Psychology Review*, *15*(1), 1–22. https://doi.org/10.1007/BF02504515

Geary, D. C. (2011). Cognitive predictors of achievement growth in mathematics: A 5-year longitudinal study. *Developmental Psychology*, *47*(6), 1539–1552. https://psycnet.apa.org/doi/10.1037/a0025510

Gentner, D. (1983). Structure-mapping: A theoretical framework for analogy. *Cognitive Science*, *7*(2), 155–170.

Gilmore, C. (2017). The interaction of procedural skill, conceptual understanding, and working memory in early mathematics achievement. *Journal of Numerical Cognition*, *3*(2), 400–411. https://doi.org/10.5964/jnc.v3i2.51

Goodman, K. S. (1967). Reading: A psycholinguistic guessing game. *Journal of the Reading Specialist*, *6*(4), 126–135. https://doi.org/10.1080/19388076709556976

Hamari, J., Koivisto, J., & Sarsa, H. (2016). Does gamification work?—A literature review of empirical studies on gamification. In *Proceedings of the 47th Hawaii international conference on system sciences (HICSS)* (pp. 3025–3034). https://doi.org/10.1109/HICSS.2014.377

Hattie, J. (2009). *Visible learning: A synthesis of over 800 meta analyses relating to achievement*. Routledge.
Hattie, J., & Timperley, H. (2007). The power of feedback. *Review of Educational Research, 77*(1), 81–112. https://doi.org/10.3102/003465430298487
Hirsch, E. D., Jr. (2006). *The knowledge deficit: Closing the shocking education gap for American children*. Houghton Mifflin.
Hirsch, E. D., Jr. (2016). *Why knowledge matters: Rescuing our children from failed educational theories*. Harvard Education Press.
Institute of Education Sciences. (2014). *Foundational skills to support reading for understanding in kindergarten through 3rd grade (NCEE 2016-4008)*. U.S. Department of Education, Institute of Education Sciences.
Kappassova, S., Abylkassymova, A., Bulut, U., Zykrina, S., Zhumagulova, Z., & Balta, N. (2025). Mathematical literacy and its influencing factors: A decade of research findings (2015–2024). *EURASIA Journal of Mathematics, Science, and Technology Education, 21*(7). https://doi.org/10.29333/ejmste/16615
Keogh, A. J., & McGillicuddy, D. (2025). The role of primary literacy education in students' later academic success. *Reading Research Quarterly*. https://doi.org/10.1002/rrq.70017
Kirschner, P. A., Sweller, J., & Clark, R. E. (2006). Why minimal guidance during instruction does not work. *Educational Psychologist, 41*(2), 75–86. https://doi.org/10.1207/s15326985ep4102_1
Mandler, J. M., & Anderson, R. C. (1971). The effects of a teacher's emphasis on the meaning or grammatical correctness of reading passages. *Journal of Educational Psychology, 62*(5), 376–380. https://psycnet.apa.org/doi/10.1037/h0031602
Meng, N. (2023). Tackle implementation challenges in project-based learning. *National Center for Biotechnology Information*. https://doi.org/10.1007/s11423-023-10202-7
Moje, E. B. (2008). Foregrounding the disciplines in secondary literacy teaching and learning: A call for change. *Journal of Adolescent & Adult Literacy, 52*(2), 96–107. https://doi.org/10.1598/JAAL.52.2.1
Mutanga, M. B. (2024). Students' perspectives and experiences in project-based learning: A qualitative study. *Trends in Higher Education, 3*(4), 903–911. https://doi.org/10.3390/higheredu3040052
National Council of Teachers of Mathematics. (1989). *Curriculum and evaluation standards for school mathematics*. https://archive.org/details/curriculumevalua00nati/page/n7/mode/1up

National Council of Teachers of Mathematics. (2000). *Principles and standards for school mathematics.* https://www.nctm.org/Standards-and-Positions/Principles-and-Standards/

National Mathematics Advisory Panel. (2008). *Foundations for success: The final report of the National Mathematics Advisory Panel.* U.S. Department of Education.

National Reading Panel. (2000). *Teaching children to read: An evidence-based assessment of the scientific research literature on reading and its implications for reading instruction.* National Institute of Child Health and Human Development.

National Research Council. (2012). *Foundations for success: The final report of the National Reading Panel.* National Academies Press. https://doi.org/10.17226/13242

Neuman, S. B., Kaefer, T., & Pinkham, A. (2014). Building background knowledge. *The Reading Teacher, 68*(2), 145–148. https://doi.org/10.1002/trtr.1314

Oakhill, J., Cain, K., & Elbro, C. (2003). Understanding and teaching reading comprehension: A handbook. In *Cognitive, linguistic, and educational foundations of Reading comprehension.* Lawrence Erlbaum Associates.

Organisation for Economic Co-operation and Development. (2023). *PISA 2022 results (volume I): The state of learning and equity in education.* OECD Publishing. https://doi.org/10.1787/53f23881-en

Paas, F. G. W. C., & Van Merriënboer, J. J. G. (1994). Variability of worked examples and transfer of geometrical problem-solving skills: A cognitive-load approach. *Journal of Educational Psychology, 86*(1), 122–133. https://psycnet.apa.org/doi/10.1037/0022-0663.86.1.122

Pane, J. F., Steiner, E.D., Baird, M.D., & Hamilton, L.S. (2015). *Promising evidence on personalized learning (Research Brief).* RAND Corporation. http://dx.doi.org/10.7249/RR1365

Pashler, H., Bain, P. M., Bottge, B. A., Graesser, A., Koedinger, K., McDaniel, M., & Metcalfe, J. (2007). *Organizing instruction and study to improve student learning (NCER 2007–2004).* National Center for Education Research, Institute of Education Sciences, U.S. Department of Education.

Peak, C. (2022, August 27). *New reading laws sweep the nation following sold a story.* APM Reports. https://www.apmreports.org/story/2025/08/27/legislators-reading-laws-sold-a-story

Polikoff, M., & Dean, J. (2019). *The supplemental curriculum bazaar: Is what's online any good?* Thomas B. Fordham Institute. https://files.eric.ed.gov/fulltext/ED601253.pdf

Pressley, M., & Afflerbach, P. (1995). *Verbal protocols of reading: The nature of constructively responsive reading.* Lawrence Erlbaum Associates.

Recht, D. R., & Leslie, L. (1988). Effect of prior knowledge on good and poor readers' memory of text. *Journal of Educational Psychology, 80*(1), 16–20. https://psycnet.apa.org/doi/10.1037/0022-0663.80.1.16

Reynolds, D., & Fisher, W. (2022). What happens when adolescents meet complex texts? Describing moments of scaffolding textual encounters. *Literacy, 56*(4), 277–287. https://doi.org/10.1111/lit.12258

Rittle-Johnson, B., & Schneider, M. (2015). Developing conceptual and procedural knowledge in mathematics. *Educational Psychology Review, 27*(4), 587–597.

Rittle-Johnson, B., Siegler, R. S., & Alibali, M. W. (2001). Developing conceptual understanding and procedural skill in mathematics: An iterative process. *Journal of Educational Psychology, 93*(2), 346–362. https://psycnet.apa.org/doi/10.1037/0022-0663.93.2.346

Rohrer, D., & Taylor, K. (2007). The shuffling of mathematics problems improves learning. *Instructional Science, 35*(6), 481–498.

Rosenshine, B. (2012). Principles of instruction: Research-based strategies that all teachers should know. *American Educator, 36*(1), 12–19.

Rosenshine, B., Meister, C., & Chapman, S. (1996). Teaching students to generate questions: A review of the intervention studies. *Review of Educational Research, 66*(2), 181–221. https://doi.org/10.3102/00346543066002181

Rumelhart, D. E. (1980). Schemata: The building blocks of cognition. In R. J. Spiro, B. C. Bruce, & W. E. Brewer (Eds.), *Theoretical issues in reading comprehension* (pp. 33–58). Erlbaum. https://doi.org/10.4324/9781315107493-4

Ryan, R. M., & Deci, E. L. (2000). Self-determination theory and the facilitation of intrinsic motivation, social development, and well-being. *American Psychologist, 55*(1), 68–78. https://psycnet.apa.org/doi/10.1037/0003-066X.55.1.68

Seidenberg, M. S. (2017). *Language at the speed of sight: How we read, why so many can't, and what can be done about it.* Basic Books.

Shanahan, T. (2015, July 16). How much comprehension strategy instruction? *Shanahan on Literacy*. https://www.readingrockets.org/blogs/shanahan-on-literacy/how-much-comprehension-strategy-instruction

Shanahan, T. (2019, March 16). Comprehension skills or strategies: Is there a difference and does it matter? *Shanahan on Literacy*. https://www.shanahanonliteracy.com/blog/comprehension-skills-or-strategies-is-there-a-difference-and-does-it-matter

Shanahan, T., & Shanahan, C. (2008). Teaching disciplinary literacy to adolescents: Rethinking content-area literacy. *Harvard Educational Review*, *78*(1), 40–59. https://doi.org/10.17763/haer.78.1.v62444321p602101

Siegler, R. S., Duncan, G. J., Davis-Kean, P., Duckworth, K., Claessens, A., Engel, M., Susperreguy, M. I., & Chen, M. (2012). *Early predictors of high school mathematics achievement.* https://doi.org/10.1177/0956797612440101

Sikorski, T. R., & Straus, A. (2025). Comparing curriculum coherence and student coherence seeking: A secondary analysis of the TIMSS video study. *Journal of Curriculum Studies*, 1–24. https://doi.org/10.1080/00220272.2025.2460482

Smith, F. (1971). *Understanding reading: A psycholinguistic analysis of reading and learning to read*. Holt, Rinehart & Winston.

Stanovich, K. E. (1986). Matthew effects in reading: Some consequences of individual differences in the acquisition of literacy. *Reading Research Quarterly*, *22*(4), 360–407.

Star, J. R. (2005). Reconceptualizing procedural knowledge. *Educational Psychologist*, *40*(2), 123–134. https://doi.org/10.2307/30034943

Sweller, J. (1988). Cognitive load during problem solving: Effects on learning. *Cognitive Science*, *12*(2), 257–285. https://doi.org/10.1207/s15516709cog1202_4

Sweller, J., Ayres, P., & Kalyuga, S. (2011a). *Cognitive load theory*. Springer. https://doi.org/10.1007/978-1-4419-8126-4

Sweller, J., van Merriënboer, J. J. G., & Paas, F. (2011b). Cognitive architecture and instructional design: 20 years later. *Educational Psychology Review*, *33*(2), 261–285. https://doi.org/10.1007/s10648-019-09465-5

Syahdia, R. R., Nuryani, H., Nuryanti, M., & Sukmayani, N. S. (2024). Challenges of implementing project-based learning models in secondary schools in various countries. *Education and Science*, *1*(6), 283–295. https://doi.org/10.62885/edusci.v6i1.340

Vogt, A., Klepsch, M., Baetge, I., & Seufert, T. (2020). Learning from multiple representations: Prior knowledge moderates the beneficial effects of signals and abstract graphics. *Frontiers in Psychology, 11*, 601125. https://doi.org/10.3389/fpsyg.2020.601125

Willingham, D. T. (2006). How knowledge helps: It speeds and strengthens reading comprehension, learning—And thinking. *American Educator, 30*(1), 30–37.

Willingham, D. T. (2009). *Why don't students like school? A cognitive scientist answers questions about how the mind works and what it means for the classroom.* Jossey-Bass.

Willingham, D. T. (2017). *The Reading mind: A cognitive approach to understanding how the mind reads.* Jossey-Bass.

3

Setting Clear Learning Intentions

At its core, the design of learning intentions is a problem of cognitive architecture. How we define, sequence, and communicate goals determines what the brain encodes, retains, and transfers. Clarity in teaching is not a matter of compliance or convenience—it's a matter of design. Current educational research overwhelmingly agrees on the power of clear learning intentions and success criteria (Brookhart, 2008; Clarke, 2001 & 2014; Hattie, 2009 & 2023; Marzano et al., 2001; Wiliam & Black, 1998). At their core, learning intentions are meant to clarify learning, not complicate teaching. While they're grounded in robust cognitive science and instructional theory, they're often misapplied in ways that undermine their purpose. Too often, these tools become about compliance—posting objectives on the board, checking boxes, and ensuring "visibility"—rather than about learning. When this happens, the focus shifts from cognitive clarity to superficial correctness. Learning intentions, or learning goals/objectives, are about making learning—and assessment—transparent. They help to guide instruction for the teacher, provide focus for students, and anchor feedback and assessment. According to Hattie (2009), teacher clarity—including clear learning intentions and success criteria—is one of the most powerful influences on student achievement (d ≈ 0.75). But when schools hyperfixate on phrasing (whether to write "I can" or "I am learning") based on sub-skills in standards, we risk disjointed learning and prioritizing compliance over cognition. Merely stating the objective doesn't improve learning; it's the mental clarity and schema activation that matter. As both Hattie (2009) and Sweller (1988) remind us, goal orientation drives impact only when it's shared, understood, and aligned with how the brain processes and manages cognitive load (Sweller, 1988; Hattie, 2009). In other words, clarity that *only* lives on the board—posted but not understood—means very little. It's the clarity that lives in the minds—for both students and teachers—that accelerates learning.

Many school districts that have embraced the importance of learning intentions and success criteria still spend unnecessary time breaking down standards into discrete, bite-sized skills—forgetting that the common core state standards (CCSS) and state standards were never intended to be curriculum. They're a staircase of increasing complexity, not a script (Hodge & Benko, 2014). Learning should be contextualized, effortful, and cumulative. When we over-fragment it, we interfere with processes—transfer and schema building—that make learning durable (Willingham, 2009). Standards define the destination—what students should know and be able to do by the end of the year. Curriculum, however, organizes the content, skills, and assessments into coherent units that help students get there. Learning intentions are the daily steps that move students along that path. Yet when teachers are handed spreadsheets of standards and are asked to unpack every line into micro-objectives and create lessons or assessments for each sub-skill, instruction quickly becomes disjointed. In literacy, this kind of atomized planning can especially fragment both instruction and thinking—reducing rich, connected learning into a checklist of tasks.

When done well, learning intentions and success criteria connect the *macro* (curriculum coherence) to the *micro* (daily learning moves). The key is calibration. Effective intentions identify the specific *thinking* that students will engage in—analyzing, comparing, evaluating—while keeping the content central. They're neither too broad ("understand character development") nor too granular ("identify three adjectives that describe the protagonist"). Instead, they balance clarity with cognitive challenge, ensuring that each lesson contributes meaningfully to long-term schema and disciplinary understanding.

In a knowledge-building approach, teachers must start with a rich curriculum, choosing meaningful texts, tasks, problems, and topics that align with grade-level standards. Standards are used to *calibrate rigor*: what should students be able to do *with these texts/tasks* to be on track with the standards? Learning intentions are crafted to support comprehension and transfer—these should help students develop the complex thinking needed for interpretation, analysis, and synthesis. Standards should be treated not as daily checklists but as long-term goals. This is especially true in literacy, where instruction should embrace complexity rather than reducing it to isolated skills. Cognitive science tells us that learning requires coherence, not isolation. The brain stores and retrieves knowledge by making meaningful connections. Teaching skills separately leads to shallow inert knowledge. Experts don't just know more facts—they know how ideas connect (Bransford et al., 2000; Willingham, 2009). Transfer depends on learning in authentic, varied contexts. Students don't apply decontextualized skills easily. Real learning must happen in *context* (i.e., analyzing theme while reading literature, not through isolated worksheets) (Detterman, 1993; Gick & Holyoak, 1983). Curriculum must provide rich contexts, and learning intentions should reflect real-world reading, writing, and thinking.

To maximize the impact of a coherent, knowledge-rich curriculum, students need more than just access to rich texts and tasks—they need clarity about what they are learning and why. This is where learning intentions and success criteria become indispensable. Clear goals act like mental spotlights. The prefrontal cortex (which is responsible for attention and executive function) becomes engaged when students know what to focus on (Posner & Rothbart, 2007). Students filter out distractions and prioritize relevant information, enhancing selective attention. Learning intentions are powerful when they clarify thinking goals, not just surface tasks. When paired with clear success criteria, they enhance the quality of feedback, foster self-regulation (Hattie & Timperley, 2007), and help students internalize what quality work looks like (Wiliam, 2011). Good intentions are about mental targets, not "I can" phrasing gymnastics. Breaking reading and writing into too many micro-objectives overloads working memory and prevents schema formation (Chi et al., 1981; Sweller, 2011). Coherence at the task level must mirror coherence at the curriculum level.

An added benefit of clear learning intentions is their ability to activate the brain's reward system. The brain releases dopamine when progress is made toward a specific goal—reinforcing learning and increasing persistence (Schunk et al., 2008). Additionally, when students know *why* they are learning something, they more effectively encode the material into long-term memory (Bransford et al., 2000; Willingham, 2009). The brain becomes more efficient when it can plan, monitor, and evaluate progress toward clear outcomes (Zimmerman, 2002).

All disciplines benefit from learning intentions that highlight *thinking*—the conceptual structures and reasoning habits that define expert performance in that field. When learning intentions emphasize intellectual work over isolated skills, students begin to see how knowledge functions within the discipline itself. Conversely, when instruction splinters into checklist skills, deep understanding and authentic engagement suffer. Preparing students for standards-based assessments—or real-world problem-solving—requires more than surface coverage; it demands alignment to disciplinary reasoning. It's about not rehearsing test formats but developing cognitive flexibility: the ability to apply ideas in new contexts. Transfer improves when students understand *why* a strategy works and how it connects to broader concepts (Bransford et al., 2000; Willingham, 2009). Neuroscientific research suggests that this process engages the prefrontal cortex—the region responsible for attention, monitoring, and executive control (Fleming & Lau, 2014; Posner & Rothbart, 2007). When goals are explicit and meaningful, students are neurologically better equipped to regulate their focus and persist through challenges. Learning endures when it is organized around meaningful concepts, not scattered tasks. Curriculum must chart a coherent path that builds mental models and disciplinary habits of mind (Bransford et al., 2000; Wiggins & McTighe, 2005). When students encounter core ideas across varied contexts, they begin to recognize patterns, make analogies, and apply learning beyond the classroom—the real measure of understanding.

Table 3.1 provides examples of learning intentions and success criteria across major disciplines, designed to align with

TABLE 3.1 Content Rich Learning Objectives

Content Area	Example Learning Intention	Example of Success Criteria
English Language Arts	I am learning to analyze how Fitzgerald uses symbolism, narrative perspective, and setting to develop themes of the American Dream and social change.	◆ I can identify key symbols (e.g., the green light, the valley of ashes) and explain their significance. ◆ I can explain how the narrator's point of view shapes the story. ◆ I can discuss how the setting reflects broader social and historical themes. ◆ I can support my ideas with evidence from the text.
Math	I am learning to understand and apply Pythagoras' theorem to solve problems involving right triangles, and to explain why the relationship between the sides holds true.	◆ I can identify the legs and hypotenuse in right triangles. ◆ I can use the theorem to calculate missing side lengths in different problems. ◆ I can explain or demonstrate why the theorem is true (e.g., through geometric proof or visual reasoning). ◆ I can solve real-world problems that involve right triangles using Pythagoras' theorem.

(Continued)

TABLE 3.1 (Continued)

Content Area	Example Learning Intention	Example of Success Criteria
Science	I am learning how the parts of a system (like a cell or an ecosystem) interact to support the whole, so I can explain how change affects function.	♦ I can identify the key parts/components of the system (e.g., organelles in a cell, species in an ecosystem). ♦ I can describe the role each part plays in maintaining the overall system's function. ♦ I can explain how the parts interact with each other to keep the system stable or functioning properly. ♦ I can analyze examples of changes or disruptions to one or more parts of the system. ♦ I can predict or explain how such changes affect the system's overall function or balance. ♦ I can use evidence from observations, experiments, or models to support my explanations.
History	I am learning to analyze the complex causes of the Civil War by evaluating multiple perspectives and understanding how economic, political, and social factors interacted.	♦ I can identify key economic, political, and social causes of the Civil War from multiple sources. ♦ I can compare and contrast perspectives from different groups (e.g., abolitionists, Southern states, enslaved people). ♦ I can explain how these factors interacted and contributed to escalating tensions before the war. ♦ I can use evidence from primary and secondary sources to support my analysis of causes. ♦ I can evaluate the reliability and bias of sources to understand differing viewpoints. ♦ I can construct a coherent written or oral explanation that integrates multiple causes and perspectives.

Examples of content-rich learning objectives across disciplines, showing aligned learning intentions and success criteria to guide student understanding and assessment.

core cognitive principles. Notice how each example emphasizes coherence (with ideas that build toward deeper conceptual understanding), transfer (through tasks that mirror authentic disciplinary thinking), metacognition (by making the learning process transparent and purposeful), and schema development (as skills are taught in rich, connected contexts). Each example is grounded in meaningful content and curricular goals, helping learners connect new knowledge to what they already know.

Well-crafted learning intentions don't need to be confined to a single class period. In fact, both cognitive science and effective instructional design suggest that many learning intentions span multiple lessons—or even an entire unit—depending on the complexity of the concept or skill. Deep understanding isn't just about spending time on a topic; it requires repeated, scaffolded practice, opportunities for reflection, and intentional revisiting to move from surface familiarity to true mastery (Bransford et al., 2000). For example, analyzing the themes in *The Great Gatsby* or understanding and applying the Pythagorean theorem are rarely achieved in a single lesson. When learning intentions are designed to anchor thinking over time—and paired with clear success criteria—they guide students toward meaningful goals, helping them see how each activity connects to larger concepts rather than just what they are doing in the moment. When students revisit a learning intention across multiple lessons, they're more likely to monitor their own progress, strengthening self-awareness and reflective thinking. Like a well-drawn map, effective learning intentions orient both teachers and students in the landscape of knowledge. They mark the destination, chart the terrain, and make visible the pathways between concepts. When the map is fragmented, learners lose their bearings—moving aimlessly between disconnected tasks.

Many schools frame success criteria at the lesson level to promote standards alignment, but this can unintentionally fragment learning. Research supports embedding success criteria within longer progressions and rich contexts (Ambrose et al., 2010; Bransford et al., 2000; National Research Council, 2012; Willingham, 2009). Professional learning and leadership can shift mindsets toward using success criteria as tools for coherence and meaningful skill development, enabling teachers to balance clarity with depth. Clear learning intentions align with principles of explicit instruction by making goals transparent and reducing ambiguity (Rosenshine, 2012). They also help manage cognitive load by minimizing distractions and clarifying expectations for novice learners (Sweller, 1988). Well-articulated intentions set the stage for teachers to model thinking processes, provide students with clear targets for success, and enable specific, aligned feedback. When students understand the why behind a task, they can monitor their learning and transfer skills to new contexts more effectively.

Not all clarity is equal. Hattie and Donoghue (2016) distinguish between surface, deep, and transfer phases of learning—each requiring different kinds of clarity. Early in a unit, clarity helps students grasp surface concepts and vocabulary. As understanding deepens, clarity should evolve to highlight relationships, principles, and transfer possibilities. When learning intentions remain static at the surface level, they fail to guide students toward flexible expertise. Without clear learning intentions, accurately assessing learning or providing actionable feedback becomes difficult. When teachers and students don't share a vision of what mastery looks like, learning can become fragmented—especially for students who are struggling, multilingual learners, or students from historically marginalized groups. These students benefit most from explicit guidance and structured support, making clear learning intentions a matter of both instructional effectiveness and educational equity. Anchored in a rich, coherent curriculum, learning goals enable scaffolding that guides all learners toward the same rigorous expectations—without lowering or altering the goals themselves

(Rosenshine, 2012; Willingham, 2009). Shared clarity helps students plan their approach, monitor progress, and engage in self-assessment, fostering essential aspects of self-regulated learning (Schunk et al., 2008; Zimmerman, 2002).

The Larger Impact of Relying Too Heavily on Standards-Based Learning Intention

Standards-based grading (SBG), while designed to clarify expectations and promote equity, can inadvertently undermine transfer learning when it fragments knowledge into isolated skills. From a cognitive-science perspective, meaningful learning depends on building integrated mental models—not practicing checklist-style standards divorced from context (Bransford et al., 2000; Chi et al., 1981). Poorly designed learning intentions, paired with atomized grading, can misrepresent what students truly know. A student may appear not to have mastered a standard due to unfamiliar content, vocabulary, or context rather than a true skill deficit. When educators treat superficial checklist items as diagnostic indicators, they risk mistaking a performance error for a conceptual gap—leading to misguided instructional decisions.

Narrowly derived learning intentions often encourage a standards-based approach to formative assessment that fragments knowledge rather than clarifying it. While SBG aims to make assessment transparent and aligned with outcomes, it frequently reduces complex disciplinary knowledge to isolated micro-skills (e.g., "can identify the theme of a passage"). This approach assumes that mastering atomized tasks equals deep understanding. Yet cognitive science shows the opposite: learning is recursive, cumulative, and context-dependent (Chi et al., 1988). True understanding emerges when knowledge is richly interconnected and embedded in meaningful contexts—conditions undermined by disjointed, surface-level indicators (Bransford et al., 2000).

These snapshot-style assessments often capture momentary fluctuations in performance rather than genuine learning gains. A student may appear to "fail" to make an inference not because they lack inference skills but because the passage introduces unfamiliar vocabulary or cultural references that overload working memory (Sweller, 1988) or concepts for which the student lacks sufficient background knowledge. Misinterpreting such performance errors as conceptual deficiencies can lead to remediation focused on isolated skills rather than the background knowledge needed to support them.

These misdiagnoses are especially harmful for multilingual learners and neurodiverse students and those from historically marginalized backgrounds. Their struggles often stem not from cognitive deficits but from gaps in cultural capital or prior exposure (Cuba & Tefera, 2024; Orionzi, 2025). Treating each standard as a diagnostic indicator risks over-pathologizing students for knowledge-based or context-dependent challenges. This is why well-crafted, coherent learning intentions are essential: they ensure that assessment reflects meaningful understanding, supports transfer, and provides a shared vision of mastery for all learners.

Additionally, the design of many micro-assessments often violates principles of effective retrieval practice. As Willingham (2009) and Zimmerman (2002) argue, durable learning depends on appropriately spaced, varied, and context-rich opportunities to recall and apply knowledge. Assessments that are too frequent, overly narrow, or contextually shallow can (1) capture noise rather than meaningful learning signals, (2) heighten test anxiety or cognitive distractibility, and (3) inadvertently incentivize teaching to the test rather than fostering transfer. Compounding the problem, rubrics often emphasize superficial "look-fors" that reward compliance, pattern recognition, or rote memorization—rather than conceptual depth, flexibility, or disciplinary thinking.

For learning intentions to meaningfully support instruction, they must be thoughtfully crafted—not merely derived from standards. Anchored in a rich, coherent curriculum, well-designed success criteria can also be sequenced or scaffolded, gradually supporting students from basic recognition of a concept to deeper analysis, synthesis, and application across contexts. When intentions are fragmented, disconnected from context, or misaligned with how learning actually works, they risk distorting both instruction and assessment—ultimately impeding the very progress they aim to measure. Ultimately, clarity is not about simplifying learning—it's about making complexity navigable. When learning intentions and success criteria mirror how knowledge is structured in the mind, they transform instruction from a checklist of standards into a map for meaning-making. In this sense, clarity is both a cognitive and moral act: it empowers all learners to see where they are, where they're going, and how to get there.

References

Ambrose, S. A., Bridges, M., DiPietro, M., Lovett, M. C., & Norman, M. K. (2010). *How learning works: Seven research-based principles for smart teaching*. Jossey-Bass.

Bransford, J. D., Brown, A. L., & Cocking, R. R. (Eds.) (2000). *How people learn: Brain, mind, experience, and school* (Expanded ed.). National Academy Press.

Brookhart, S. M. (2008). *How to give effective feedback to your students*. ASCD.

Chi, M. T. H., Feltovich, P. J., & Glaser, R. (1981). Categorization and representation of physics problems by experts and novices. *Cognitive Science*, 5(2), 121–152. https://doi.org/10.1207/s15516709cog0502_2

Chi, M. T. H., Glaser, R., & Farr, M. J. (1988). *The nature of expertise*. Lawrence Erlbaum Associates, Inc.

Clarke, S. (2001). *Unlocking formative assessment: Practical strategies for enhancing pupils' learning in the primary classroom*. Hodder & Stoughton.

Clarke, S. (2014). *Outstanding formative assessment: Culture and practice*. Hodder Education.

Cuba, M. J., & Tefera, A. A. (2024). Contextualizing multilingual learner disproportionality in special education: A mixed-methods approach. *Teachers College Record: The Voice of Scholarship in Education, 126*(1), 29–60. https://doi.org/10.1177/01614681241233877

Detterman, D. K. (1993). The case for the prosecution: Transfer as an epiphenomenon. In D. K. Detterman & R. J. Sternberg (Eds.), *Transfer on trial: Intelligence, cognition, and instruction* (pp. 1–24). Ablex.

Fleming, S. M., & Lau, H. C. (2014). How to measure metacognition. *Frontiers in Human Neuroscience, 8*, 443. https://doi.org/10.3389/fnhum.2014.00443

Gick, M. L., & Holyoak, K. J. (1983). Schema induction and analogical transfer. *Cognitive Psychology, 15*(1), 1–38. https://doi.org/10.1016/0010-0285(83)90002-6

Hattie, J. (2009). *Visible learning: A synthesis of over 800 meta analyses relating to achievement*. Routledge.

Hattie, J. (2023). *Visible learning: The sequel: A synthesis of over 2,100 meta-analyses relating to achievement*. Routledge.

Hattie, J. A. C., & Donoghue, G. M. (2016). Learning strategies: A synthesis and conceptual model. *npj Science of Learning, 1*(1). https://doi.org/10.1038/npjscilearn.2016.13

Hattie, J., & Timperley, H. (2007). The power of feedback. *Review of Educational Research, 77*(1), 81–112. https://doi.org/10.3102/003465430298487

Hodge, E., & Benko, S. L. (2014). A "common" vision of instruction? An analysis of English/language arts professional development materials related to the common Core state standards. *English Teaching: Practice and Critique, 13*(1), 169–196.

Marzano, R. J., Pickering, D. J., & Pollock, J. E. (2001). *Classroom instruction that works: Research-based strategies for increasing student achievement*. ASCD.

National Research Council. (2012). *A framework for K-12 science education: Practices, crosscutting concepts, and Core ideas*. National Academies Press. https://doi.org/10.17226/13165

Orionzi, B. (2025). Neurodiversity in children from historically marginalized communities. *Pediatric Annals, 54*(8), e257–e260. https://doi.org/10.3928/19382359-20250612-05

Posner, M. I., & Rothbart, M. K. (2007). *Educating the human brain*. American Psychological Association. https://psycnet.apa.org/doi/10.1037/11519-000

Rosenshine, B. (2012). Principles of instruction: Research-based strategies that all teachers should know. *American Educator, 36*(1), 12–19.

Schunk, D. H., Pintrich, P. R., & Meece, J. L. (2008). *Motivation in education: Theory, research, and applications* (3rd ed.). Pearson Merrill Prentice Hall.

Sweller, J. (1988). Cognitive load during problem solving: Effects on learning. *Cognitive Science, 12*(2), 257–285.

Sweller, J. (2011). Cognitive load theory. *Psychology of Learning and Motivation, 55*, 37–76. https://doi.org/10.1016/B978-0-12-387691-1.00002-8

Wiggins, G., & McTighe, J. (2005). *Understanding by design* (Expanded 2nd ed.). Alexandria, VA: ASCD.

Wiliam, D. (2011). *Embedded formative assessment*. Solution Tree Press.

Wiliam, D., & Black, P. (1998). Inside the black box: Raising standards through classroom assessment. *Phi Delta Kappan, 80*(2), 139–148.

Willingham, D. T. (2009). *Why don't students like school? A cognitive scientist answers questions about how the mind works and what it means for the classroom*. Jossey-Bass.

Zimmerman, B. J. (2002). Becoming a self-regulated learner: An overview. *Theory Into Practice, 41*(2), 64–70. https://doi.org/10.1207/s15430421tip4102_2

4

Teacher Clarity and Credibility

Among the hundreds of influences studied in education, few are as foundational as teacher clarity and credibility—the degree to which students understand what they are learning and believe their teacher is trustworthy, competent, and invested in their success. Teacher clarity is one of the highest-impact strategies used to improve student understanding, retention, and performance. Research consistently shows that students benefit when they know what they are learning, why it matters, and how to succeed (Hattie, 2009). Similarly, teacher credibility is a powerful, evidence-based construct in education that refers to the extent to which students believe their teacher is trustworthy, competent, caring, and passionate. These perceptions directly shape how students attend, engage, and learn. According to John Hattie's research, teacher clarity (0.75) and teacher credibility (0.90) are two of the highest-impact strategies on teaching and learning (Hattie, 2009). These are well supported by cognitive science when we consider how (1) clarity helps reduce extraneous load and helps student organize knowledge through schema and dual coding, while building metacognition and self-regulation, and (2) credibility ensures that we gain attention by trust and relevance. Interestingly, credibility is built, not assumed; it is earned through consistency, competence, caring, and passion—all of which are observable signals that students use to determine whether to invest their attention and cognitive effort (Bandura, 1986; Hattie, 2009; McCroskey, 2000; Ryan & Deci, 2000; Sweller, 1988). Actually, clarity and credibility are deeply interconnected—and cognitive science shows that clarity is one of the most powerful ways that a teacher *builds credibility*.

Students judge credibility in part by how well a teacher seems to understand and explain content. When teachers present ideas logically, provide clear goals, and scaffold tasks well, students perceive them as knowledgeable and well prepared. McCroskey and Teven (1999) illustrate competence as one of the three key factors defining teacher credibility. Students feel more secure when instruction is consistent and transparent. When a teacher explains what, why, and how every day, students learn they can count on the teacher to guide their learning effectively. Confusing or disorganized instruction, by contrast, erodes trust and increases anxiety (Hattie, 2009; Meyer & Turner, 2007; Ryan & Deci, 2000). Additionally, clarity supports fairness and believability. Students are more likely to perceive a teacher as fair and credible when (1) expectations are explicit, (2) success criteria are clear, and (3) feedback is tied directly to communicated learning goals (Black & Wiliam, 2010; Brookhart, 2017; McCroskey, 1997). Finally, clarity enhances teacher presence. Clear teachers command attention and convey confidence, strengthening their credibility (Bandura, 1986; Hamre & Pianta, 2006; Marzano, Marzano, & Pickering, 2003).

In some pedagogical approaches, credibility is seen less as teacher expertise communicated through clarity and more as facilitation skill or the teacher's ability to co-construct knowledge with students. Ambiguity undermines perceived credibility, which depends heavily on clear, consistent communication

(Hattie, 2009; McCroskey, 1997). Clear learning goals and success criteria foster trust in assessment and teacher fairness, where lack of transparency reduces student motivation and trust (Black & Wiliam, 2010; Brookhart, 2017). Learners model and follow credible authority figures; when teacher roles blur, their perceived authority weakens, which in turn impacts student motivation and engagement (Bandura, 1986; Marzano et al., 2003). Furthermore, when teachers lack clarity, feedback is often delayed, and this reduces trust in teacher competence (Hattie & Timperley, 2007; Rosenshine, 2012).

How Student-Centered Approaches Devalue Teacher Clarity and Undermine Credibility

Student-centered approaches encourage students to take charge of their learning, which often means that teachers step back from delivering clear, direct explanations. This can lead to less structured, less explicit communication of learning goals, success criteria, and steps to mastery. When teachers offer less clear guidance, students may become confused or uncertain about expectations which can reduce perceptions of the teacher as a clear and competent expert. Similarly, when the teacher role is shifted from expert to facilitator, teacher authority, expertise, and clarity are reduced, leading to ambiguity and confusing expectations (Biesta, 2010; McLeskey & Waldron, 2011). Again, this impacts assessments. Student-centered learning often relies on open-ended tasks, projects, or inquiry, which can make success criteria less explicit—and when success criteria are unclear, feedback is harder to target and act upon (Brookhart, 2013, 2017; Wiliam & Thompson, 2008). Crucially, cognitive science distinguishes between guided and unguided inquiry. Unguided inquiry—where students are expected to discover complex concepts independently—often fails to support deep learning, especially for novices (Hattie, 2009; Kirschner et al., 2006; Sweller, 1988).

Even when students appear engaged in such tasks, they may not be thinking deeply or productively. Without structured support, inquiry learning can inadvertently increase cognitive load and exacerbate achievement gaps. Research consistently shows that open-ended, constructivist environments are most effective when paired with direct instruction and explicit scaffolding to ensure that all students can access and build conceptual understanding. But timing matters: if students lack clarity on the learning goals, they won't get much out of discovery or inquiry-based activities.

In classrooms where a teacher has clarity and credibility, the following practices are usually in place:

1. Learning objectives and success criteria are posted, referred to, and explained (i.e., internalized by students).
2. Lessons follow a clear sequence—review, input, guided practice, feedback, check for understanding, and independent practice. That final step is critical: independent practice shows whether students can apply their learning on their own and reveals the depth of their understanding.
3. Verbal directions are concise, repeated visually, and clarified as needed.
4. Concepts are broken into chunks; the teacher uses examples, non-examples, and models and checks for understanding.
5. Feedback is immediate, specific, and actionable; students know where they stand and how to improve.
6. Teacher asks both low- and high-level questions, uses cold calling strategically (not as a "gotcha"), and follows up with appropriate scaffolds.
7. The teacher is clear, fair, and consistent; redirects are calm and predictable—not personal or reactive.
8. Students feel safe to ask questions because the teacher responds respectfully and helps them think through misunderstandings.

9. The teacher is calm, warm, and passionate about content and smiles, uses names, and listens attentively.
10. There's mutual respect; students engage because they trust the teacher and see the value in the work.

Throughout each of the steps above, the teacher is constantly formatively assessing and adjusting instruction, through checks for understanding. In a classroom where teachers have clarity and credibility, lectures are interactive, with visuals and guided notes; modeled annotation and writing tasks; exit tickets with feedback returned the next day; whole-class discussions with cold calling and scaffolding; and quick teaching at the start of the next class based on misunderstandings. You will also see the teacher making quite a few adjustments during instruction, after checks for understanding, to meet the needs of students in real time (i.e., providing additional modeling, cues and prompts, etc.). Teachers who know the impact of clarity value clear instructional explanations and expectations for success and have logical lesson structure and transitions. Coherence in lesson design builds teacher credibility because it signals to students that the teacher is competent, intentional, and trustworthy—and curriculum is the foundation that supports this coherence. A strong curriculum gives teachers clear learning goals, vetted materials, and structured sequences, allowing them to focus on delivering the content well, *not* improvising. It also provides the vertical alignment of concepts helping teachers build lessons that connect yesterday's learning to today's. Consistently, research supports that teachers working from strong curricula are more likely to implement effective instructional practices while maintaining instructional consistency (Steiner, 2017).

Addressing the Curricula

While clarity and credibility begin at the classroom level, they are sustained—or undermined—by the curriculum that frames what and how teachers teach. When the curriculum is coherent and knowledge-rich, students experience instruction that feels purposeful, connected, and trustworthy. When it is fragmented or overloaded, teacher explanations can seem inconsistent or confusing—undermining both clarity and credibility. Reviews of commercial textbooks and curriculum materials consistently reveal several shortcomings. First, many lack instructional guidance that aligns with cognitive science principles. Second, topics are often presented in a fragmented manner, with superficial repetition rather than deep, cumulative coverage. Third, there is an excessive emphasis on engaging activities at the expense of developing cumulative knowledge. Additionally, most commercial and open-source curricula tend to be overpacked, assuming ideal conditions within the school day. When instructional time is constrained, pacing inevitably suffers (Schmidt et al., 2005). This tension between depth and coverage frequently results in an emphasis on moving forward to maintain pace, even when students have not yet mastered essential concepts (Wiggins & McTighe, 2005). When teachers are forced to rush content or pivot prematurely, students often perceive gaps in logic or coherence. Even strong explanations can lose credibility when learners sense that understanding is being sacrificed for coverage. Likewise, the strongest instructional materials fail to produce desired outcomes if teachers cannot implement them effectively in real classroom settings (Steiner, 2017). Rich curricula often require teachers to orchestrate complex tasks, such as multi-day investigations, collaborative problem-solving, or blended learning incorporating technology. Successfully managing these complex tasks demands significant preparation and instructional skill.

Curricula that are coherent, knowledge-building, and informed by teacher expertise tend to perform better. Such curricula prioritize content knowledge as the foundation upon which reading, writing, and critical thinking skills are built (Hirsch, 2016; Willingham, 2006). They are intentionally designed to reflect how students learn most effectively, incorporating evidence-based strategies, including retrieval practice, spaced repetition, and worked examples.

Furthermore, these curricula provide sufficient flexibility for teachers to exercise professional judgment and adapt to student needs without compromising overall coherence or progression. When curricula are aligned with cognitive science principles regarding learning and memory, they consistently outperform more superficial, commercially produced alternatives. Involving teachers in the curriculum design process yields materials that are more relevant to classroom realities and better aligned with student needs and local pacing constraints and engender greater teacher investment through a clearer understanding of the rationale behind the content.

While challenges related to time, professional development, and systemic trust often impede the development and implementation of such curricula, these obstacles are not insurmountable. It is imperative that school districts prioritize providing teachers with protected time for deliberate planning, vertical alignment, and research-based curriculum decision-making to ensure effective and equitable instruction. Table 4.1 provides a framework for designing cognitively aligned pacing in an ELA classroom.

Many teachers and district leaders are trained to start with the standard, break it into subskills, and then create lessons targeting just that skill (i.e., determine theme). When standards are treated as isolated skills rather than outcomes of rich content,

TABLE 4.1 Step-by-Step Framework for a Cognitively Aligned Semester Pacing in ELA

Steps	Guiding Questions	Why It Matters
Step 1: Clarify Core Understandings and End Goals	What themes, content knowledge, and text structures do we want students to deeply understand by the end of the semester? What end-of-semester performance tasks or writing should students be able to produce? What big ideas will unify the semester?	Coherent knowledge builds schema. Students retain more when ideas are logically connected (Hirsch, 2016; Willingham, 2006).

(Continued)

TABLE 4.1 (Continued)

Steps	Guiding Questions	Why It Matters
Step 2: Select & Sequence Core Texts Intentionally	Choose anchor texts (novels, plays, essays) that support the semester's central ideas. Layer in short texts (poems, speeches, articles) that build or challenge prior texts. Map out how texts will increase in complexity over time. *Consider*: Are texts ordered to help build knowledge and vocabulary cumulatively? Are different genres and voices represented to promote literacy transfer?	Building knowledge across domains (i.e., civil rights rhetoric) makes reading more efficient and deeper (Wexler, 2019)
Step 3: Map Key Knowledge, Vocabulary & Concepts	Identify tiered vocabulary for each unit (Tier 2 academic and Tier 3 domain-specific). Articulate the literary, rhetorical, and grammatical concepts students must revisit. Develop a vertical map of ideas (i.e., how "theme" builds from short stories to full novels to literary arguments)	Students cannot analyze what they do not understand. Vocabulary and content knowledge enable high-order thinking (Beck et al., 2002; Marzano, 2004)
Step 4: Create a Pacing Map with Spacing & Retrieval in Mind	Interleave concepts (revisit tone, syntax or characterization across units) Study weekly retrieval practice (warm-ups connected to prior day's/weeks'/months' learning), quizzes, short responses recalling prior texts Build in spiral review before each major assessment Leave space for adjustment weeks or re-teaching	Retrieval and spacing improves retention and transfer (Roediger & Butler, 2011; Rohrer et al., 2015)
Step 5: Align Assessments to Knowledge & Transfer, *NOT Just Skills*	Design performance tasks that require application of cumulative knowledge (i.e., synthesis essay on voice and justice). Use checkpoints that require retrieval of earlier content (i.e., refer to a text from September in December argument). Incorporate open-ended formative assessments (i.e., low-stakes essays, discussion protocols, exit tickets).	Deep understanding shows through transfer, not isolated skills. Backward design keeps learning meaningful (Wiggins & McTighe, 2005)

(Continued)

TABLE 4.1 (Continued)

Steps	Guiding Questions	Why It Matters
Step 6: Plan for Instructional Routines that Support Learning	Embed routines like: Warm-ups, Vocabulary notebooks, annotation protocols, retrieval lessons & guided practice, collaborative analysis & daily reading & writing	These routines create predictability and reduce cognitive load (Clark et al., 2012; Rosenshine, 2012).

Step-by-step framework for cognitively aligned semester pacing in ELA, including guiding questions and rationale for each step to support knowledge building, retrieval, and transfer.

instruction becomes superficial (Hirsch, 2016; Willingham, 2006). Standards often assume that knowledge is in place—particularly in reading. High-leverage skills like evaluating, comparing and contrasting, determining theme or author's purpose, and constructing arguments without foundational knowledge will prove challenging to students because they can't apply the skill to something they don't fully understand (Hirsch, 2016; Recht & Leslie, 1988; Schmidt et al., 2005; TNTP, 2018; Willingham, 2006). This principle holds across all academic disciplines. In math, science, history, and even the arts, standards assume prior knowledge and conceptual foundations (Chi et al., 1981; Krajcik & Blumenfeld, 2006; Steiner, 2017; Sweller et al., 2011; Willingham, 2018; Wineburg, 1991). Additionally, we must look at standards as the framing of what students should be able to *do*—not a curriculum to teach. To build skill, students need a rich knowledge base to think with; when standards are embedded in content-rich curricula, students learn skills in authentic contexts (Steiner, 2017).

This approach is a difficult sell for districts required to administer standards-based assessments. Many districts face intense pressure to boost test scores quickly, which leads to over-reliance on test-aligned subskill practice and skills-based instruction (TNTP, 2018; Wexler, 2019). There is also still a foundational misunderstanding of the standards, from teachers to district leaders that results in fragmented instruction (Hirsch, 2016).

Commercial curricula are marketed around standards alignment, not coherence or knowledge building, and districts purchase these programs thinking they are rigorous because they match the standards documents. Because many teachers and instructional leaders have not been exposed to the power behind cognitive science research, professional learning often emphasizes engagement strategies rather than evidence-based approaches to how students learn.

Yet there is strong, well-documented evidence showing that schools using knowledge-building curricula—where standards are not the sole starting point—still outperform on standardized assessments. In a landmark randomized controlled trial, the University of Virginia conducted a comparison between students admitted via lottery to Core Knowledge–based charter schools versus applicants who were not admitted. From grades 3–6, treatment groups scored 16 percentile points higher on reading, translating to roughly 0.47 standard deviations (SD). Science improvements were around 0.30 SD, and math gains approached 0.16 SD (though not always statistically significant). Notably, these gains were enough to eliminate income-related achievement gaps in reading (Grissmer et al., 2023). In Louisiana, statewide implementation of knowledge-rich ELA curricula—such as the Core Knowledge Language Arts (CKLA) program and Louisiana Guidebooks—has been associated with notable gains in early literacy. According to the Louisiana Department of Education (2024), K–3 reading proficiency increased by 10 percentage points on the state's first universal literacy screener, reflecting the impact of systematic, content-based instruction on foundational reading outcomes.

Outside of the United States, in England, Schools Minister Nick Gibb championed reforms grounded in cognitive science and evidence-based practice from 2010 to 2023. Drawing on the work of scholars such as E.D. Hirsch, Daniel Willingham, and Barak Rosenshine, Gibb advanced a knowledge-rich curriculum that emphasized the role of long-term memory and domain knowledge as the foundation for higher-order thinking. His policies promoted explicit instruction, systematic phonics, deliberate practice, and teacher clarity, challenging decades of student-led or discovery-based approaches.

Rooted in cognitive load theory and research on how the brain learns, Gibb's reforms sought to ensure that students first master essential knowledge and skills before engaging in complex inquiry or problem-solving. Supporters view this shift as a transformative alignment of curriculum, pedagogy, and assessment with how learning actually occurs, while critics caution that it risks narrowing creativity and undervaluing inquiry if implemented too rigidly (Australian Education Research Organisation, n.d.; de Jong, 2024; NSW Education, 2017). Nonetheless, Gibb's influence has reshaped teacher training, curriculum design, and classroom practice across England—making cognitive science a central driver of educational policy and classroom reform. Since the introduction of Gibb's cognitive science–informed reforms, England has seen measurable gains in both literacy and mathematics. The Phonics Screening Check, introduced in 2012, led to a dramatic rise in early reading proficiency, with the proportion of Year 1 pupils meeting the expected standard climbing from 58% in 2012 to over 80% by 2019, and significant catch-up among disadvantaged students (Department of Education, 2019). These gains carried through to later stages: by 2015, roughly 80% of primary pupils achieved the expected standard in reading, writing, and math, compared with 62% in 2009 (Department of Education, 2022). International assessments show similar upward trends. England achieved its highest-ever reading score in the 2016 PIRLS (Progress in International Reading Literacy Study) study and ranked fourth globally in 2023, while PISA (Programme for International Student Assessment) results reveal steady improvement in mathematics, moving from 27th place in 2009 to 11th in 2022 (Department for Education, 2023; Organisation for Economic Co-operation and Development [OECD], 2023). Recent Key Stage 2 data also show continued progress, with 73%

of students meeting expected standards in math and 71% in writing in 2023 (Department of Education, 2023). Together, these outcomes suggest that the shift toward a knowledge-rich curriculum, explicit instruction, and systematic phonics—grounded in cognitive science—has strengthened foundational literacy and numeracy across England's schools.

Taken together, these findings suggest a promising direction for district leaders in the United States who are reconsidering how curriculum sequences are designed, even as the evidence may not yet warrant large-scale, wholesale shifts. Districts don't widely adopt knowledge-rich approaches not because they don't work but because the system isn't designed to support them. Shifting the focus from covering standards to building knowledge for understanding requires changes in mindset, policy, training, and leadership priorities. Many teachers, under pressure to align with standards and district expectations, genuinely believe they are providing the best instruction. Because the system presents these mandates as authoritative, teachers often assume that compliance with standards equates to effective teaching. However, without exposure to cognitive science principles and research on how students learn, even well-intentioned instruction can become fragmented, superficial, and less credible in the eyes of learners. Ultimately, teachers earn credibility not only through their delivery but through the coherence and effectiveness of the learning experiences they design. When instruction aligns with cognitive science, students perceive their teachers as competent guides who make learning make sense.

Recognizing the Secondary Gap

While great gains have been made in this area in both the United States and the UK, these trends do not always carry over into secondary education. One of the key challenges in secondary education is ensuring that students can transfer the foundational knowledge and skills gained in primary school to more complex tasks and new contexts. Gibb's reforms have strengthened this foundation through explicit instruction, scaffolding, and mastery of core content—reducing cognitive load and freeing working memory for higher-order thinking. However, mastery alone does not guarantee transfer. Students often struggle to apply arithmetic to real-world problems, or reading fluency to critical analysis of complex texts, without deliberate opportunities to practice and extend their skills. Additionally, retention of knowledge over time is essential for transfer; without spaced practice, review, and application in secondary contexts, early gains risk becoming context-dependent. To fully capitalize on primary-level improvements, secondary instruction must provide structured challenges, interdisciplinary applications, and consistent reinforcement, ensuring that students not only retain what they have learned but also can apply it flexibly and effectively across subjects.

Teacher Mindsets

Another factor impacting teacher credibility and clarity is a fixed mindset about student ability. This can not only undermine teacher credibility but also significantly affect the quality of the learning opportunities available to students. Teacher credibility is directly impacted by a teacher's care in student learning, their knowledge of the content, and their belief that students can succeed (Hattie, 2012; Rosenthal & Jacobson, 1968). Students sense low expectations, even if they are never stated outright (Rubie-Davies, 2006). The teacher may offer less feedback or less rigorous work, or "leveled" texts, or packets that are "differentiated" to "be on the student's instructional level." Teacher expectations are a key influence on student achievement—students often rise or fall to match their teacher's belief in them (Hattie & Clarke, 2019). Students perceive high expectations when a teacher engages them in challenging tasks with scaffolding and feedback and provides affirming messages of high standards and belief in students' ability to meet them, equitable participation in classroom activities, cold calling, and consistent rigor across all groups of students.

While elements like novelty or student choice can enhance engagement, studies suggest that clear expectations, purposeful work, and meaningful feedback have a deeper and more sustained impact on student motivation and achievement (Eccles & Wigfield, 2002; Hattie, 2012). While many classrooms employ strategies such as choice boards, gamification, technology-rich projects, and interest surveys to boost engagement, these approaches often assume that motivation hinges primarily on personal interest or external novelty. However, motivation is complex and shaped by students' beliefs about their capabilities, their role in learning, and the value they attach to the task (Eccles & Wigfield, 2002). Interest represents only one dimension of task value; other critical components include attainment value, utility value, and cost—or the perceived effort and risk involved. Without a sense of efficacy and clear meaning, even enjoyable tasks may fail to sustain student effort. Moreover, research shows that providing students with challenging, constructive feedback significantly enhances motivation to revise and persist, particularly for those who might otherwise disengage (Yeager et al., 2014). Fostering motivation, therefore, requires helping students understand how tasks connect to their learning goals and broader curriculum progression, reinforcing that effort produces improvement, and ensuring that they feel capable and supported throughout the process.

When we talk about motivation and engagement, we often invoke *student agency*—frequently equated with giving students control over their learning. Agency can indeed be empowering but only when learners possess the cognitive resources to make meaningful choices. Without sufficient background knowledge or guidance, too much autonomy can lead to confusion and cognitive overload (Kirschner et al., 2006). While agency correlates with higher performance, it is not the causal factor. Motivation and agency emerge when students understand their goals, believe they possess the knowledge and skills to reach them, and perceive that effort leads to success—that is, when clarity, competence, and perceived control are present (Bandura, 1997; Schunk & Zimmerman, 2006). In this sense, agency is best viewed not as the *starting point* of learning but as its *outcome*—a product of effective instruction that cultivates confidence, competence, and purpose.

Increasing Rigor—and Defining What That Means

Rigor is one of the most misunderstood and overused terms in education, often treated as a buzzword without a clear or consistent definition. However, research and cognitive science provide a more precise understanding: rigor means engaging students in challenging thinking that requires deep understanding and meaningful application of knowledge. Teacher clarity and credibility are central to achieving this balance. When teachers communicate expectations explicitly, structure lessons logically, and provide support for both foundational and complex skills, students perceive the teacher as competent, caring, and trustworthy. Clear instruction ensures that fluency becomes a tool for deeper reasoning rather than an end in itself, allowing students to tackle cognitively demanding tasks with confidence. In this way, rigor is not merely about difficulty—it is about designing learning experiences that are challenging, meaningful, and accessible, ultimately strengthening both student learning and teacher credibility.

Unfortunately, many teachers equate rigor with simply giving students more work, removing scaffolds or teacher-led instruction, increasing student choice or agency, or accelerating pacing. These approaches may have the illusion of rigor but often lack the cognitive depth needed to truly challenge students and promote meaningful learning. Common instructional frameworks like Bloom's Taxonomy and Webb's Depth of Knowledge

(DOK) are frequently misapplied in ways that contribute to this confusion. Bloom's Taxonomy categorizes types of thinking, from remembering to creating, but a "create" task can be surface-level if it lacks disciplinary knowledge, while a "remember" task may be rigorous if it is foundational for later complex applications. Webb's DOK focuses on the kind of thinking required (e.g., recall versus reasoning), the depth of understanding needed, and the complexity of the context in which content is applied. Importantly, DOK does not measure task difficulty based on wording, time, or perceived "hardness." Assigning a high DOK level does not guarantee intellectual rigor or challenge.

True rigor depends not only on *what* we ask students to do but on *when* we ask them to do it. Cognitive science emphasizes that students must first develop sufficient schema before they can engage in complex reasoning or creative application (Chi, 2009; Sweller, 1988). Rigor, therefore, should be sequenced intentionally: tasks should progress from guided practice toward independent transfer as fluency and understanding solidify (Hattie & Donoghue, 2016; Rosenshine, 2012). When teachers calibrate timing—introducing challenge at the moment when prior knowledge can support new learning—they move students through the "sweet spot" of desirable difficulty (Bjork & Bjork, 2011). In this sense, rigor is not a fixed level of difficulty but a dynamic balance between cognitive demand, support, and readiness. True rigor arises when learners integrate knowledge, apply reasoning, and sustain meaningful cognitive engagement.

Rigor matters because deep cognitive engagement promotes better transfer of learning, long-term retention, and real-world problem-solving (Bransford et al., 2000; Willingham, 2009). Yet rigor must also be equitable. When misunderstood as "harder" or "less guided" work, it often excludes rather than empowers learners. Effective rigor balances challenge with explicit instruction and strategic scaffolding, ensuring that all students can access complex thinking without cognitive overload (Rosenshine, 2012). Without this balance, rigor risks becoming a gatekeeping mechanism that widens opportunity gaps. Defining rigor as intellectually demanding, well-supported engagement with core disciplinary ideas allows teachers to promote both deep understanding and equity.

At the end of the day, rigorous thinking is not the automatic result of asking "rigorous questions." It emerges from intentionally designed instruction that builds a strong foundation of knowledge, creates meaningful and relevant tasks, and provides structured opportunities for students to explain, apply, and connect what they've learned—with appropriate support. Rigor is most effectively increased through the interplay of four key factors: the substance of the task, the cognitive demand it imposes, the requirement for justification and evidence, and the presence of scaffolding to ensure accessibility. The questions that educators should ask when designing for rigor are not simply about phrasing or format but about intellectual depth: Is there rich content to think about? Does the task require reasoning, synthesis, or transfer? Are students expected to support claims with evidence? And, crucially, are they supported in meeting these demands—or simply left to struggle on their own?

Rigor, then, is best defined by the quality of thinking that students must engage in—not by the verb in a question stem or a label affixed to an activity. Unfortunately, standardized testing often distorts our understanding of what constitutes a "rigorous" task, particularly in math and literacy. These assessments are designed to maximize efficiency, reliability, and comparability of scores and, as a result, tend to rely on decontextualized tasks, narrowly defined multiple-choice formats, and abstract, syntactically complex question wording. Research indicates that test items may appear challenging due to surface features like syntax or vocabulary yet fail to engage the higher-order thinking they purport to measure (Kendeou et al., 2012), reflecting a broader trend in standardized assessments to prioritize efficiency and comparability over cognitive depth.

In literacy, it is a common misconception that the structural or lexical complexity of a test item equates to genuine comprehension work. Tasks with high Lexile levels or dense vocabulary can easily be mistaken for rigorous reading, when, in fact, deep comprehension involves synthesizing ideas across texts, evaluating an author's claims, or inferring tone and intent on the basis of subtle textual evidence. Many so-called comprehension questions on standardized assessments more accurately measure test-taking strategies than actual understanding (Shanahan, 2018, 2023). The pattern is similarly evident in mathematics, where standardized tests tend to emphasize procedural fluency and computational accuracy over reasoning, problem-solving, and disciplinary thinking (Koretz, 2008). In response, instructional focus often narrows to the most frequently tested skills, leaving out higher-level conceptual content and richer problem-solving experiences (Blazar & Pollard, 2017).

This narrowing of focus leads to an illusion of proficiency: students may perform well on questions that emphasize speed or rote procedures but struggle when asked to engage in tasks that require conceptual reasoning, transfer, or application (Hiebert & Grouws, 2007). As Au (2007) argues, such test formats often disguise the absence of deep mathematical understanding, since success on narrowly defined tasks does not translate into broader thinking skills. Even multi-step word problems—often used to signal difficulty—may fail to demand true rigor if they merely replicate procedural steps in longer form (Wiliam, 2011). Authentic mathematical learning requires the integration of procedural fluency with conceptual understanding, a balance that is frequently undermined by test-driven instruction (National Mathematics Advisory Panel, 2008).

Superficial rigor, test-focused instruction, and misinterpretations of standards don't just affect learning outcomes. They also deeply affect teacher credibility in the eyes of students. Misaligned instruction undermines credibility, so if students perceive that the teacher is assigning busywork or disconnected drills, they're less likely to view that teacher as competent or caring (Hattie, 2012). When teachers do not truly stretch students or invite them to think deeply, it communicates that they have low expectations for their students, particularly adolescents (Ferguson, 2003). Adolescents are especially sensitive to whether instruction is meaningful, coherent, and challenging. They are expected to transfer foundational knowledge from primary school into new subjects and problem-solving contexts, and without carefully sequenced instruction, scaffolding, and application opportunities, even well-intentioned lessons can seem shallow. Ensuring rigor and credibility at this stage requires instruction that is deliberate, structured, and cognitively engaging.

To counteract this narrowing of focus, teachers can leverage writing as a powerful tool for cognitive engagement—an approach that also strengthens teacher credibility. In secondary classrooms, discipline-specific writing tasks require students to articulate reasoning, synthesize knowledge, and justify conclusions—supporting both transfer and retention. Writing tasks require students to organize their thinking, connect concepts, and make their reasoning explicit. When teachers provide clear instructions, model, and offer success criteria for these tasks, students perceive the teacher as competent, intentional, and trustworthy (Hattie, 2009; McCroskey, 2000). This effect is amplified when students receive targeted feedback on their reasoning. In mathematics, explaining the steps and logic behind a solution deepens both conceptual understanding and procedural fluency. In literacy and history, constructing written arguments compels students to integrate evidence, evaluate claims critically, and communicate insights clearly. By embedding frequent, discipline-specific writing opportunities with transparent guidance, teachers signal credibility while ensuring that students are synthesizing, reasoning, and demonstrating genuine understanding.

Sustaining Learning through Credible Teaching

By holding high expectations, scaffolding rigor, providing explicit modeling, maintaining consistency, guiding practice with checks for understanding, and delivering a coherent, knowledge-rich curriculum, teachers signal to students that they are competent and credible. When teachers also demonstrate passion, empathy, and responsiveness, they show that they understand and care about their students' needs while maintaining high expectations for learning. These teachers communicate that they believe in their students' ability to rise to challenges, and they prioritize learning in clear, intentional ways that are visible to students. In secondary classrooms, teacher credibility and clarity are particularly critical. To ensure that the gains achieved in elementary school carry over, secondary instruction must include strategic practices—such as scaffolding, explicit modeling, guided practice, and consistent feedback—that reinforce learning, support transfer, and sustain student engagement.

Ultimately, clarity and creativity are not opposing forces but complementary dimensions of meaningful learning. Cognitive science reminds us that the mind cannot think creatively about what it does not yet understand. When students possess well-organized knowledge and fluent foundational skills, they can engage in higher-order inquiry, transfer, and innovation with confidence. Far from stifling creativity, explicit instruction and structured practice establish the mental architecture that makes creative and critical thinking possible. The challenge for educators, then, is not to choose between clarity and curiosity but to design instruction that builds both—ensuring that knowledge serves as a springboard, not a ceiling, for imagination.

References

Au, W. (2007). High-stakes testing and curricular control: A qualitative metasynthesis. *Educational Researcher*, *36*(5), 258–267. https://doi.org/10.3102/0013189X07306523

Australian Education Research Organisation. (n.d.). *Mastery learning*. https://www.edresearch.edu.au/summaries-explainers/explainers/mastery-learning

Bandura, A. (1997). *Self-efficacy: The exercise of control*. W. H. Freeman.
Bandura, A., & National Inst of Mental Health. (1986). *Social foundations of thought and action: A social cognitive theory*. Prentice-Hall, Inc.
Beck, I. L., McKeown, M. G., & Kucan, L. (2002). *Bringing words to life: Robust vocabulary instruction*. Guilford Press.
Biesta, G. (2010). *Good education in an age of measurement: Ethics, politics, democracy*. Routledge.
Bjork, R. A., & Bjork, E. L. (2011). Making things hard on yourself, but in a good way: Creating desirable difficulties to enhance learning. In M. A. Gernsbacher, R. W. Pew, L. M. Hough, & J. R. Pomerantz (Eds.), *Psychology and the real world: Essays illustrating fundamental contributions to society* (pp. 56–64). Worth Publishers.
Black, P., & Wiliam, D. (2010). Inside the black box: Raising standards through classroom assessment. *Phi Delta Kappan, 92*(1), 81–90. https://doi.org/10.1177/003172171009200119
Blazar, D., & Pollard, C. (2017). Does test preparation mean low-quality instruction? *Educational Researcher, 46*(8), 420–433. https://doi.org/10.3102/0013189X17732753
Bransford, J. D., Brown, A. L., & Cocking, R. R. (Eds.) (2000). *How people learn: Brain, mind, experience, and school* (Expanded ed.). National Academy Press.
Brookhart, S. M. (2013). *How to give effective feedback to your students*. ASCD.
Brookhart, S. M. (2017). *How to give effective feedback to your students* (2nd ed.). ASCD.
Chi, M. T. H. (2009). Topics in active-constructive-interactive: A conceptual framework for differentiating learning activities. *Cognitive Science, 1*(1), 73–105. https://doi.org/10.1111/j.1756-8765.2008.01005.x
Chi, M. T. H., Feltovich, P. J., & Glaser, R. (1981). Categorization and representation of physics problems by experts and novices. *Cognitive Science, 5*(2), 121–152. https://doi.org/10.1207/s15516709cog0502_2
Clark, R. E., Kirschner, P. A., & Sweller, J. (2012). Putting students on the path to learning: The case for fully guided instruction. *American Educator, 36*(1), 6–11.
de Jong, T. (2024). Beyond inquiry or direct instruction: Pressing issues for researchers and practitioners. *Educational Research Review, 42*(2), 100611. https://doi.org/10.1016/j.edurev.2024.100623

Department for Education. (2019, September 26). *Free schools leading the way with top primary school results.* https://www.gov.uk/government/news/free-schools-leading-the-way-with-top-primary-school-results

Department for Education. (2022, December 10). *National curriculum assessments at key stage 2 in England, 2015 (revised).* https://assets.publishing.service.gov.uk/media/5a805284e5274a2e87db9269/SFR47_2015_text.pdf

Department for Education. (2023, May 16). *England moves to fourth in international rankings for reading.* https://www.gov.uk/government/news/england-moves-to-fourth-in-international-rankings-for-reading

Eccles, J. S., & Wigfield, A. (2002). Motivational beliefs, values, and goals. *Annual Review of Psychology, 53*(1), 109–132. https://doi.org/10.1146/annurev.psych.53.100901.135153

Ferguson, R. F. (2003). Teachers' perceptions and expectations and the Black–White test score gap. *Urban Education, 38*(4), 460–507. https://doi.org/10.1177/0042085903038004006

Grissmer, D., White, T., Buddin, R., Berends, M., Willingham, D., DeCoster, J., Duran, C., Hulleman, C., Murrah, W., & Evans, T. (2023). *A kindergarten lottery evaluation of Core knowledge charter schools: Should building general knowledge have a central role in educational and social science research and policy?*

Hamre, B. K., & Pianta, R. C. (2006). Student–teacher relationships. In G. G. Bear & K. M. Minke (Eds.), *Children's needs III: Development, prevention, and intervention* (pp. 59–71). National Association of School Psychologists.

Hattie, J. (2009). *Visible learning: A synthesis of over 800 meta analyses relating to achievement.* Routledge.

Hattie, J. (2012). *Visible learning for teachers: Maximizing impact on learning.* Routledge.

Hattie, J., & Clarke, S. (2019). *Visible learning: Feedback.* Routledge.

Hattie, J., & Donoghue, G. (2016). Learning strategies: A synthesis and conceptual model. *npj Science of Learning, 1*(1), 16013. https://doi.org/10.1038/npjscilearn.2016.13

Hattie, J., & Timperley, H. (2007). The power of feedback. *Review of Educational Research, 77*(1), 81–112. https://doi.org/10.3102/003465430298487

Hiebert, J., & Grouws, D. A. (2007). The effects of classroom mathematics teaching on students' learning. In F. K. Lester, Jr. (Ed.), *Second handbook of research on mathematics teaching and learning* (pp. 371–404). Information Age Publishing.

Hirsch, E. D. (2016). *Why knowledge matters: Reshaping the American curriculum*. Harvard Education Press.

Kendeou, P., Papadopoulos, T. C., & Spanoudis, G. (2012). Processing demands of reading comprehension tests in young readers. *Learning and Instruction*, *22*(5), 354–367. https://doi.org/10.1016/j.learninstruc.2012.02.001

Kirschner, P. A., Sweller, J., & Clark, R. E. (2006). Why minimal guidance during instruction does not work: An analysis of the failure of constructivist, discovery, problem-based, experiential, and inquiry-based teaching. *Educational Psychologist*, *41*(2), 75–86. https://doi.org/10.1207/s15326985ep4102_1

Koretz, D. (2008). *Measuring up: What educational testing really tells us*. Harvard University Press.

Krajcik, J. S., & Blumenfeld, P. C. (2006). Project-based learning. In R. K. Sawyer (Ed.), *The Cambridge handbook of the learning sciences* (pp. 317–334). Cambridge University Press.

Louisiana Department of Education. (2024, July 9). *Louisiana K-3 reading scores jump 10 percent on state's first universal literacy screener*. https://doe.louisiana.gov/about/newsroom/news-releases/release/2024/07/09/louisiana-k-3-reading-scores-jump-10-percent-on-state-s-first-universal-literacy-screener

Marzano, R. J. (2004). *Building background knowledge for academic achievement: Research on what works in schools*. ASCD.

Marzano, R. J., Marzano, J. S., & Pickering, D. J. (2003). *Classroom management that works: Research-based strategies for every teacher*. Alexandria, VA: Association for Supervision and Curriculum Development (ASCD).

McCroskey, J. C. (1997). Willingness to communicate, communication apprehension, and self-perceived communication competence: Conceptualizations and perspectives. In J. A. Daly, J. C. McCroskey, J. Ayres, T. Hopf, & D. M. Sonandre (Eds.), *Avoiding communication: Shyness, reticence, and communication apprehension* (2nd ed., pp. 21–34). Hampton Press.

McCroskey, J. C. (2000). *An introduction to rhetorical communication* (8th ed.). Allyn & Bacon.

McCroskey, J. C., & Teven, J. J. (1999). Goodwill: A reexamination of the construct and its measurement. *Communication Monographs, 66*(1), 90–103. https://doi.org/10.1080/03637759909376464

McLeskey, J., & Waldron, N. L. (2011). Educational programs for elementary students with learning disabilities: Can they be both effective and inclusive? *Learning Disabilities Research & Practice, 26*(1), 48–57. https://doi.org/10.1111/j.1540-5826.2010.00324.x

Meyer, D. K., & Turner, J. C. (2007). Scaffolding emotions in classrooms. In P. Schutz & R. Pekrun (Eds.), *Emotion in education* (pp. 243–258). Academic Press.

National Mathematics Advisory Panel. (2008). *Foundations for success: The final report of the National Mathematics Advisory Panel.* U.S. Department of Education.

NSW Department of Education. (2017). *Cognitive load theory: Research that teachers really need to understand.* Centre for Education Statistics and Evaluation (CESE).

Organisation for Economic Co-operation and Development. (2023). *PISA 2022 results (Volume I): Excellence and equity in education.* https://www.oecd.org/en/publications/pisa-2022-results-volume-i_53f23881-en.html

Recht, D. R., & Leslie, L. (1988). Effect of prior knowledge on reading comprehension. *Journal of Educational Psychology, 80*(4), 468–474. https://doi.org/10.1037/0022-0663.80.1.16

Roediger, H. L., & Butler, A. C. (2011). The critical role of retrieval practice in long-term retention. *Trends in Cognitive Sciences, 15*(1), 20–27. https://doi.org/10.1016/j.tics.2010.09.003

Rohrer, D., Dedrick, R. F., & Stershic, S. (2015). Interleaved practice improves mathematics learning. *Journal of Educational Psychology, 107*(3), 900–908. https://doi.org/10.1037/edu0000001

Rosenshine, B. (2012). Principles of instruction: Research-based strategies that all teachers should know. *American Educator, 36*(1), 12–19.

Rosenthal, R., & Jacobson, L. (1968). *Pygmalion in the classroom: Teacher expectation and pupils' intellectual development.* Holt, Rinehart & Winston.

Rubie-Davies, C. M. (2006). Teacher expectations and student self-perceptions: Exploring relationships. *British Journal of Educational Psychology*, *76*(3), 429–450.

Ryan, R. M., & Deci, E. L. (2000). Self-determination theory and the facilitation of intrinsic motivation, social development, and well-being. *American Psychologist*, *55*(1), 68–78. https://psycnet.apa.org/doi/10.1037/0003-066X.55.1.68

Schmidt, W. H., Wang, H. C., & McKnight, C. C. (2005). Curriculum coherence: An examination of US mathematics and science content standards from an international perspective. *Journal of Curriculum Studies*, *37*(5), 525–559. https://doi.org/10.1080/0022027042000294682

Schunk, D. H., & Zimmerman, B. J. (Eds.) (2006). *Self-regulated learning: Theory, research, and applications*. Mahwah, NJ: Lawrence Erlbaum Associates.

Shanahan, T. (2018). *Where questioning fits in comprehension instruction: Skills and strategies, part II*. Shanahan on Literacy.

Shanahan, T. (2023). *Knowledge or comprehension strategies — What should we teach?*. Shanahan on Literacy. https://www.shanahanonliteracy.com/blog/knowledge-or-comprehension-strategies-what-should-we-teach

Steiner, D. (2017). *High-quality curriculum implementation: Connecting what to teach with how to teach it*. National Institute for Excellence in Teaching.

Sweller, J. (1988). Cognitive load during problem solving: Effects on learning. *Cognitive Science*, *12*(2), 257–285.

Sweller, J., Ayres, P., & Kalyuga, S. (2011). *Cognitive load theory*. Springer. https://doi.org/10.1007/978-1-4419-8126-4

The New Teacher Project (TNTP). (2018). *The opportunity myth: What students can show us about how school is letting them down and how to fix it*. https://tntp.org/our-work

Wexler, J. (2019). *The knowledge gap: The hidden cause of America's broken education system—And how to fix it*. Avery.

Wiggins, G., & McTighe, J. (2005). *Understanding by design* (Expanded 2nd ed.). ASCD.

Wiliam, D. (2011). *Embedded formative assessment*. Solution Tree Press.

Wiliam, D., & Thompson, M. (2008). Integrating assessment with learning: What will it take to make it work? In C. A. Dwyer (Ed.), *The future of assessment: Shaping teaching and learning* (pp. 53–82). Routledge. https://doi.org/10.4324/9781315086545-3

Willingham, D. T. (2006). How knowledge helps: It speeds and strengthens reading comprehension, learning—And thinking. *American Educator, 30*(1), 30–37.

Willingham, D. T. (2009). *Why don't students like school? A cognitive scientist answers questions about how the mind works and what it means for the classroom.* Jossey-Bass.

Willingham, D. T. (2018). Unlocking the science of how kids think: A new proposal for reforming teacher education. *Education Next, 18*(3), 42–49.

Wineburg, S. S. (1991). Historical problem solving: A study of the cognitive processes used in the evaluation of documentary and pictorial evidence. *Journal of Educational Psychology, 83*(1), 73–87. https://psycnet.apa.org/doi/10.1037/0022-0663.83.1.73

Yeager, D. S., et al. (2014). Breaking the cycle of mistrust: Wise interventions to provide critical feedback across the racial divide. *Journal of Experimental Psychology: General, 143*(2), 804–824.

5

Scaffolding and Worked Examples

Although Soviet psychologist Lev Vygotsky never used the term scaffolding, his work laid the conceptual foundation for what Wood, Bruner, and Ross would later formalize in 1976. As early as the 1930s, Vygotsky introduced the idea of the Zone of Proximal Development (ZPD), which reframed learning as most effective when it occurs just beyond a learner's current level of competence—challenging but attainable with appropriate support. This was a revolutionary departure from dominant learning theories of the time. Vygotsky emphasized the social nature of learning, the role of more knowledgeable others, and the idea that development follows instruction—not the other way around. Scaffolding, as later defined, builds directly on these ideas by describing how temporary instructional supports help learners reach higher levels of understanding and performance.

Scaffolding is often described as "meeting learners where they are," but more accurately, it involves providing structured, temporary supports that help students progress from guided to independent performance (van de Pol et al., 2010; Wood et al., 1976).

Cognitive science grounds scaffolding in the understanding of how *the mind processes and stores information*. From this view, scaffolding consists of intentional external supports—such as teacher guidance, tools, or structured strategies—that reduce cognitive load and help learners connect new information to prior knowledge, improving retention and transfer across contexts. Intentional teacher design is central to effective scaffolding in explicit instruction. Teachers carefully structure tasks using a gradual release of responsibility model, breaking content into manageable chunks, and providing clear, explicit instructions, along with modeling and examples before independent practice (Rosenshine, 2012). This deliberate sequencing and scaffolding not only make complex tasks more accessible by reducing cognitive demand (Sweller et al., 2011) but also ensure that foundational knowledge is firmly established before advancing to more challenging content. Importantly, scaffolding can be delivered effectively even when teaching an entire class simultaneously, as teachers guide students step by step through the learning process while gradually releasing responsibility.

This intentional scaffolding approach is especially crucial for equity in the classroom. Students come with diverse backgrounds, prior knowledge, and cognitive resources, and many benefit from carefully designed supports that provide access to rigorous, grade-level content without diluting expectations. While fostering independence and critical thinking is a vital goal, these skills cannot be developed in isolation from foundational understanding and adequate support. Balancing scaffolding with opportunities for autonomy enables all learners to engage meaningfully and build confidence, ensuring that independence grows alongside competence. Effective scaffolding thus empowers students to progress from supported learning toward independent mastery, making deep, transferable understanding attainable for every learner.

Unfortunately, the classroom translation of Vygotsky's ideas has often drifted from their original intent. Rather than using the

ZPD to stretch students toward greater complexity, many modern frameworks have used it to justify keeping students in simplified or leveled work. Chief among them is the over-reliance on reading levels to determine what content students are "ready" to access. Chaiklin (2003) argues that many contemporary uses of Vygotsky's ZPD have departed from his original conception—shifting toward simplified or leveled work rather than genuine stretching of learners toward greater complexity. Though Vygotsky advocated for supporting students through challenging material, not reducing its complexity, many classrooms still limit students to texts at their so-called "instructional reading level"—often determined by informal assessments or commercial leveling systems such as Fountas and Pinnell. The rationale is typically to prevent frustration, particularly for struggling readers. However, over time, this approach can have the opposite effect, restricting students' exposure to rich vocabulary, complex syntax, and grade-level ideas—especially for those from disadvantaged backgrounds (Hiebert, 2014, 2017). In the long run, such practices constrain the very cognitive and linguistic development they intend to support.

Timothy Shanahan, a leading reading researcher and former Director of Reading for Chicago Public Schools, has been a vocal critic of instructional text leveling. He contends that students benefit more from exposure to grade-level texts—even when those texts are challenging—so long as teachers provide appropriate scaffolding through vocabulary instruction, rereading, and guided questioning (Shanahan, 2025a). According to Shanahan (2025a), restricting access to complex texts on the basis of reading level underestimates students' capacity to learn and limits their academic growth. He cites extensive research demonstrating that text difficulty is a poor predictor of learning and that reading comprehension improves most when students engage with complex materials—not when texts are simplified to match students' current proficiency (Shanahan, 2014; Shanahan & Shanahan, 2008).

Historically, students developed literacy by grappling with demanding texts, rich in complex syntax and advanced vocabulary. Comprehension, vocabulary, and background knowledge grow through sustained exposure, even when full understanding is not immediate. Productive struggle builds cognitive structures: it fosters schema development, inference-making, elaboration, and retrieval (Neuman et al., 2023). These are essential processes for deep, transferable literacy. Thus, the key to supporting struggling readers is not simplification but scaffolding. With effective support, students can access and learn from rigorous content—an approach that ultimately accelerates, rather than hinders, long-term reading success.

This confusion and challenge around effective scaffolding often run parallel to widespread misunderstandings of differentiation. While Carol Tomlinson originally emphasized that differentiation is meant to help all students reach the same rigorous academic goals, the model she proposes includes adjusting content, process, and product (Tomlinson, 2005). In practice, this has frequently led educators to differentiate content—for example, by assigning simpler texts to struggling readers or reserving advanced materials only for high-achieving students. Though well intentioned, this approach often reinforces internal tracking, reduces access to complex ideas, and undermines equity (Gamoran, 1992; Oakes, 2005; Cunningham et al., 2005; Dzaldov & Peterson, 2005). Such interpretations misapply Vygotsky's ZPD, suggesting that struggling students must be given easier materials to avoid frustration. But Vygotsky never advocated reducing cognitive demand—he argued for supporting students through challenging tasks with the help of a more knowledgeable other. In reality, what students need is not easier content but more *effective* scaffolding.

Effective scaffolds—like chunking complex texts, providing vocabulary support, modeling, guided questions, and graphic organizers—allow students to engage with the same rich material as their peers, regardless of their starting point. When we shift our focus from simplifying content to supporting access to it, we maintain high expectations for all learners. Scaffolding, not content differentiation, is where instructional impact and long-term learning gains are made. In contrast to the leveling-down that often accompanies differentiation, scaffolding offers a temporary framework that leads students toward independence and deeper understanding.

The key to effective scaffolding lies not only in providing support but in knowing when and where to provide it—and, just as importantly, when to fade it. Scaffolds should be responsive, temporary, and purposefully aligned to a learner's current level of competence (van de Pol et al., 2010). When supports are introduced too early, they can reduce productive struggle and limit opportunities for cognitive engagement; when withdrawn too soon, students may become frustrated or disengaged. Cognitive science emphasizes that the timing and calibration of scaffolds are central to managing cognitive load—teachers must ensure that students have enough guidance to process new information without becoming overwhelmed but also enough independence to consolidate learning and transfer it to new contexts (Rosenshine, 2012; Sweller, 1988). Effective scaffolding therefore requires ongoing formative assessment: teachers must continually monitor student performance to determine whether to maintain, adjust, or remove supports. As learners gain fluency and schema become more automated, scaffolds are gradually faded to promote autonomy and durable learning. This dynamic process—sometimes described as the "art" of instruction—ensures that support serves as a bridge to independence rather than a permanent crutch.

Whole-Group vs. Small-Group Instruction

While whole-group, explicit instruction offers a powerful opportunity for scaffolding—through modeling, think-alouds, guided practice, and shared discussion—this approach is often underutilized, particularly in student-centered learning models that emphasize small-group activities over explicit, whole-group instruction. In progressive teaching models, teachers are encouraged to minimize direct instruction in favor of student-driven discovery and peer collaboration. As a result, whole-group time is rarely used to build shared knowledge or model cognitive processes explicitly. Critically, instruction that could be delivered efficiently to the entire class is often fragmented into small-group lessons, the benefits of which are seldom enough to offset the loss of instructional time, reduced teacher modeling, and content fragmentation (Shanahan, 2025b). Students may be asked to engage in tasks before they have the necessary background knowledge, reflecting a fundamental principle: learners cannot think critically about content they do not yet understand (Willingham, 2009). While peer discussion and inquiry may appear engaging, research indicates that *mental engagement*—not just active participation—is what drives long-term learning (Bjork & Bjork, 2011; Clark & Mayer, 2008). Many of the purported advantages of small-group instruction can be realized more efficiently through well-structured whole-group teaching. Teachers often use small groups to deliver the same modeling, guided practice, or strategy instruction that could be conducted with the entire class without sacrificing coherence or instructional time. Empirical evidence supports this approach: when lessons are explicit, interactive, and carefully paced, whole-group instruction can produce gains that are equal to or greater than those of small-group formats (Kamil & Rauscher, 1990; Taylor et al., 2000). In these instances, small-group activities may simply repackage whole-class tasks, dividing what could otherwise be collective cognitive work into fragmented pieces.

At the secondary level, the benefits of whole-group instruction remain particularly pronounced, despite the greater complexity of content and skills that students encounter. Adolescents must engage with abstract reasoning, disciplinary knowledge, and interdisciplinary problem-solving, but they still require sufficient background knowledge and scaffolding to do so effectively (Rosenshine, 2012; Willingham, 2009). Whole-class instruction allows teachers to efficiently build shared schema, model higher-order thinking, and provide guided practice in a coherent, consistent manner. When lessons are fragmented into small groups, content can become disjointed. Moreover, explicit modeling of complex skills—whether analyzing historical arguments, solving multi-step algebra problems, or interpreting literature—can often be delivered more efficiently through whole-class instruction. When they present clear explanations and worked examples to all students, teachers reduce redundant instruction, maintain coherence, and free cognitive capacity for focused practice. This approach aligns with research demonstrating that well-designed instruction, which minimizes extraneous cognitive load and integrates guided modeling, promotes deeper learning and more efficient knowledge transfer (Clark & Mayer, 2008).

What matters most is the *quality* of whole-group instruction. It is not inherently better simply because a teacher is leading the class; effectiveness depends on focus, clarity, and alignment with students' prior knowledge. When students engage in collaboration, or group problem-solving without first mastering core content or skills, cognitive engagement suffers—students may appear active, but their thinking remains superficial (Kirschner et al., 2006; Willingham, 2009). Similarly, elevating student choice as the primary route to engagement can exacerbate shallow learning. True engagement is measured not by visible signs like raised hands or group participation but by a serious emotional and cognitive investment in learning—intellectual engagement—requiring deep thinking, elaboration, and deliberate practice (Willms et al., 2009).

In an effective Gradual Release of Responsibility (GRR) framework, students progress systematically from "I do" (explicit modeling), to "We do" (guided practice), to "You do together" (collaborative application), and finally to "You do alone" (independent practice). Small-group or collaborative work, therefore, still represents a guided stage of learning—not full independence. A true GRR framework is also dynamic and responsive: teachers move fluidly between phases based on ongoing formative assessment and real-time checks for understanding. It is important for administrators, instructional coaches, and district leaders—as well as those who assess teacher effectiveness—to recognize that some of the most cognitively engaged students *may appear quiet*, internally processing complex ideas rather than speaking frequently. Observable activity is not synonymous with cognitive engagement. Overemphasis on group work, discourse, or project-based learning that minimizes the teacher's role as the primary source of expert knowledge and scaffolded guidance can inadvertently reduce learning outcomes (Kirschner et al., 2006; Willingham, 2009). High-quality whole-group instruction blends clear, content-rich explanations with intentional scaffolding and structured opportunities for purposeful discussion, guided collaboration, or strategic choice, ensuring that students grapple with substantive ideas and develop both understanding and transferable skills (Archer & Hughes, 2011; Fisher & Frey, 2014a; Rosenshine, 2012).

Scaffolding in Whole-Group Instruction

In a well-scaffolded, whole-group lesson, teachers use think-alouds often to make their cognitive processes explicit (Archer & Hughes, 2011). By verbalizing their reasoning, teachers guide students in how to approach problems, helping them organize their thinking and internalize effective problem-solving strategies. This modeling phase is followed by guided practice, where students actively engage with the task while receiving targeted prompts, guiding questions, and feedback from the teacher. Throughout this stage, teachers closely monitor progress and adjust support dynamically to meet learners' needs. In this way, scaffolding is maintained even during whole-group instruction, as teachers use questions, prompts, and visual cues to help students access prior knowledge and make sense of new information, effectively reducing cognitive load and fostering deeper comprehension (Hattie, 2009).

Even within whole-group, explicit instruction, teachers can strategically organize students into brief, scaffolded small-group interactions. These moments allow students to discuss ideas or solve problems together before returning to the full class, reinforcing learning while the teacher monitors and adjusts support as needed (Johnson & Johnson, 2009; Sweller, 1988; Ryan & Deci, 2000; Roediger & Butler, 2011). Throughout the lesson, the teacher continuously monitors and provides feedback, dynamically adjusting scaffolding on the basis of student responses. When students struggle, the teacher can offer additional explanations, guide learners through further examples, or modify how content is presented. This ongoing feedback loop ensures that students remain focused, clearly understand areas for improvement, and receive the necessary tools to succeed, while enabling the teacher to tailor support to the evolving needs of the class. Perhaps most crucial to effective scaffolding is knowing when to release students to independent practice—fading supports at the right moment so they can consolidate learning and demonstrate true understanding. Table 5.1 provides a view of the difference between progressive and explicit models of scaffolding instruction.

While most instructional models agree that scaffolding should be gradually withdrawn as learners gain expertise, cognitive science emphasizes helping students automate cognitive processes and independently manage their thinking. Cognitive Load Theory posits that learning is most effective when instructional methods reduce unnecessary or distracting mental effort, allowing learners to devote their working memory to processing and organizing information in ways that promote understanding and long-term retention. As learners gain expertise, they can automate cognitive processes, transferring them from working memory to long-term memory, thereby reducing the cognitive load required for task execution. This process of automation is

TABLE 5.1 Key Differences Between Student-Centered and Cognitive-Science Views on Scaffolding

Area of the Scaffold	Student-Centered Approaches	Cognitive Science
Role of the Teacher	♦ Facilitator who supports student's exploration and discovery ♦ Teacher provides guidance and feedback but allows students significant autonomy in their learning process. ♦ Creates opportunities for students to construct knowledge through interaction and engagement	♦ Teacher's role is more directive, providing clear instruction and explicit guidance, especially in the initial stages of learning. ♦ Tasks are organized by the teacher, who provides tools and frameworks for students to build and store knowledge efficiently, using structured practices like retrieval practice and spaced repetition.
Task Design & Complexity	♦ Tasks are typically designed to be open-ended, with a focus on inquiry-based learning and problem solving. ♦ Scaffolding is used to help students navigate these tasks, but the emphasis is on self-directed learning and collaboration with peers.	♦ Tasks are designed to ensure that learners are presented with appropriate levels of complexity based on their prior knowledge. ♦ Scaffolding is about structuring the task in a way that prevents cognitive overload, such as breaking complex problems into small chunks, and providing step-by-step guidance or visual aids.
Fading the Scaffold	♦ The gradual removal of support is an essential part of scaffolding. Once the learner has demonstrated competence, the teacher reduces their involvement, encouraging independent learning.	♦ While fading the scaffold is important, cognitive scientists emphasize spaced practice and review for long-term retention and transfer. ♦ After initial support is removed, periodic review or retrieval practice may continue to aid in transferring knowledge to new contexts.

(Continued)

TABLE 5.1 (Continued)

Area of the Scaffold	Student-Centered Approaches	Cognitive Science
Assessment of Learning	♦ Assessment is often more formative, focusing on process of learning and student's ability to construct and apply knowledge. ♦ Emphasis on self-assessment and peer feedback	♦ Stress the importance of summative assessments and checks for mastery of core concepts. ♦ Retrieval-based assessments to ensure that knowledge is retained in long-term memory and can be applied flexibly

Key differences between student-centered and cognitive-science perspectives on scaffolding, highlighting contrasts in teacher role, task design, scaffold fading, and assessment practices.

essential for developing expertise and independent thinking (Sweller et al., 1998). Independence remains a shared goal, but cognitive science focuses more on equipping students with strategies to solve problems efficiently and effectively on their own.

While small-group instruction is often considered a cornerstone of effective teaching, its integration into core, whole-group lessons does not consistently translate to improved student achievement, in either literacy or math (Shanahan, 2025b; Bonesrønning et al., 2022). These findings underscore the importance of ensuring that students have mastered core content *before* engaging in small-group activities—and that administrators, instructional coaches, and district leaders are aware of evidence-based practices with the strongest evidence for effectiveness. Without this foundational knowledge, small-group work can create the illusion of impact: students may appear engaged, but their learning remains shallow.

A Word on Skill-Based Grouping in Reading: For Intervening on Deficits

Recognizing that small-group instruction is not a replacement for high-quality whole-class teaching is the first step toward using it effectively. Grouping should occur only at key points in the learning cycle—when students need targeted guidance or support to close gaps in understanding, typically outside of core instruction. This challenge extends beyond core instruction. Many teachers are encouraged to "differentiate" by forming flexible groups around discrete comprehension skills—such as main idea, cause and effect, or compare and contrast—as a way to scaffold learning. This approach often reflects a standards-based model, where skills are "unpacked" into isolated learning targets. Students are then assigned differentiated, leveled texts, aligned with each group's perceived "reading level." These texts are usually short passages accompanied by targeted strategy instruction. Students rotate among groups on the basis of identified "skill deficits." However, research indicates that this approach is largely ineffective for improving reading comprehension because it isolates surface-level strategies rather than addressing the deeper cognitive and linguistic capacities—namely word reading and language comprehension—that underlie true understanding (Gough & Tunmer, 1986; Storch & Whitehurst, 2002). According to the Simple View of Reading (Gough & Tunmer, 1986), comprehension is the product of decoding and language comprehension; weaknesses in either component constrain overall reading development. Skills-based grouping often ignores this reality, focusing narrowly on comprehension strategies without addressing underlying constraints.

As addressed in previous chapters, reading comprehension is not a collection of discrete skills to be mastered in isolation. Evidence supporting grouping solely by standards-based "skill deficits" is weak, as it does not reliably improve comprehension outcomes (Connor et al., 2014). Moreover, this practice often obscures the more fundamental challenges: poor word reading and limited language comprehension are the true bottlenecks to understanding (Bowers, 2020). Research shows that interventions targeting both decoding and language comprehension yield greater learning gains than those focusing on comprehension strategies alone (Barth et al., 2016). When teachers rely on skills-based grouping or text-leveling systems such as Fountas and

Pinnell to assign groups by "reading ability," they may inadvertently limit students' access to complex syntax, rich vocabulary, and grade-level ideas—key drivers of long-term reading growth (Cabell & Hwang, 2020; Hiebert, 2020). Over time, this can lead to fragmented instruction, lowered expectations, and widening achievement gaps, especially for students who most need exposure to rigorous, knowledge-building texts. In contrast, research suggests that students benefit far more from explicit vocabulary, syntax, and content instruction within whole-class reading of complex, content-rich texts, where teachers provide embedded supports to make challenging material accessible without diluting it (Cabell & Hwang, 2020; Shanahan, 2024a; Willingham, 2009).

When Small-Group Instruction in Literacy Shows Impact

When used purposefully, small-group instruction can be highly effective for reteaching misunderstood concepts, strengthening background knowledge, and scaffolding understanding of specific texts—not generic skills. It's especially valuable for younger readers still mastering foundational skills and for older students who need explicit support with vocabulary, syntax, and comprehension strategies. In most classrooms, these groups are most effective in targeted intervention settings, where teaching is guided by diagnostic data—such as assessments of phonological awareness, phonics, fluency, vocabulary, and syntax—rather than by isolated comprehension skills (Dubé et al., 2014). By continuously monitoring students' responses and adjusting supports—modeling, guided practice, or strategic prompts—teachers are actively scaffolding each learner toward independent mastery. Grouping informed by foundational skill assessments, language comprehension data, curriculum-aligned assessments, and student writing or discussion is far more beneficial for improving reading comprehension than arbitrary standards-based skill grouping.

This approach is particularly important for older students. Despite the focus on higher-level comprehension skills, many struggling readers—including adolescents—still lack mastery of foundational reading skills like decoding and fluency. Unfortunately, this critical gap is often overlooked in secondary settings, where educators assume that all students can decode proficiently when, in reality, a substantial group still struggle with word recognition, decoding, weaker fluency, or limited vocabulary (Kilpatrick, 2015; Torgesen et al., 2007; Wexler et al., 2008). Strong reading comprehension relies on well-developed language networks, including vocabulary, syntactic awareness, and background knowledge (Cain & Oakhill, 2007; Catts & Kamhi, 2017; Gough & Tunmer, 1986; Snow, 2002). This becomes especially critical at the secondary level, where students encounter increasingly complex academic vocabulary and sentence structures. Flexible, targeted small groups focused on vocabulary and syntax development allow teachers to scaffold learning by providing structured practice, modeling strategies, and guided discussion, gradually transferring responsibility to students as they develop skill and confidence. Instruction in morphology, context clue strategies, sentence unpacking, and structured listening and speaking activities—combined with graphic organizers and discussion—benefits students across elementary and secondary grades (Biemiller, 2005; Cain & Oakhill, 2007; Snow, 2002).

Building on these targeted strategies, comprehension instruction depends heavily on content knowledge and vocabulary, not just isolated skills. Even students who decode proficiently can struggle to retain or analyze what they read, facing challenges with text structure, using evidence, literal and inferential comprehension, reading stamina, and engagement (Kilpatrick, 2015; Recht & Leslie, 1988; Torgesen et al., 2007; Wexler et al., 2008). Curriculum-based assessments tied to complex texts help teachers see whether students can handle grade-level demands when confronted with unfamiliar vocabulary, syntax, or ideas. Many students thrive with instruction that targets close reading, text structure recognition, inferencing, and reasoning—core processes that strengthen both reading and writing—especially when paired with support for background knowledge and vocabulary (Applebee & Langer, 2011; Shanahan, 2020; Willingham, 2009). Flexible comprehension-focused groups are inherently scaffolded, emphasizing modeling, guided practice, and attention to text structure. Lessons might begin by activating background knowledge with brief pre-reading activities, like advanced organizers, pre-teaching key vocabulary, and previewing text structures such as cause-effect, compare-contrast, or narrative patterns (Beck et al., 2013; Duke & Pearson, 2002). During reading, students work with short, purposeful excerpts, annotating for structure, noting shifts in tone, identifying key ideas, paraphrasing, making inferences from evidence, and answering text-dependent questions (Duke & Pearson, 2002; Fisher & Frey, 2014b). Post-reading activities might include guided discussion, retrieval practice focused on author intent, theme, or tone, and writing or speaking tasks using sentence stems. Follow-up activities like one-paragraph retells the next day help strengthen long-term retention (Karpicke & Blunt, 2011; Weinstein et al., 2018). At every stage, teachers gradually fade support, allowing students to practice independence while still providing guidance when needed, exemplifying the core principles of scaffolding.

Just as flexible small groups can target the underlying skills that support reading comprehension, they can also be highly effective for helping students translate understanding into written expression. Comprehension is only part of the equation; students must also learn to organize, articulate, and elaborate on their ideas in writing. Targeted instruction in writing ensures that students can communicate their thinking clearly and accurately, building on the language skills they develop through reading. Adolescent writers facing these challenges benefit most from explicit instruction in planning and structuring their writing, developing sentence-level fluency, and integrating evidence (Graham & Perin, 2007). By structuring lessons to model strategies, provide guided practice, and progressively remove support, teachers can scaffold students' writing development in a way that parallels reading instruction. In practice, this can look like targeted lessons on paragraph structure, embedding and citing evidence, and strategies for elaboration or sentence combining to make writing more fluent, coherent, and sophisticated.

One powerful approach is modeling strong versus weak responses. By providing teacher-created or peer exemplars, teachers enable students to see exactly what effective writing looks like before attempting it independently (Fisher & Frey, 2014a). Guided practice with immediate feedback, breaking tasks into manageable steps, using sentence frames, and providing checklists or rubrics for self-monitoring all support stronger writing outcomes—far more than simply assigning tasks and hoping for improvement (Graham et al., 2012). Teachers can scaffold sentence-level challenges by guiding students through combining simple ideas into complex sentences, using transitions like "because" or "although," and gradually reducing prompts as students internalize the strategies. Practice with relative clauses, appositives, and other sentence structures also strengthens both writing development and reading comprehension (Berninger & Abbott, 2010).

When Small-Group Instruction in Math Shows Impact

The same principles apply in mathematics. Just as reading comprehension cannot be reduced to isolated skills, mathematical understanding depends on connecting concepts, procedures, and reasoning. When small-group instruction in math focuses narrowly on discrete standards rather than conceptual relationships, it risks fragmenting learning in much the same way that skills-based reading groups do. It has long been well established that rigid "low" or "high" math tracks can lower expectations for struggling learners and restrict access to challenging content (Boaler, 2016; National Council of Teachers of Mathematics [NCTM], 2014). However, research indicates that thoughtfully implemented homogeneous grouping—particularly for *advanced* learners—can provide opportunities for targeted, appropriately challenging instruction that supports deeper mathematical reasoning and skill development (Steenbergen-Hu et al., 2016; Preckel et al., 2019). The nuance here is that the benefits of any grouping strategy—homogenous or heterogenous—are mediated by teacher skill, scaffolding, curriculum rigor, and the opportunities that students have to engage deeply with content (Černilec et al., 2023). Ultimately, this underscores that teacher scaffolding and instructional design, rather than the grouping structure itself, are the most powerful determinants of student growth.

Practically speaking, scaffolding in math mirrors the same cognitive principles seen in literacy instruction: teachers provide supports that help students bridge what they already know to what they are learning, gradually fading those supports as confidence and competence grow. Students benefit most when teachers use formative assessments—like exit tickets, error analyses, or quick checks—to spot patterns in understanding. Grouping students by shared misconceptions, revisiting key prerequisite concepts, or extending learning for those ready to move ahead allows instruction to *build from students' current thinking* (Rosenshine, 2012). Research consistently shows that learning gains are strongest when teachers adjust instruction, materials, and pacing to match the needs of each group—confirming that it's the instructional response, not the grouping itself, that makes the difference (Lou et al., 1996; Wang et al., 2023).

Misconceptions often reflect deeply held mental models that can block new learning. By using guided examples, step-by-step modeling, and targeted prompts, teachers can help students surface and revise these models while supporting working memory and reducing cognitive load (Hattie & Timperley, 2007; Shute, 2008; Sweller et al., 1998). Research on conceptual change shows that durable learning happens when instruction activates prior knowledge, directly confronts misconceptions, and helps students reconstruct more accurate understandings (Chi & Wylie, 2014; Schroeder & Kucera, 2022; Will et al., 2019; Li et al., 2023). Studies of refutation texts and misconception-based instruction find that when learners are guided to examine and revise their existing beliefs, they achieve deeper conceptual understanding (Broughton et al., 2010; Schroeder & Kucera, 2022). Grouping students by shared misconceptions is one practical way to make this process more intentional, enabling teachers to design discussions and tasks that directly address common misunderstandings (National Association for Research in Science Teaching [NARST], 1989/2025).

Another effective way to flexibly group students in math is for targeted practice that incorporates teacher guidance and scaffolding, typically implemented after explicit instruction. Once a concept has been clearly taught to the whole class, students can be temporarily organized into flexible groups designed to reinforce and consolidate new learning through carefully structured opportunities to process and apply information. This small-group time allows the teacher to diagnose where cognitive load may be overwhelming, provide additional worked examples, and use guiding questions, prompts, or cues to gradually release responsibility to the students. Rather than practicing identical problems repetitively, students benefit most from interleaved practice, which mixes different problem types or concepts together—enhancing discrimination and facilitating transfer of learning (Rohrer & Taylor, 2007).

In addition to targeted practice, flexible grouping can support peer collaboration focused on reasoning and problem-solving. Ideally, these mixed-ability groups use clear roles or protocols to ensure equitable participation and prevent stronger students from dominating, allowing learners to explain their reasoning, justify solutions, and apply multiple representations or strategies (Chi & Wylie, 2014; Webb et al., 2014). Unlike practice groups aimed at correcting errors or building fluency, these collaboration groups emphasize articulating and defending thinking, exploring diverse solution paths, and engaging in rich mathematical discourse while reinforcing retrieval and elaboration. When structured intentionally, this kind of guided collaboration functions as a bridge between teacher-led instruction and independent application—helping students consolidate and extend new learning within their ZPD (Hogan & Pressley, 1997; van de Pol et al., 2010). Formed after explicit instruction, these groups are intended not to replace teacher modeling or guided practice but rather to complement them by providing application-focused support. Research shows that when students generate, explain, and elaborate on ideas—key components of active constructive learning—they engage in effortful thinking that strengthens memory consolidation (Webb et al., 2014; Weinstein et al., 2018). To maximize effectiveness, such groups require deliberate structure, including defined roles, protocols, and active teacher monitoring—ensuring that collaboration functions as a scaffold for deeper reasoning rather than an unstructured activity.

Scaffolding does not end once students reach proficiency; rather, it evolves to include enrichment and transfer opportunities. Flexible grouping in math should not be limited to remediation—extension opportunities are equally critical. When students demonstrate mastery of a concept or skill (via formative assessments or performance tasks), they benefit from engaging in extension activities that challenge them to apply their knowledge to novel problems, explore real-world connections, and participate in rich mathematical discourse. Encountering concepts in new and varied contexts strengthens mental schemas and promotes deeper encoding (Anderson & Pearson, 1984; Willingham, 2009). As Barnett and Ceci (2002) explain, transfer—the ability to apply knowledge in unfamiliar situations—is more likely to occur when students engage with non-routine problems, make connections across representations, and reflect on the "why" behind strategies, not just the "how." Once fluency is achieved, continued repetition without increased challenge can lead to stagnation. Thus, advancing students to independent or extended applications after successful guided practice is essential for continued growth (Ericsson & Pool, 2016; Rosenshine, 2012). Higher-level tasks and collaborative discussions also promote metacognitive awareness, as students justify, revise, and reflect on their strategies (Desoete & Roeyers, 2006).

Importantly, mathematical proficiency is not a fixed or general trait—it is domain-specific (Geary, 2004; Siegler, 2000). A student may demonstrate strength in geometry while struggling with fractions, which is both common and expected. Grouping based on current understanding—rather than permanent labels—enables instruction to remain responsive and adaptive. In this way, grouping becomes fluid rather than tracked, avoiding the harmful consequences often associated with rigid ability grouping. Empirical studies also highlight that differences in teacher expectations and access to rigorous content—not inherent ability—largely explain why rigid grouping systems widen achievement gaps (Boaler, 2016; Oakes, 2005). Flexible grouping mitigates these risks by ensuring that all students engage with challenging, conceptually rich tasks supported by appropriate scaffolds. This approach should not be confused with traditional "ability grouping" or tracking models. Whereas fixed tracks tend to entrench inequities and limit access to rich mathematical thinking, flexible grouping guided by formative assessment functions as an adaptive scaffolding tool—allowing teachers to respond to students' evolving understanding while maintaining shared access to rigorous content. At the same time, research indicates that homogeneous grouping can be beneficial for advanced learners when it includes curriculum acceleration or enrichment rather than simply grouping by ability level (Steenbergen-Hu et al., 2016). Such contexts emphasize depth, complexity, and challenge, aligning instruction with students' readiness rather than reinforcing static labels.

Whole versus Small Groupings in Literacy and Math

Across subjects, the effectiveness of small-group instruction depends not on the grouping structure itself but on the intentional design of the learning experience. Strong whole-class instruction remains the most powerful lever for learning; small-group work is most effective when it builds on, reinforces, or extends this foundation rather than replacing it. Whether in math or literacy, grouping works best when it is flexible, temporary, and guided by evidence of student thinking—not fixed labels like "ability" or reading level. Whether the goal is targeted support, extension, or collaborative problem-solving, group work should come after explicit, guided instruction so that students have a clear foundation to build on. Asking learners to collaborate or apply skills before they have received adequate instruction can easily lead to confusion or reinforce misconceptions. Similarly, isolated, standards-based skill practice—whether identifying a main idea in reading or multiplying fractions in math—tends to fragment learning and limits transfer. Skills are context-bound, and students need opportunities to connect them to meaningful content. Research shows that practices such as retrieval, elaboration, and interleaving are key to building long-term retention and deeper understanding; without these, students might perform well in the moment but quickly forget, lacking the durable connections that make learning stick (Cepeda et al., 2006; Dunlosky et al., 2013; Karpicke & Blunt, 2011). Together, these findings reinforce that effective grouping is fundamentally an instructional design decision—one that succeeds only when guided by ongoing evidence of student thinking.

What Does This Mean for RTI and MTSS?

These findings have important implications for how we structure support in frameworks like Response to Intervention (RTI) and Multi-Tiered System of Support (MTSS). Both models aim to provide targeted interventions through small-group instruction for students who need extra help. But if these groups aren't strategic—grounded in clear diagnostic data, aligned with meaningful content, and connected to core instruction—they can easily become fragmented and ineffective. Too often, Tier 2 and Tier 3 interventions focus narrowly on general "skills" without integrating the language, content, and background knowledge that students need to truly understand texts.

Research helps clarify why this matters. A 2017 meta-analysis of small-group reading interventions found a moderate overall effect size (0.54), but the story becomes more nuanced when we look closer. Interventions targeting a single, well-defined skill—such as foundational word reading, vocabulary, or fluency—produced stronger effects (around 0.60) than broader, less focused comprehension approaches (around 0.35) (Hall & Burns, 2018). Yet the effectiveness of interventions tends to decline at the secondary level. Meta-analyses of adolescent literacy instruction reveal that middle and high school interventions generally yield small gains, with typical effect sizes ranging from 0.15 to 0.30 for comprehension outcomes (Scammacca et al., 2007; Vaughn et al., 2010). In mathematics, interventions delivered by teachers or other professionals have been proven to yield larger average effects than interventions delivered by technology—or computer-based instruction (Williams et al., 2022). Yet computer-based pathway programs, such as i-Ready, MATHia, or Math Pathways & Pitfalls, are frequently used by schools to address instructional gaps in mathematics, despite evidence that these tools alone produce modest gains compared with teacher-led interventions (Williams et al., 2022). These findings highlight that the quality and alignment of instruction matter far more than the mere presence of interventions or software.

Interventions in an MTSS are designed as a tiered, data-driven framework to provide early, flexible academic or behavioral support and ensure access to grade-level learning. When implemented well, it is preventative and responsive. However, in practice, it is often misapplied. Attempts to replicate elementary-style interventions in secondary classrooms often prove unimpactful, with effect sizes dropping sharply and empirical evidence for sustained gains largely lacking (Hall & Burns, 2018; Scammacca et al., 2007; Cabell & Hwang, 2020). Isolating skills from meaningful content diminishes learning. For example, pulling students for practice on RI.2.6 (author's point of view) using short, decontextualized passages does little to support deep comprehension of grade-level texts. To be effective, Tier 2 interventions, whether in elementary or secondary settings, should be short-term and diagnostic, tightly aligned with Tier 1 instruction, and focused on building vocabulary, knowledge, and strategic thinking through explicit instruction, retrieval practice, and scaffolded work with authentic, grade-level tasks.

To ensure that Tier 2 supports are both effective and equitable, instructional decisions must be rooted in diagnostic evidence and aligned with the demands of grade-level learning. This means shifting away from generic skill practice and toward targeted scaffolds that support access to rich content. In reading, decoding-focused interventions should be used only when a demonstrated need exists, while comprehension supports should keep students engaged with grade-level texts, supplemented by pre-teaching key vocabulary, sentence frames for writing or speaking, and retrieval practice to reinforce text knowledge. In math, small groups should follow explicit whole-class instruction, be driven by diagnosed conceptual misunderstandings rather than surface-level errors, and provide targeted support through visual models, worked examples, and spaced practice. By intentionally connecting intervention to core instruction, Tier 2 scaffolds strengthen learning coherence instead of fragmenting it. Tables 5.2 and 5.3 illustrate how RTI supports in reading and math can be structured to align with cognitive-science principles—prioritizing explicit instruction, retrieval practice, and cumulative knowledge-building over isolated skill drills.

TABLE 5.2 Interventions in Reading (Grades 3–12 Example)

Step	Component	Details
1	Identify Need	Use data from universal screeners, comprehension checks, writing samples, and oral responses tied to *grade-level texts*. **Tip**: Focus on identifying where students struggle in context, not just raw scores.
2	Analyze the Breakdown	Is it: ♦ Decoding/Fluency? ♦ Vocabulary/Language? ♦ Knowledge Gaps? ♦ Strategic Comprehension (i.e., connecting ideas, summarizing, making inferences)?
3	Design Tier 2 Support	♦ Supplement—not replace—core text ♦ Keep the same anchor text or content but add ♦ Pre-teaching critical vocabulary ♦ Use retrieval prompts to reinforce prior knowledge ♦ Provide graphic organizers to reduce cognitive load ♦ Modeled think-alouds and use sentence stems to guide responses
4	Structure	♦ 15–25 mins, 3x/week ♦ Small Group (3–5 students) ♦ Group based on *specific misunderstanding*, not broad skill label ("main idea group")
5	Sample Activity	After reading a shared passage: ♦ **Retrieval Practice**: "What happened in the scene before this?" ♦ **Text-Based Discussion**: "What claim can we make about the character?" ♦ **Written Response**: Supported short answer using stem + evidence
6	Progress Monitor	Use curriculum-embedded formative checks (brief written response, verbal answer tied to core reading) not isolated skill quizzes
7	Exit Criteria	Student independently applies scaffolded comprehension skill in Tier 1 task (i.e., answers text-based questions, writes with evidence)

Example step-by-step framework for reading interventions (Grades 3–12), outlining identification, analysis, tiered support design, implementation, and progress monitoring to support targeted comprehension development.

TABLE 5.3 Interventions in Math (Grades 3–12 Example)

Step	Component	Details
1	Identify Misunderstanding	Use error analysis: is it conceptual (i.e., fractions as quantities), procedural (i.e., steps of multiplication), or factual (math facts)?
2	Design Tier 2 Support	Use similar problem types from Tier 1 lesson but ♦ Provide worked examples and step-by-step guidance ♦ Use visual models (number lines, area models, manipulatives) ♦ Encourage verbal explanation of reasoning ♦ Include retrieval practice on related prior content
3	Structure	15–25 mins, 2–4×/week Group by specific misunderstanding Groups flex weekly, based on formative data
4	Sample Activity	For misunderstandings of fraction multiplication: ♦ Worked example breakdown with teacher prompts ♦ Use real-world scenario modeled with an area diagram ♦ Apply learning in a Tier 1-aligned word problem in a word problem ♦ Use verbal explanation protocol (i.e., I multiplied because…")
5	Monitor Progress	Same problem types as Tier 1 with fading scaffolds (remove visuals, reduce prompts)
6	Exit Criteria	Student solves independently in whole-group with accuracy and reasoning

Example step-by-step framework for math interventions (Grades 3–12), detailing identification of misunderstandings, design of tiered support, structured implementation, sample activities, progress monitoring, and exit criteria to promote targeted skill development.

Designing effective RTI supports at the secondary level requires more than simply scaling up elementary practices. Many secondary RTI/MTSS models fail precisely because they attempt to replicate elementary structures without adapting to the realities of middle and high school. Common pitfalls include (1) insufficient attention to adolescent developmental needs, (2) limited focus on domain-specific knowledge, (3) rigid or constrained scheduling, and (4) over-reliance on isolated skills practice with older students. In secondary settings, strong Tier 1 instruction—anchored in rich content and explicit teaching—is essential. This means using high-quality curriculum rather than worksheets and embedding evidence-based strategies grounded in cognitive science. When Tier 1 is weak, Tier 2 and Tier 3 supports become overburdened and lose their impact (Vaughn et al., 2010; Wanzek et al., 2015).

Tier 2, in this model, should provide short-term, integrated supports that enable students to access grade-level material rather than isolating them from it. These supports might include (1) pre-teaching vocabulary and background knowledge tied to core instruction, (2) retrieval practice connected to texts or concepts taught in Tier 1, (3) additional worked examples and scaffolded problem-solving in math, and (4) comprehension instruction using authentic, content-rich texts. Crucially, Tier 2 should not function as a generic "comprehension skills" group; it must directly support students' success in core content areas such as English Language Arts (ELA), science, or history (Shanahan, 2024b; Wanzek et al., 2013). Tier 3, in contrast, should be reserved for students with the most intensive needs and delivered by specialists using targeted, evidence-based programs. These interventions should focus on decoding and fluency, explicit writing instruction, or numeracy support that combines procedural practice with conceptual models. When Tier 3 instruction is tightly aligned to students' gaps and delivered with structure and intensity, it promotes transfer, builds durable knowledge, and helps prevent fragmentation and cognitive overload common in less guided, skill-only approaches (Table 5.4).

SCENARIO: HIGH-QUALITY, GRADE-LEVEL INSTRUCTION IN ENGLISH GRADE 11 CLASSROOM

Ms. Thomas is teaching her 11th-grade ELA class the 1920s novel, *The Great Gatsby*. Her Tier 1 instruction includes the following:

- Explicit instruction on themes like the American Dream and disillusionment and Socratic discussions around Nick's reliability as a narrator
- Vocabulary instruction for words like "supercilious," "riotous," and "ephemeral"
- Reading comprehension tasks focused on interpreting symbolism and inferences (i.e., the green light, Dr. T.J. Eckleburg)
- Use of retrieval practice (i.e., daily low-stakes questions on key plot points and themes)
- Scaffolded writing tasks, analyzing character motivations and author's craft

During these lessons, Ms. Thomas notices that three students—Malik, Oliver, and Ashleigh—are struggling to make sense of the text independently. They can't keep up with in-class readings (their reading rate is slow), they are having difficulty writing about abstract concepts like symbolism, and they often give surface-level responses in discussion or reading checks. Ms. Thomas gives a brief fluency and vocabulary check and realizes that these three students (1) decode multisyllabic words slowly, (2) don't know key Tier 2 vocabulary (like "gaudy," "incessant," and "vitality"), and (3) lack background knowledge about the 1920s or the novel's social commentary. Malik, Oliver, and Ashliegh need Tier 2 support but not remediation or "main idea" practice. They need help accessing *The Great Gatsby* more effectively. Ms. Thomas designs the following instructional plan to help these three students access the grade-level text, as an ongoing support for 6 to 9 weeks, with progress monitoring every 2 or 3 weeks. She will meet with them during a built-in intervention block 3x/week for 20–30 minutes.

TABLE 5.4 Tier 2 Intervention Progression for *The Great Gatsby*

Instructional Focus: Vocabulary, Fluency, Background Knowledge, and Deep Comprehension

Student: Malik, Oliver, Ashliegh

Week	Tier 2 Focus	Instructional Strategies	Goal / Rationale
Week 1	Build Context & Vocabulary	♦ Introduce *Gatsby* background: 1920s, class, prohibition, American Dream (via short articles + visuals) ♦ Pre-teach 5–7 Tier 2 words (e.g., *lavish, decadent, illusion*) ♦ Use Frayer models & sentence stems ♦ Read and annotate short adapted Gatsby passage	Build semantic and world knowledge to reduce cognitive load and increase comprehension (Willingham, 2006)
Week 2	Vocabulary + Fluency	♦ Revisit Tier 2 words using spaced practice ♦ Guided oral reading of a Gatsby passage (e.g., Chap. 3 party scene) with feedback ♦ Fluency drills (prosody, punctuation, unfamiliar words) ♦ Retrieval practice on plot/events	Strengthen orthographic mapping (Ehri, 2014) and fluency to allow more focus on meaning
Week 3	Comprehension Scaffolds	♦ Use graphic organizer to analyze setting, tone, and symbolism (e.g., green light, Valley of Ashes) ♦ Teacher models how to answer "What does the green light represent?" with sentence starters ♦ Practice constructing short written responses with support	Support working memory by using scaffolds and worked examples (Clark et al., 2012; Sweller, 1988)

(Continued)

TABLE 5.4 (Continued)

Instructional Focus: Vocabulary, Fluency, Background Knowledge, and Deep Comprehension

Student: Malik, Oliver, Ashliegh

Week	Tier 2 Focus	Instructional Strategies	Goal / Rationale
Week 4	Practice Analyzing Characters & Themes	◆ Reread and annotate key scenes ◆ Structured peer discussion using question stems: "Why does Gatsby lie about his past?" ◆ Use retrieval quizzes (Who? What? Why?) to reinforce narrative structure	Promote deeper processing and retrieval-enhanced learning (Roediger & Karpicke, 2006)
Week 5	Partial Transfer to Tier 1 Tasks	◆ Analyze a new passage independently (e.g., confrontation scene, Chapter 7) ◆ Apply vocabulary in writing (e.g., "Write how Gatsby's dream is *illusory*") ◆ Reflect on how Gatsby's choices relate to the American Dream	Encourage application and schema development in the context of original text
Week 6	Independent Practice & Re-integration	◆ Complete short literary analysis paragraph with sentence frames and tiered vocabulary ◆ Conduct oral presentation on a theme or symbol ◆ Monitor comprehension through Tier 1 discussion and writing	Show transfer of learning to Tier 1 tasks; scaffold withdrawal begins

Tier 2 intervention progression for *The Great Gatsby*, detailing weekly instructional focus, strategies, and goals to support vocabulary, fluency, background knowledge, and deep comprehension for small-group instruction.

The belief that MTSS/RTI is most effective when tied to isolated standards or discrete skills has gained traction—particularly in schools under pressure to raise test scores. But this belief reflects outdated models and common misconceptions, not what current research in cognitive science supports.

Mastering a standard in isolation does not guarantee comprehension or transfer to authentic reading or problem-solving contexts (Shanahan, 2020; Willingham, 2006). Yet many schools rely on computer-based intervention programs that reinforce this checklist approach—remediating one standard or skill at a time. These platforms appear "data-driven" and easy to monitor, making them attractive Tier 2 solutions. However, they often show little to no long-term impact, especially at the secondary level (Lipsey et al., 2018; Slavin et al., 2009; Williams et al., 2022). Progress-monitoring tools in many new, digital curriculums, frequently report performance per standard, giving the illusion of diagnostic precision. These scores rarely reflect deep understanding or the ability to apply knowledge in real tasks, yet educators feel pressured to "fix" each low standard individually.

Curriculum companies contribute to this issue. Because they design materials to align with state standards and testing blueprints, many prioritize compliance and surface-level usability over alignment to cognitive science, reading research, or evidence-based instructional design. This approach may prioritize meeting external requirements over incorporating evidence-based instructional design principles. Buzzwords like differentiation, inquiry-based, and data-driven often drive purchasing decisions. Even widely used review platforms like EdReports.org, while useful in assessing alignment to college- and career-readiness standards, do not evaluate whether materials reflect learning theory or cognitive science. As a result, materials that are well aligned with standards but lack a strong foundation in cognitive science may still receive positive evaluations. The emphasis on compliance and surface-level usability can lead educators to adopt materials that appear effective based on standardized criteria but may not support deep learning. To promote more effective instruction, it is essential to consider both alignment to standards and adherence to principles of cognitive science in the selection and design of instructional materials. This approach can help ensure that materials not only meet external requirements but also support meaningful learning experiences.

To improve MTSS at both the elementary and secondary levels, we need a fundamental shift away from compliance-driven, standard-by-standard intervention models. Instead, schools must ground their approach in the science of learning, domain-specific knowledge, and authentic academic tasks. The most effective way to strengthen MTSS is to start by strengthening Tier 1: deliver explicit instruction, use a high-quality curriculum, and build lessons around rich content rather than watered-down skills. Abandon the practice of differentiating by "level" and instead *scaffold* students toward rigorous goals. Use formative checks, retrieval practice, and cumulative review regularly and prioritize language development and knowledge-building—not just standard mastery. Tier 2, likewise, must be intentionally designed and delivered by skilled teachers—not outsourced to software. Supports should align to Tier 1 content and address the underlying barriers to comprehension or application rather than reacting to individual test items. Ultimately, remembering that MTSS is a system for ensuring access to Tier 1—not a permanent remediation track—is key to avoiding the very practices that undermine student growth. MTSS succeeds not when students are tracked into endless remedial groups but when every tier scaffolds them toward meaningful, grade-level learning—anchored in rich content, guided practice, and the deliberate building of knowledge and skills.

Worked Examples: Reducing Cognitive Load and Building Schema

Worked examples are among the most effective, research-backed instructional strategies available—and yet they remain underused, especially in secondary classrooms. Rooted in Cognitive

Load Theory (Sweller, 1988), worked examples reduce unnecessary cognitive load, allowing students to focus on reasoning, structure, and strategy before applying concepts independently (Clark et al., 2012). A worked example is simply a completed—or partially completed—problem, model, or task that shows students exactly how to solve it step by step, often with annotated reasoning. In Tier 1 instruction, teachers model everything from analyzing a text to solving a math problem or conducting a lab experiment. These demonstrations make thinking visible, guiding students through the process. In Tier 2, struggling students benefit from even more structured support: multiple worked examples, sentence stems for writing, or fill-in-the-step problems that help them focus on underlying patterns (Booth et al., 2013; Graham & Perin, 2007).

But using worked examples effectively matters. Research cautions against assuming that students will simply "pick up" the strategy by watching. Teachers must explicitly walk through the example, make thinking visible, and gradually release responsibility. For example, asking students to compare two worked examples and explain which is more effective—using visual scaffolds or reflection prompts—can deepen metacognition while still supporting cognitive load. Teachers are often surprised by how powerful worked examples can be—but also prone to underestimating their value. This stems from several misconceptions: the false belief that students must always be "doing" something active to learn or that observing is passive and therefore ineffective. Particularly in secondary classrooms, teachers often suffer from expert blind spot—forgetting how complex a task is for a novice once it has become automatic for the expert (Nathan & Koedinger, 2000). As a result, instruction often jumps too quickly to independent problem-solving, skipping the modeling and guided practice that students actually need.

Worked examples are especially potent in writing and math—two domains with high cognitive demands. Writing requires planning, vocabulary, syntax, structure, and reasoning—all at once. By reducing cognitive load early in the writing process, worked examples allow students to focus on application and schema-building (Sweller et al., 2011). Teachers can model how to write a paragraph using the hero's journey, revise weak topic sentences, or annotate a model essay with success criteria. Over time, students internalize expectations and build transferable structures across genres (Graham & Perin, 2007). The benefits of worked examples may not be flashy—but they are cumulative and profound. When used consistently, they help students build the background knowledge and cognitive strategies needed to succeed with independent tasks. They support access to rigorous content in Tier 1 and provide meaningful, structured support in Tier 2—aligning perfectly with the principles of MTSS grounded in learning science.

In math, worked examples show step-by-step problem-solving processes, making thinking visible. Effective ones include each step written out clearly, often pair visuals with verbal reasoning (to support dual coding), and highlight common misconceptions or errors. Math heavily taxes working memory—especially when students are still learning procedures and concepts—so novices benefit from seeing how and why steps are taken. Paired with deliberate practice, worked examples lead to more robust schema development and better transfer. This is precisely where scaffolding and worked examples intersect. Worked examples are not just a strategy—they are a form of scaffolding designed to support students as they move from novice to proficient learners. By showing students how to do something and providing concrete references, we reduce problem-solving demands, freeing up cognitive resources for pattern recognition and conceptual understanding. While scaffolding is the broader principle, worked examples are among the most effective tools to provide that support. When used thoughtfully and phased out over time, they allow students to move from observing a process to completing it independently—with confidence and clarity.

The effectiveness of worked examples lies not in their flash but in their consistency and alignment with how learning actually happens. They support equity in Tier 1 by giving all students access to rigorous content, and they strengthen Tier 2 by offering guided, structured opportunities for skill-building. When teachers let go of the myth that students must always struggle to learn and instead embrace modeling as a way to make thinking visible, students are more likely to succeed—not because the task is easier but because the path to mastery is clearer.

The Power of Effective Scaffolding

Scaffolding is the most impactful, efficient, and responsive way to meet student needs while keeping all learners engaged with rich, grade-level content. It's proactive—allowing teachers to maintain coherence and rigor for the entire class. Unlike small-group instruction, which often consumes time, relies heavily on differentiation and personalization, and separates students by perceived ability, effective scaffolding ensures that all students receive structured supports—such as worked examples, guided practice, and gradual release—that build schema efficiently and reduce the guesswork and frustration of premature independence. These strategies benefit every learner—not only those who struggle—because they align with how the brain actually acquires and organizes complex information. When implemented skillfully, scaffolding is equity in action: it gives every learner a clear pathway toward mastery without lowering expectations or fragmenting instruction. When done well, it doesn't just close gaps—it prevents them from widening in the first place.

References

Anderson, R. C., & Pearson, P. D. (1984). A schema-theoretic view of basic processes in reading comprehension. In P. D. Pearson, R. Barr, M. L. Kamil, & P. Mosenthal (Eds.), *Handbook of reading research* (pp. 255–291). Longman.

Applebee, A. N., & Langer, J. A. (2011). *Writing instruction that works: Proven methods for middle and high school classrooms.* Teachers College Press.

Archer, A. L., & Hughes, C. A. (2011). *Explicit instruction: Effective and efficient teaching.* Guilford Press.

Barnett, S. M., & Ceci, S. J. (2002). When and where do we apply what we learn? A taxonomy for far transfer. *Psychological Bulletin, 128*(4), 612–637. https://doi.org/10.1037/0033-2909.128.4.612

Barth, A. E., Vaughn, S., Capin, P., Cho, E., Stillman-Spisak, S., Martinez, L., & Kincaid, H. (2016). Effects of a text-processing comprehension intervention on struggling middle school readers. *Topics in Language Disorders, 36*(4), 368–389. https://doi.org/10.1097/TLD.0000000000000101

Beck, I. L., McKeown, M. G., & Kucan, L. (2013). *Bringing words to life: Robust vocabulary instruction* (2nd ed.). The Guilford Press.

Berninger, V. W., & Abbott, R. D. (2010). Relationship of word- and sentence-level working memory to reading and writing in second, fourth, and sixth grade. *Language, Speech, and Hearing Services in Schools, 41*(2), 179–193. https://doi.org/10.1044/0161-1461(2009/08-0002)

Biemiller, A. (2005). Addressing developmental patterns vocabulary: Implications for choosing words for primary grade vocabulary instruction. In E. H. Hiebert & M. Kamil (Eds.), *Bringing scientific research to practice: Vocabulary* (pp. 223–242). Erlbaum.

Bjork, R. A., & Bjork, E. L. (2011). Making things hard on yourself, but in a good way: Creating desirable difficulties to enhance learning. In M. A. Gernsbacher & R. W. Pew (Eds.), *Psychology and the real world: Essays illustrating fundamental contributions to society* (pp. 56–64). Worth Publishers.

Boaler, J. (2016). *Mathematical mindsets: Unleashing students' potential through creative math, inspiring messages, and innovative teaching.* JosseyBass.

Bonesrønning, H., Finseraas, H., Hardoy, I., Iversen, J. M. V., Nyhus, O. H., Opheim, V., Salvanes, K. V., Sandsør, A. M. J., & Schøne, P. (2022). Small-group instruction to improve student performance in mathematics in early grades: Results from a randomized field experiment. *Journal of Public Economics*, *216*, 104765. https://doi.org/10.1016/j.jpubeco.2022.104765

Booth, J. L., Lange, K. E., Koedinger, K. R., & Newton, K. J. (2013). Using example problems to improve student learning in algebra: Differentiating between correct and incorrect examples. *Learning and Instruction*, *25*, 24–34. https://doi.org/10.1016/j.learninstruc.2012.11.002

Bowers, J. S. (2020). Reconsidering the evidence that systematic phonics is more effective than alternative methods of reading instruction. *Educational Psychology Review*, *32*, 681–705. https://doi.org/10.1007/s10648-019-09515-y

Broughton, S. H., Sinatra, G. M., & Reynolds, R. E. (2010). The nature of the refutation text effect: An investigation of attention allocation. *The Journal of Educational Research*, *103*(6), 407–423. https://doi.org/10.1080/00220670903383101

Cabell, S. Q., & Hwang, H. (2020). Building content knowledge to boost comprehension in the primary grades. *The Reading Teacher*, *74*(1), 17–25. https://doi.org/10.1002/trtr.1905

Cain, K., & Oakhill, J. (2007). *Children's comprehension problems in oral and written language: A cognitive developmental perspective*. The Guilford Press.

Catts, H. W., & Kamhi, A. G. (2017). Prologue: Reading comprehension is not a single ability. *Language, Speech, and Hearing Services in Schools*, *48*(1), 16–24. https://doi.org/10.1044/2017_LSHSS-16-0033

Cepeda, N. J., Pashler, H., Vul, E., Wixted, J. T., & Rohrer, D. (2006). Distributed practice in verbal recall tasks: A review and quantitative synthesis. *Psychological Bulletin*, *132*(3), 354–380. https://doi.org/10.1037/0033-2909.132.3.354

Černilec, B., Cotič, M., Darjo, F., & Doz, D. (2023). Differences in students' mathematics knowledge in homogenous and heterogenous groups. *European Journal of Science and Mathematics Education*, *11*(1), 15–32.

Chaiklin, S. (2003). The zone of proximal development in Vygotsky's analysis of learning and instruction. In A. Kozulin, B. Gindis, V. S. Ageyev, & S. M. Miller (Eds.), *Vygotsky's educational theory in cultural context* (pp. 39–64). Cambridge University Press. https://doi.org/10.1017/CBO9780511840975.004

Chi, M. T. H., & Wylie, R. (2014). The ICAP framework: Linking cognitive engagement to active learning outcomes. *Educational Psychologist, 49*(4), 219–243. https://doi.org/10.1080/00461520.2014.965823

Clark, R. E., Kirschner, P. A., & Sweller, J. (2012). Putting students on the path to learning: The case for fully guided instruction. *American Educator, 36*(1), 6–11, 38.

Clark, R. C., & Mayer, R. E. (2008). Learning by viewing versus learning by doing: Evidence-based guidelines for principled learning environments. *Performance Improvement, 47*(9), 5–13. https://doi.org/10.1002/pfi.20028

Connor, C. M., Alberto, P. A., Compton, D. L., & O'Connor, R. E. (2014). *Improving reading outcomes for students with or at risk for reading disabilities: A synthesis of the contributions from the Institute of Education Sciences research centers (NCSER 2014-3000)*. U.S. Department of Education, Institute of Education Sciences, National Center for Special Education Research.

Cunningham, J. W., Spadorcia, S. A., Erickson, K. A., Koppenhaver, D. A., Sturm, J. M., & Yoder, D. E. (2005). Investigating the instructional supportiveness of leveled texts. *Reading Research Quarterly, 40*(4), 410–427. https://doi.org/10.1598/RRQ.40.4.2

Desoete, A., Roeyers, H., & Huylebroeck, A. (2006). Metacognitive skills in Belgian third grade children (age 8 to 9) with and without mathematical learning disabilities. *Metacognition and Learning, 1*(2), 119–135. https://doi.org/10.1007/s11409-006-8152-9

Dubé, F., Dorval, C., & Bessette, L. (2014). Flexible grouping and explicit reading instruction in elementary school. *Journal of Instructional Pedagogies, 10*.

Duke, N. K., & Pearson, P. D. (2002). Effective practices for developing reading comprehension. In A. E. Farstrup & S. J. Samuels (Eds.), *What research has to say about reading* (3rd ed., pp. 205–242). International Reading Association.

Dunlosky, J., Rawson, K. A., Marsh, E. J., Nathan, M. J., & Willingham, D. T. (2013). Improving students' learning with effective learning techniques: Promising directions from cognitive and educational psychology. *Psychological Science in the Public Interest, 14*(1), 4–58. https://doi.org/10.1177/1529100612453266

Dzaldov, B. S., & Peterson, S. (2005). Book leveling and readers. *Journal of Adolescent & Adult Literacy, 48*(1), 66–76.

Ehri, L. C. (2014). Orthographic mapping in the acquisition of sight word reading, spelling memory, and vocabulary learning. *Scientific Studies of Reading, 18*(1), 5–21. https://doi.org/10.1080/10888438.2013.819356

Ericsson, K. A., & Pool, R. (2016). *Peak: Secrets from the new science of expertise.* Houghton Mifflin Harcourt.

Fisher, D., & Frey, N. (2014a). *Better learning through structured teaching: A framework for the gradual release of responsibility* (3rd ed.). ASCD.

Fisher, D., & Frey, N. (2014b). *Text-dependent questions, grades 6–12: Pathways to close and critical Reading.* Corwin.

Gamoran, A. (1992). Is ability grouping equitable? *Educational Leadership, 50*(2), 11–17.

Geary, D. C. (2004). Mathematics and learning disabilities. *Journal of Learning Disabilities, 37*(1), 4–15. https://doi.org/10.1177/00222194040370010201

Gough, P. B., & Tunmer, W. E. (1986). Decoding, reading, and reading disability. *Remedial and Special Education, 7*(1), 6–10. https://doi.org/10.1177/074193258600700104

Graham, S., McKeown, D., Kiuhara, S., & Harris, K. R. (2012). A meta-analysis of writing instruction for students in the elementary grades. *Journal of Educational Psychology, 104*(4), 879–896. https://doi.org/10.1037/a0029185

Graham, S., & Perin, D. (2007). *Writing next: Effective strategies to improve writing of adolescents in middle and high schools.* Carnegie Corporation of New York.

Hall, M. S., & Burns, M. K. (2018). Meta-analysis of targeted small-group reading interventions. *Journal of School Psychology, 66,* 54–66. https://doi.org/10.1016/j.jsp.2017.11.002

Hattie, J. (2009). *Visible learning: A synthesis of over 800 meta analyses relating to achievement.* Routledge.

Hattie, J., & Timperley, H. (2007). The power of feedback. *Review of Educational Research, 77*(1), 81–112. https://doi.org/10.3102/003465430298487

Hiebert, E. H. (2014). *What's complex in text complexity? What's new in literacy teaching? E-ssentials.* International Reading Association. https://www.researchgate.net/profile/Elfrieda-Hiebert/publication/

275696670_What's_Complex_in_Text_Complexity/links/55d157f208ae118c85c01b8e/Whats-Complex-in-Text-Complexity.pdf

Hiebert, E. H. (2017). The texts of literacy instruction: Obstacles to or opportunities for educational equity? *Literacy Research: Theory, Method, and Practice, 66*, 117–134. https://doi.org/10.1177/2381336917718521

Hiebert, E. H. (2020). The core vocabulary: The foundation of proficient comprehension. *The Reading Teacher, 73*(6), 757–768. https://doi.org/10.1002/trtr.1894.Hogan, K., & Pressley, M. (Eds.) (1997). *Scaffolding student learning: Instructional approaches and issues.* Brookline.

Johnson, D. W., & Johnson, R. T. (2009). An Educational Psychology success story: Social interdependence theory and cooperative learning. *Educational Researcher, 38*(5), 365–379. https://doi.org/10.3102/0013189X09339057

Kamil, M. L., & Rauscher, W. C. (1990). Effects of grouping and difficulty of materials on reading achievement. *National Reading Conference Yearbook, 39*, 121–127.

Karpicke, J. D., & Blunt, J. R. (2011). Retrieval practice produces more learning than elaborative studying with concept mapping. *Science, 331*(6018), 772–775. https://doi.org/10.1126/science.1199327

Kilpatrick, D. A. (2015). *Essentials of assessing, preventing, and overcoming reading difficulties.* Wiley.

Kirschner, P. A., Sweller, J., & Clark, R. E. (2006). Why minimal guidance during instruction does not work: An analysis of the failure of constructivist, discovery, problem-based, experiential, and inquiry-based teaching. *Educational Psychologist, 41*(2), 75–86. https://doi.org/10.1207/s15326985ep4102_1

Li, X., Li, Y., & Wang, W. (2023). Long-lasting conceptual change in science education. *Science & Education, 32*, 123–168. https://doi.org/10.1007/s11191-021-00288-x

Lipsey, M. W., Pion, G. M., & Durkin, K. G. (2018). *Effects of the Tennessee voluntary prekindergarten program on children's achievement and behavior through third grade.* Vanderbilt University

Lou, Y., Abrami, P. C., Spence, J. C., Poulsen, C., Chambers, B., & d'Apollonia, S. (1996). Within-class grouping: A meta-analysis. *Review of Educational Research, 66*(4), 423–458. https://doi.org/10.3102/00346543066004423

Nathan, M. J., & Koedinger, K. R. (2000). An investigation of teachers' beliefs of students' algebra development. *Cognition and Instruction, 18*(2), 209–237. https://doi.org/10.1207/S1532690XCI1802_03

National Association for Research in Science Teaching. (1989). *Enhancing learning through conceptual change teaching* (Research Matters, #8902). https://narst.org/research-matters/enhancing-learning-through-conceptual-change-teaching

National Council of Teachers of Mathematics. (2014). *Access and equity in mathematics education.* https://www.nctm.org/standards-and-positions/position-statements/access-and-equity-in-mathematics-education/

Neuman, S. B., Kaefer, T., & Pinkham, A. (2023). Building background knowledge. *Reading Rockets.* https://www.readingrockets.org/topics/background-knowledge/articles/building-background-knowledge

Oakes, J. (2005). *Keeping track: How schools structure inequality.* Yale University Press.

Preckel, F., Schmidt, I., Stumpf, E., Motschenbacher, M., Vogl, K., Scherrer, V., & Schneider, W. (2019). High-ability grouping: Benefits for gifted students' achievement development without costs in academic self-concept. *Child Development*, 90(4), 1185–1201. https://doi.org/10.1111/cdev.12996

Recht, D. R., & Leslie, L. (1988). Effect of prior knowledge on reading comprehension. *Journal of Educational Psychology*, 80(4), 468–474. https://doi.org/10.1037/0022-0663.80.1.16

Roediger, H. L., & Butler, A. C. (2011). The critical role of retrieval practice in long-term retention. *Trends in Cognitive Sciences*, 15(1), 20–27. https://doi.org/10.1016/j.tics.2010.09.003

Roediger, H. L., & Karpicke, J. D. (2006). Test-enhanced learning: Taking memory tests improves long-term retention. *Psychological Science*, 17(3), 249–255. https://doi.org/10.1111/j.1467-9280.2006.01693.x

Rohrer, D., & Taylor, K. (2007). The shuffling of mathematics problems improves learning. *Instructional Science*, 35(6), 481–498. https://doi.org/10.1007/s11251-007-9015-8

Rosenshine, B. (2012). Principles of instruction: Research-based strategies that all teachers should know. *American Educator*, 36(1), 12–19.

Ryan, R. M., & Deci, E. L. (2000). Self-determination theory and the facilitation of intrinsic motivation, social development, and well-being. *American Psychologist*, 55(1), 68–78.

Scammacca, N., Vaughn, S., Roberts, G., Wanzek, J., & Torgesen, J. K. (2007). *Interventions for adolescent struggling readers: A meta-analysis with implications for practice* (NCEE 2008-4023). RMC Research Corporation, Center on Instruction. https://eric.ed.gov/?id=ED521837

Schroeder, N. L., & Kucera, A. C. (2022). Refutation text facilitates learning: A meta-analysis of between-subjects experiments. *Educational Psychology Review, 34*(2), 957–987. https://doi.org/10.1007/s10648-021-09656-z

Shanahan, T. (2014, September 2). Building up to frustration-level text. *Literacy Worldwide.* https://www.literacyworldwide.org/blog/literacy-now/2014/09/02/building-up-to-frustration-level-text

Shanahan, T. (2020). What constitutes a science of reading instruction? *Reading Research Quarterly, 55*(S1), S235–S2547. https://doi.org/10.1002/rrq.349

Shanahan, T. (2024a, March 23). *The instructional level concept revisited: Teaching with complex text.* Shanahan on Literacy. https://www.shanahanonliteracy.com/blog/the-instructional-level-concept-revisited-teaching-with-complex-text-1

Shanahan, T. (2024b, May 04). *Ensuring success: Pre-remediation as a valuable alternative.* Shanahan on Literacy. https://www.shanahanonliteracy.com/blog/ensuring-success-pre-remediation-as-a-valuable-alternative

Shanahan, T. (2025a). *Leveled Reading, Leveled lives.* Harvard Education Press.

Shanahan, T. (2025b, June 14). *Should reading be taught whole class or small group? Shanahan on Literacy.* https://www.shanahanonliteracy.com/blog/should-reading-be-taught-whole-class-or-small-group-1

Shanahan, T., & Shanahan, C. (2008). Teaching disciplinary literacy to adolescents: Rethinking content-area literacy. *Harvard Educational Review, 78*(1), 40–59. https://doi.org/10.17763/haer.78.1.v62444321p602101

Shute, V. J. (2008). Focus on formative feedback. *Review of Educational Research, 78*(1), 153–189. https://doi.org/10.3102/0034654307313795

Siegler, R. S. (2000). The rebirth of children's learning. *Developmental Psychology, 36*(5), 539–550.

Slavin, R. E., Lake, C., & Groff, C. (2009). Effective programs in middle and high school mathematics: A best-evidence synthesis. *Review of Educational Research, 79*(2), 139–179.

Snow, C. E. (2002). *Reading for understanding: Toward an R&D program in reading comprehension.* RAND Corporation.

Steenbergen-Hu, S., Makel, M. C., & Olszewski-Kubilius, P. (2016). What one hundred years of research says about the effects of ability grouping and acceleration on K–12 students' academic achievement: Findings of two second-order meta-analyses. *Review of Educational Research*, *86*(4), 849–899. https://doi.org/10.3102/0034654316675417

Storch, S. A., & Whitehurst, G. J. (2002). Oral language and code-related precursors to reading: Evidence from a longitudinal structural model. *Developmental Psychology*, *38*(6), 934–947.

Sweller, J. (1988). Cognitive load during problem solving: Effects on learning. *Cognitive Science*, *12*(2), 257–285.

Sweller, J., van Merriënboer, J. J., & Paas, F. (1998). Cognitive architecture and instructional design. *Educational Psychology Review*, *10*, 251–296. https://doi.org/10.1023/A:1022193728205

Sweller, J., van Merriënboer, J. J. G., & Paas, F. G. W. C. (2011). Cognitive architecture and instructional design: 20 years later. *Educational Psychology Review*, *23*(2), 261–292. https://doi.org/10.1007/s10648-019-09465-5

Taylor, B. M., Pearson, D. P., Clark, K. F., & Walpole, S. (2000). Effective schools and accomplished teachers: Lessons about primary-grade reading instruction in low-income schools. *Elementary School Journal*, *101*(2), 121–165. https://www.journals.uchicago.edu/doi/abs/10.1086/499662

Tomlinson, C. A. (2005). *How to differentiate instruction in mixed-ability classrooms* (2nd ed.). ASCD.

Torgesen, J. K., Houston, D. D., Rissman, L. M., Decker, S. M., Roberts, G., Vaughn, S., Wexler, J., Francis, D. J., Rivera, M. O., & Lesaux, N. (2007). *Academic literacy instruction for adolescents: A guidance document from the Center on instruction*. Portsmouth, NH: RMC Research Corporation, Center on Instruction.

van de Pol, J., Volman, M., & Beishuizen, J. (2010). Scaffolding in teacher–student interaction: A decade of research. *Educational Psychology Review*, *22*(3), 271–296. https://doi.org/10.1007/s10648-010-9127-6

Vaughn, S., Cirino, P. T., Wanzek, J., Wexler, J., Fletcher, J. M., Denton, C. A., Barth, A. E., Romain, M., & Francis, D. J. (2010). Response to intervention for middle school students with reading difficulties: Effects of a primary and secondary intervention. *School Psychology Review*, *39*(1), 3–21.

Wang, H., King, R. B., & McInerney, D. M. (2023). Ability grouping and student performance: A longitudinal investigation of teacher support as a mediator and moderator. *Research Papers in Education, 38*(2), 121–142. https://doi.org/10.1080/02671522.2021.1961293

Wanzek, J., Vaughn, S., & Scammacca, N. (2015). Meta-analyses of the effects of tier 2 type reading interventions for students in grades K–3. *Journal of Learning Disabilities, 48*(6), 547–560. https://doi.org/10.1007/s10648-015-9321-7

Wanzek, J., Vaughn, S., Scammacca, N. K., Metz, K., Murray, C. S., Roberts, G., & Danielson, L. (2013). Extensive Reading interventions for students with Reading difficulties after grade 3. *Review of Educational Research, 83*(2), 163–195. https://doi.org/10.3102/0034654313477212

Webb, N. M., Franke, M. L., Ing, M., Wong, J., Fernandez, C., Shin, N., & Turrou, A. C. (2014). Engaging with others' mathematical ideas: Interrelationships among student participation, teachers' instructional practices, and learning. *International Journal of Educational Research, 63*, 79–93. https://doi.org/10.1016/j.ijer.2013.02.001

Weinstein, Y., Madan, C. R., & Sumeracki, M. A. (2018). Teaching the science of learning. *Cognitive Research, 3*(2). https://doi.org/10.1186/s41235-017-0087-y

Wexler, J., Vaughn, S., Edmonds, M., & Reutebuch, C. K. (2008). A synthesis of fluency interventions for secondary struggling readers. *Reading and Writing, 21*(4), 317–347. https://doi.org/10.1007/s11145-007-9085-7

Will, K. K., Masad, A., Vlach, H. A., & Kendeou, P. (2019). The effects of refutation texts on generating explanations. *Learning and Individual Differences, 69*, 108–115. https://doi.org/10.1016/j.lindif.2018.12.002

Williams, R., Citkowicz, M., Miller, D., Lindsay, J., & Walters, K. (2022). *Understanding the varied effects of mathematics interventions through meta-analysis*. American Institutes for Research.

Willingham, D. T. (2006). How knowledge helps: It speeds and strengthens reading comprehension, learning—And thinking. *American Educator, 30*(1), 30–37.

Willingham, D. T. (2009). *Why don't students like school? A cognitive scientist answers questions about how the mind works and what it means for the classroom*. Jossey-Bass.

Willms, J. D., Friesen, S., & Milton, P. (2009). *What did you do in school today? Transforming classrooms through social, academic, and intellectual engagement (first findings from the what did you do in school today? Study)*. Canadian Education Association.

Wood, D. J., Bruner, J. S., & Ross, G. (1976). The role of tutoring in problem solving. *Journal of Child Psychology and Psychiatry, 17*(2), 89–100. https://doi.org/10.1111/j.1469-7610.1976.tb00381.x

6

Formative Assessments and Checks for Understanding

Teachers sometimes forget the power of quick, informal checks for understanding (CFUs) as a key to guiding instruction. Responsive teachers continuously monitor student thinking through micro-checks—such as nods, thumbs-up, or brief responses—throughout the class while conducting slightly longer formative checks, such as exit tickets or one-minute papers, three to five times per class period. When teachers respond in the moment, they prevent confusion, reinforce accuracy, and increase instructional efficiency. This is the heart of responsive teaching—where small moves lead to a big impact. The power lies in a teacher's ability to then adjust instruction in real time on the basis of what teachers observe students need (Dataworks, 2020; Wiliam, 2011). But what do these adjustments look like? Mini-adjustments in instruction are often not explicitly planned for, yet they require a teacher to have deep content knowledge and an understanding of common misconceptions in their subject. The adjustments may include rephrasing, providing additional examples or scaffolding, modeling problem-solving steps, or asking more strategic questions to guide student thinking. Formative assessments and adjustments are extremely powerful because they address misconceptions immediately. Unlike end-of-unit evaluations, formative tools are diagnostic and flexible—enabling timely instructional decisions. Cognitive science underscores formative assessment as a key feedback loop that strengthens learning by (1) reinforcing retrieval practice (Roediger & Karpicke, 2006), (2) guiding self-regulation (Hattie & Timperley, 2007; Zimmerman, 2002), and (3) managing cognitive load (Sweller et al., 2011). Additionally, strategically spaced and interleaved checks can enhance long-term retention and transfer of learning (Bjork & Bjork, 2011; Cepeda et al., 2006). When feedback is immediate, specific, and aligned to goals, it clarifies misconceptions before they become entrenched. Research shows that its impact is greatest when grounded in clear objectives, timely feedback, and teacher responsiveness (Black & Wiliam, 1998; Hattie, 2012). It's no surprise that feedback ranks among the top five influences on student achievement.

Checks for Understanding: Core Principles

CFUs are not about grading—they're about responsiveness. These quick, in-the-moment tools help teachers actively gauge student thinking and adapt instruction as needed. Backed by decades of cognitive science and formative assessment research (Black & Wiliam, 1998; Hattie & Timperley, 2007; Roediger & Karpicke, 2006) as well as research on deliberate practice and feedback (Ericsson & Pool, 2016), CFUs align with how memory, attention, and learning works. Effective strategies include cold calling (Lemov, 2010), think-pair-share (Lyman, 1981), mini whiteboards (Wiliam, 2011), and exit tickets (Angelo & Cross, 1993). These strategies not only provide immediate feedback to teachers but also encourage students to actively retrieve, rehearse, and apply knowledge, consistent with the principles of desirable difficulties (Bjork, 1994). Small in size but large in impact, these techniques help teachers catch misconceptions early, provide timely feedback, and keep instruction tightly aligned to student needs.

A Brief Word on Cold Calls and Turn-and-Talks

It is important to note that while cold-calling and turn-and-talk are frequently used strategies to assess student understanding, neither should be implemented without clear intention and support (Learning Scientists, 2024). In many secondary classrooms, cold-calling can devolve into an "I'll get you" tactic—calling on a student the teacher suspects is not paying attention—rather than a purposeful learning interaction. Yet, for students to feel safe and confident sharing their thinking, the classroom must foster a culture in which they believe their teacher values their voices and trusts their contributions. Research shows that students are more willing to participate when they perceive their teacher as credible and supportive (Liu et al., 2023; McCroskey & Young, 1981; Rocca, 2007). Additionally, turn-and-talks risk falling flat if they are unguided, lacking in clear expectations, modelling, and rehearsal. Without that scaffolding, these partner-talk routines may not function as an opportunity to practice a concept learned in whole-group instruction but instead may become idle chatter or momentary distractions.

Using Checks for Understanding During Explicit Instruction

CFUs during interactive lectures—particularly within an explicit instruction model—can dramatically improve learning and help students transfer knowledge beyond the immediate lesson. When instruction is broken into chunks (5–10 minutes) and teachers pose quick questions or prompts to assess understanding, it becomes possible to respond to student thinking in real time. CFUs such as recall questions, application tasks, predictions, and intentional think-pair-shares engage different cognitive processes and allow teachers to identify gaps early. Immediate feedback corrects misconceptions, while alignment with learning intentions and success criteria helps students monitor their own progress and generalize their learning (Anderson, 1990; Sweller et al., 2011).

Unlike traditional models of differentiation—which are often resource-intensive and inconsistently applied—CFUs are efficient, scalable, and repeatable. They don't require redesigning curriculum or materials, and they offer real-time insight that can guide reteaching or targeted support. CFUs also allow teachers to implement spaced retrieval and interleaved practice within a lesson, increasing long-term retention (Cepeda et al., 2006). While differentiation has mixed evidence of impact and can increase teacher workload without reliably improving outcomes (Deunk et al., 2018; Huebner, 2010; Pozas et al., 2021; Reis et al., 2011), formative evaluation and feedback—including regular CFUs—rank among the most powerful influences on student learning (Hattie, 2009), and CFUs support retrieval-based learning, reduce cognitive overload, and help build coherent mental models (Pashler et al., 2007).

CFUs are especially powerful during explicit instruction because they align directly with how the brain learns—reinforcing key ideas, surfacing misconceptions, and sustaining cognitive engagement. Contrary to misconceptions about direct instruction being passive, effective explicit teaching requires students to actively think, retrieve, and make meaning. CFUs also support metacognition, enable students to monitor their understanding, recognize gaps, and regulate their learning strategies (Zimmerman, 2002). Techniques such as turn-and-talks, cold calls, and quick written or verbal responses promote retrieval, rehearsal, and connection to prior knowledge (Roediger & Karpicke, 2006). These repeated, low-stakes opportunities help solidify learning and support generalization—the ability to apply knowledge or skills across contexts (Bransford et al., 2000). When students understand what success looks like and receive timely feedback, they are more likely to stay motivated, focused, and confident in their progress (Schunk et al., 2008).

Formative Assessment in the Disciplines

Across all disciplines, formative assessments are most effective when they are low-stakes, frequent, and embedded within explicit instruction, targeting thinking rather than guessing. These assessments provide feedback that fosters metacognition and reduces ambiguity and cognitive overload (Bjork & Bjork, 2011; Hattie & Timperley, 2007; Rosenshine, 2012) while allowing teachers to adjust instruction in real time. Importantly, they help students develop the cognitive skills that transfer across subjects. For example, in English Language Arts, CFUs support text-based reasoning, the activation of background knowledge, and repeated engagement with complex ideas, such as summarizing a paragraph in one sentence or identifying an author's argument. In mathematics, formative assessments guide step-by-step problem-solving, conceptual understanding, and error detection through worked examples, strategic questioning, and error analysis (Kirschner et al., 2006). In science, CFUs promote systems thinking, causal reasoning, and conceptual transfer using models, simulations, and explanatory prompts (Bransford et al., 2000; Chi, 2009), such as predicting outcomes in an experiment before running it. In history, assessments emphasize sourcing, contextualization, and evidence-based argumentation—moving beyond surface-level fact recall (Willingham, 2009; Wineburg, 1991), like identifying the perspective of a primary source and justifying it with evidence. Across all these disciplines, the power of formative assessment lies not just in measuring what students know but in shaping learning in real time—clarifying misconceptions, reinforcing retrieval, guiding self-regulation, and supporting meaningful engagement with content (Hattie, 2012; Roediger & Karpicke, 2006; Sweller et al., 2011; Zimmerman, 2002). By integrating CFUs with spaced and interleaved practice, teachers can further strengthen retention and promote flexible, transferable learning.

Questioning Paired with Feedback and Formative Assessment

Effective questioning is intentional, responsive, and strategic. When done well, it enhances metacognition, deepens learning, and provides real-time insight into student understanding. Teacher questioning aligns directly with core principles of cognitive science: it promotes retrieval and strengthens retention, prompts students to explain their reasoning and connect new learning to prior knowledge (Chi et al., 1989; Weinstein et al., 2018), encourages self-monitoring (Schraw & Dennison, 1994; Zimmerman, 2002), and helps identify misconceptions during guided practice (Archer & Hughes, 2011).

In explicit instruction classrooms, questioning is used to clarify, reinforce, and correct, serving as a scaffold for building accurate and connected knowledge. In contrast, progressive teaching models often prioritize student-driven meaning-making, with teachers responding to ideas with additional questions rather than direct feedback. Research shows that structured classroom discussions, guided by carefully sequenced questions, have a high impact on learning (Hattie, 2023). These findings underscore the importance of intentional questioning design in scaffolding learning and managing cognitive load. Teachers may begin with closed questions to promote factual recall and gradually move to open-ended prompts that require students to connect and apply knowledge. This approach assumes that students need explicit scaffolding before they can express complex disciplinary ideas. When questioning is paired with immediate, actionable feedback, it not only maintains engagement but strengthens memory consolidation and formation of accurate mental models.

Webb's Depth of Knowledge and How They've Been Misused

As noted in Chapter 4, Norman Webb's Depth of Knowledge (DOK) levels are frequently misunderstood—not as indicators of the kind of thinking required but as a scale of how "hard" a question seems. Webb's DOK framework (Webb, 2002) was designed to categorize tasks on the basis of the complexity of thinking that students must engage in—not the surface-level difficulty of the task or how "hard" it feels. DOK levels aim to measure cognitive demand—the type of mental processing required to complete a task successfully. Webb emphasized that high-quality learning tasks should go beyond simple recall or rote memorization to include reasoning, analysis, and application. The framework was originally developed to align standards, curriculum, instruction, and assessment with the intended level of thinking required. Crucially, Webb (2007) noted that cognitive demand is contextual: the same task could be DOK 1 in one setting and DOK 3 in another, depending on factors such as text complexity, prior knowledge, and task expectations.

In practice, however, DOK levels have often been misapplied. Teachers are frequently told to aim for "higher DOK questions" to meet college- and career-ready standards, and some administrators use DOK levels to judge instructional rigor during classroom walkthroughs. But as Shanahan (2025a) and others have argued, question level alone does not guarantee deeper understanding. Even "low-DOK" tasks can challenge students if they require connection to complex prior knowledge, and "high DOK" questions may be superficial if background knowledge is missing. Without solid background knowledge, students struggle even with low-DOK tasks; with well-developed knowledge structures, they can navigate high-DOK tasks more effectively (Bransford et al., 2000; Chi, 2009; Willingham, 2009).

True depth of learning is achieved not by chasing "higher-order questions" but by embedding purposeful, successive questioning within rich content. This includes frequent CFUs, metacognitive prompts, and scaffolded tasks aligned to clear goals. Teachers should focus less on labeling questions by DOK level and more on crafting meaningful instructional sequences that build understanding over time. Without this foundation, efforts to "raise rigor" through question complexity alone can be ineffective—or even frustrating—for students (Shanahan, 2025b).

The Formative Feedback Loop

Formative assessment during learning enhances retention and understanding by promoting retrieval practice, diagnosing misconceptions, and allowing for timely correction. However, quick checks are effective only when paired with meaningful, actionable feedback. Without it, misconceptions may go unnoticed, and students may become confused or discouraged. Feedback must be timely, specific, and actionable to help learners make adjustments and move forward. When CFUs are frequent, low-pressure, and normalized as part of the learning process, they strengthen metacognition, reduce test anxiety, and foster a classroom culture that values learning over performance (Agarwal et al., 2014; Khanna, 2015; Putnam et al., 2016; Roediger & Karpicke, 2006). These checks also provide valuable information for teachers, allowing them to adapt instruction, reteach or clarify as needed, and adjust the pacing or depth of their lessons accordingly. While often contrasted with summative assessment, formative assessment is not a separate event but an ongoing, embedded process of instruction. It is assessment *for* learning, not *of* learning, and its value lies not in recording student performance but in illuminating student thinking and guiding both teacher and student decisions. For formative checks to serve their purpose, they must result in action. This might mean that the teacher reteaches a concept, slows or increases the pace, or adjusts instruction in other ways to increase the probability of student mastery. It also requires the students to engage with the feedback—reconsidering a response, revising an idea, or asking a clarifying question. Without this responsive loop, formative assessment becomes inert: a diagnostic tool that identifies misunderstanding but does not correct it. Black and Wiliam (1998) argue that formative assessment must produce evidence that both teachers and students can use to make decisions about next steps. Students may need explicit instruction on how to interpret and use feedback to guide their own learning. Ultimately, formative assessment is not a moment on a timeline—it is the engine of effective instruction, continuously driving improvement for both teacher and learner.

From Feedback to Feedforward

Formative assessments and CFUs are not ancillary tasks—they are central to effective, evidence-based teaching. By embedding frequent, low-stakes checks throughout instruction, teachers can dynamically gauge student thinking, correct misconceptions in real time, and reinforce learning through retrieval and rehearsal. Coupled with intentional, structured questioning, these practices support cognitive processes such as self-regulation, metacognition, and the management of cognitive load, all of which are critical for durable, transferable learning. Across disciplines, formative assessments provide actionable insights for both teachers and students, guiding instruction, scaffolding understanding, and fostering engagement with complex ideas. Importantly, these strategies demonstrate that high-quality learning is measured not solely by summative outcomes but by the ongoing interplay between feedback, student thinking, and responsive teaching. When implemented consistently and thoughtfully, formative assessment transforms the classroom into a dynamic learning environment—one in which students are active participants, misconceptions are addressed before they take root, and teachers make informed instructional decisions grounded in research and cognitive science. In short, formative assessment is not merely a tool; it is the engine that drives learning forward.

References

Agarwal, P. K., Roediger, H. L., McDaniel, M. A., & McDermott, K. B. (2014). Classroom-based programs of retrieval practice reduce test anxiety and improve learning. *Journal of Applied Research in Memory and Cognition*, *3*(2), 131–139. https://psycnet.apa.org/doi/10.1016/j.jarmac.2014.07.002

Anderson, J. R. (1990). *Cognitive psychology and its implications* (3rd ed.). W. H. Freeman.

Angelo, T. A., & Cross, K. P. (1993). *Classroom assessment techniques: A handbook for college teachers* (2nd ed.). Jossey-Bass.

Archer, A. L., & Hughes, C. A. (2011). *Explicit instruction: Effective and efficient teaching*. Guilford Press.

Bjork, R. A. (1994). Memory and metamemory considerations in the training of human beings. In J. Metcalfe & A. Shimamura (Eds.), *Metacognition: Knowing about knowing* (pp. 185–205). MIT Press.

Bjork, R. A., & Bjork, E. L. (2011). Making things hard on yourself, but in a good way: Creating desirable difficulties to enhance learning. In M. A. Gernsbacher & R. W. Pew (Eds.), *Psychology and the real world: Essays illustrating fundamental contributions to society* (pp. 56–64). Worth Publishers.

Black, P., & Wiliam, D. (1998). Inside the black box: Raising standards through classroom assessment. *Phi Delta Kappan*, *80*(2), 139–148.

Bransford, J. D., Brown, A. L., & Cocking, R. R. (Eds.) (2000). *How people learn: Brain, mind, experience, and school* (Expanded ed.). National Academy Press.

Cepeda, N. J., Pashler, H., Vul, E., Wixted, J. T., & Rohrer, D. (2006). Distributed practice in verbal recall tasks: A review and quantitative synthesis. *Psychological Bulletin, 132*(3), 354–380. https://doi.org/10.1037/0033-2909.132.3.354

Chi, M. T. H. (2009). Active-constructive-interactive: A conceptual framework for differentiating learning activities. *Topics in Cognitive Science, 1*(1), 73–105. https://doi.org/10.1111/j.1756-8765.2008.01005.x

Chi, M. T. H., Bassok, M., Lewis, M.W., Reimann, P., & Glaser, R. (1989). Self-explanations: How students study and use examples in learning to solve problems. *Cognitive Science, 13*(2), 145–182. https://doi.org/10.1207/s15516709cog1302_1

Dataworks Education. (2020). *Checking for understanding: Why and how*. https://dataworks-ed.com/checkingunderstanding/

Deunk, M. I., Jacobse, A. E., de Boer, H., Doolaard, S., & Bosker, R. J. (2018). Effective differentiation practices: A systematic review and meta-analysis of studies on the cognitive effects of differentiation practices in primary education. *Educational Research Review, 24*, 31–54. https://doi.org/10.1016/j.edurev.2018.02.002

Ericsson, K. A., & Pool, R. (2016). *Peak: Secrets from the new science of expertise*. Houghton Mifflin Harcourt.

Hattie, J. (2009). *Visible learning: A synthesis of over 800 meta analyses relating to achievement*. Routledge.

Hattie, J. (2012). *Visible learning for teachers: Maximizing impact on learning*. Routledge.

Hattie, J. (2023). *Visible learning: The sequel: A synthesis of over 2,100 meta-analyses relating to achievement*. Routledge.

Hattie, J., & Timperley, H. (2007). The power of feedback. *Review of Educational Research, 77*(1), 81–112. https://doi.org/10.3102/003465430298487

Huebner, T. A. (2010, February). What research says about… differentiated learning. *Educational Leadership, 67*(5), 79–81. https://www.ascd.org/el/articles/differentiated-learning

Khanna, M. M. (2015). Ungraded pop quizzes: Test-enhanced learning without all the anxiety. *Teaching of Psychology, 42*(2), 174–178. https://doi.org/10.1177/0098628315573144

Kirschner, P. A., Sweller, J., & Clark, R. E. (2006). Why minimal guidance during instruction does not work: An analysis of the failure of constructivist, discovery, problem-based, experiential, and inquiry-based teaching. *Educational Psychologist, 41*(2), 75–86. https://doi.org/10.1207/s15326985ep4102_1

Learning Scientists. (2024, April 4). Cold calling in the classroom: Why it's not as scary as you think. *The Learning Scientists*. https://www.learningscientists.org/blog/2024/4/4

Lemov, D. (2010). *Teach like a champion: 49 techniques that put students on the path to college*. Jossey-Bass.

Liu, J., Wang, M., & Ryan, T. (2023). Factors influencing student engagement: A meta-analysis. *Behavioral Sciences*, *13*(1), 59. https://doi.org/10.3390/bs13010059

Lyman, F. (1981). The responsive classroom discussion: The inclusion of all students. In A. S. Anderson (Ed.), *Mainstreaming digest* (pp. 109–113). University of Maryland College of Education.

McCroskey, J. C., & Young, T. J. (1981). Ethos and credibility: The construct and its measurement after three decades. *Central States Speech Journal*, *32*(1), 24–34. https://doi.org/10.1080/10510978109368075

Pashler, H., Bain, P. M., Bottge, B. A., Graesser, A., Koedinger, K., McDaniel, M., & Metcalfe, J. (2007). *Organizing instruction and study to improve student learning (NCER 2007–2004)*. National Center for Education Research, Institute of Education Sciences, U.S. Department of Education.

Pozas, M., Letzel, V., Lindner, K.-T., & Schwab, S. (2021). DI (differentiated instruction) does matter! The effects of DI on secondary school students' well-being, social inclusion, and academic self-concept. *Frontiers in Education*, *6*. https://doi.org/10.3389/feduc.2021.729027

Putnam, A. L., Sungkhasettee, V. W., & Roediger, H. L. (2016). Optimizing learning in college: Tips from cognitive psychology: Tips from cognitive psychology. *Perspectives on Psychological Science*, *11*(5), 652–660. https://doi.org/10.1177/1745691616645770

Reis, S. M., McCoach, D. B., Little, C. A., Muller, L. M., & Kaniskan, R. B. (2011). *American Educational Research Journal*, *48*(2), 462–501. https://doi.org/10.3102/0002831210382891

Rocca, K. A. (2007). Immediacy in the classroom: Research and practical implications. *Communication Education*, *56*(1), 32–48.

Roediger, H. L., & Karpicke, J. D. (2006). Test-enhanced learning: Taking memory tests improves long-term retention. *Psychological Science*, *17*(3), 249–255. https://doi.org/10.1111/j.1467-9280.2006.01693.x

Rosenshine, B. (2012). Principles of instruction: Research-based strategies that all teachers should know. *American Educator*, *36*(1), 12–19.

Schraw, G., & Dennison, R. S. (1994). Assessing metacognitive awareness. *Contemporary Educational Psychology*, *19*(4), 460–475. https://doi.org/10.1006/ceps.1994.1033

Schunk, D. H., Pintrich, P. R., & Meece, J. L. (2008). *Motivation in education: Theory, research, and applications* (3rd ed.). Pearson Education.

Shanahan, T. (2025a). *Leveled reading, leveled lives*. Harvard Education Press.

Shanahan, T. (2025b, August 23). Rejecting instructional level theory. *Shanahan on Literacy*. https://www.shanahanonliteracy.com/blog/rejecting-instructional-level-theory-1

Sweller, J., van Merriënboer, J. J. G., & Paas, F. G. W. C. (2011). Cognitive architecture and instructional design: 20 years later. *Educational Psychology Review*, *23*(2), 261–292. https://doi.org/10.1007/s10648-019-09465-5

Webb, N. L. (2002). *Depth-of-knowledge levels for four content areas (research report)*. Wisconsin Center for Educational Research.

Webb, N. L. (2007). Issues related to judging the alignment of curriculum standards and assessments. *Applied Measurement in Education*, *20*(1), 7–25. https://doi.org/10.1080/08957340709336728

Weinstein, Y., Madan, C. R., & Sumeracki, M. A. (2018). Teaching the science of learning. *Cognitive Research*, *3*, 2. https://doi.org/10.1186/s41235-017-0087-y

Wiliam, D. (2011). *Embedded formative assessment*. Solution Tree Press.

Willingham, D. T. (2009). *Why don't students like school? A cognitive scientist answers questions about how the mind works and what it means for the classroom*. Jossey-Bass.

Wineburg, S. S. (1991). Historical problem solving: A study of the cognitive processes used in the evaluation of documentary and pictorial evidence. *Journal of Educational Psychology*, *83*(1), 73–87.

Zimmerman, B. J. (2002). Becoming a self-regulated learner: An overview. *Theory Into Practice*, *41*(2), 64–70. https://doi.org/10.1207/s15430421tip4102_2

7

The Power of Feedback

Feedback is one of the most powerful tools for learning—but only when it's timely, specific, and actionable (Hattie & Timperley, 2007; Shute, 2008). Too often, feedback is thought of as something teachers *give*—a one-way delivery of information in small doses, sometimes even unintentional. But effective feedback—the kind that actually changes learning—is a two-way street. When feedback happens close to the learning event, it helps the brain connect cause and effect. When it's specific, it highlights *what* was done well and *what* needs improvement rather than offering vague praise or general criticism. And when it's actionable, it gives learners a clear path forward—a concrete next step for improvement. Importantly, feedback works in a loop: it informs teachers' next instructional moves while helping students understand their own next steps in the learning process. In that sense, feedback isn't an endpoint—it's a conversation that drives learning forward.

That said, not all feedback helps. Too much, or overly detailed, feedback can actually backfire. It might feel intuitive to think that the more we comment on a student's work, the more they'll grow—but the opposite often happens. When feedback is excessive, students become overwhelmed and unsure where to begin. Similarly, over-scaffolding—providing constant, high-frequency feedback—can prevent learners from engaging in deeper thinking or productive struggle (Sweller, 1988; Van Merriënboer & Sweller, 2005). As learners gain experience, the nature of effective feedback shifts. While *all* students benefit from clear, timely guidance, the amount and type of support should be adjusted as their competence grows. For more proficient learners, excessive guidance can become redundant or even counterproductive—a phenomenon known as the expertise reversal effect (Van Merriënboer & Sweller, 2005). In these cases, feedback that emphasizes self-monitoring, goal setting, and reflection promotes continued growth without reducing cognitive engagement (Kluger & DeNisi, 1996; Nicol & Macfarlane-Dick, 2006). Finally, not all feedback that feels encouraging is actually effective. Praise, for instance, can be tricky. Person-based praise ("You're so smart") often promotes a fixed mindset, while process-oriented feedback ("You used a strong strategy here") reinforces effort, strategy use, and ongoing growth.

Why Teacher Feedback Matters More Than Computer-Based Feedback

While teachers are often busy—and frequently cite the difficulty of providing individual feedback to every student, especially in secondary classrooms, where class sizes are large—the impact of tailored feedback that prompts reflection is substantial (Shute, 2008). Effective teachers don't just give answers; they offer strategic prompts that help students monitor their own thinking, evaluate their work, and adjust their strategies (Nicol & Macfarlane-Dick, 2006). Teacher feedback carries power not only because it supports cognitive processes but because it builds relational trust. It signals to students that someone is invested in their learning and can adjust feedback to support both motivation and confidence—key ingredients in fostering the belief that improvement is possible (Hattie & Timperley, 2007). Since deeper learning happens when students actively engage with content, teachers are uniquely positioned to ask probing questions, prompt self-explanation, and guide students to elaborate on their reasoning—something that automated systems cannot do effectively. Learning improves when students try, fail, and revise—a process strengthened by timely, corrective feedback that clarifies both the *why* and the *how* behind errors (Roediger & Butler, 2011).

Teachers who have established trust and credibility have an even greater impact. According to Hattie (2012), teacher credibility is built on four elements: trust, competence, dynamism, and immediacy. When students perceive their teacher as credible, they are more likely to value the feedback, act on it, and feel safe taking academic risks. The effect size of teacher credibility is remarkable—0.90, more than double the average of most teacher interventions (Hattie, 2012). Credibility is reinforced when feedback is consistent, accurate, fair, matched to individual needs, and accompanied by follow-up support. When feedback is both instructional and relational, it sends a powerful message: *you matter, and your learning matters too.*

Still, even credible teachers often feel that their carefully crafted feedback goes unnoticed. This frustration is understandable—cognitive science reminds us that attention is selective and guided by perceived relevance. Students are more likely to engage with feedback from someone they view as trustworthy, knowledgeable, and supportive. When a teacher is credible, feedback is seen as worth considering—not something to resist or ignore (Krashen, 1982; Willingham, 2009). High-credibility teachers are more effective at offering feedback that students reflect on rather than resist (Nicol & Macfarlane-Dick, 2006).

When students perceive their teacher as credible and caring, they are more intrinsically motivated—believing that their effort matters (Dweck, 2006). Positive teacher–student relationships enhance not only motivation but also memory: emotionally safe classrooms activate the brain systems that strengthen attention and long-term retention (Lieberman, 2013).

This broad understanding of feedback is crucial when distinguishing formative feedback from summative assessment. While summative assessments offer a snapshot of student learning at a point in time—typically for grading or accountability purposes—formative feedback is an ongoing, interactive process designed to advance learning. As discussed in Chapter 6, effective formative feedback informs both the learner and the teacher about progress relative to learning goals and provides specific guidance on how to improve. This distinction is critical because summative scores alone rarely yield actionable insights for students or educators. By clearly separating formative feedback from summative judgment, teachers can foster a classroom culture where mistakes are viewed as opportunities rather than failures. Formative feedback guides instructional decisions and helps students understand their strengths and areas for improvement before final evaluations. When formative feedback is systematically integrated into teaching, assessments become a tool for learning—not just a measure of it (Black & Wiliam, 1998; Sadler, 1989).

Feedback and Writing Instruction

Writing is one of the most complex cognitive tasks that students face—it requires memory, planning, self-regulation, attention to conventions, and metacognition. Because of this, effective writing instruction depends heavily on thoughtful, personalized feedback—the kind that only a credible teacher can provide. Writing requires deep, effortful processing—and feedback guides that process. Craik and Lockhart (1972) showed that learning is strengthened when students reflect, revise, and elaborate—core features of the writing process. Teacher feedback prompts this deeper processing, helping students see how and why to improve their thinking and structure—not just whether they got it right. Because writing is personal, students are more willing to take risks, revise deeply, and persist through multiple drafts when feedback comes from a teacher they trust and respect (Hattie, 2012). Although artificial intelligence (AI) tools have been introduced to assist with grading, automated systems cannot provide the contextualized, motivating, and instructionally rich feedback that helps students meaningfully improve their writing. Formative feedback must be goal-oriented, explanatory, and elaborative (Shute, 2008)—and that requires human insight, relationships, and pedagogical judgment.

Cognitive science offers clear guidance on what kinds of feedback support writing growth, without overwhelming either students or teachers. When providing feedback on writing, teachers can focus on a few high-impact principles. First, feedback should be task-focused—anchored in skills, strategies, and next steps rather than vague praise or personal evaluation (Dweck, 2006). This type of feedback promotes application because it is directly tied to actionable steps students can take. Second, feedback should prompt metacognition by asking students to reflect on their choices and reasoning, rather than simply correcting errors (Wiliam, 2011). For instance, asking students to identify their areas of strength and potential growth in their writing encourages them to take ownership of their growth and transforms feedback into feedforward. Finally, feedback should target just one or two goals *per draft*, since students can process only limited information at once. Prioritizing major elements like organization or clarity helps writers focus their efforts where it matters most. Because students often don't read or act on lengthy end comments, feedback should also be *manageable and interactive*. Quick, margin-based codes or comments are easier to digest and act on. Some effective approaches include the following:

- **Margin codes or symbols**: Use short, targeted comments or symbols (e.g., "C" for clarity, "E" for evidence) to help students focus on specific areas without overwhelming them with lengthy notes.
- **Focused feedback goals**: Limit comments to one or two high-impact areas per assignment to reduce cognitive overload and increase uptake.
- **Use of exemplars and models**: Pair feedback with examples of strong work to clarify expectations and guide revision.
- **Conferencing and one-on-one feedback**: Hold brief, targeted conversations to provide personalized guidance and boost motivation.
- **Incorporating technology judiciously**: Use tools like audio feedback or learning management systems to save time while maintaining a personal connection.
- **Peer feedback protocols**: Teach students to give constructive, criterion-based comments to foster a supportive and reflective classroom culture.
- **Timely follow-up**: Provide structured opportunities for students to act on feedback—through revision, editing, or reflection—so it leads to visible improvement rather than being passively received.

Feedback in Mathematics Instruction

Just as in writing, feedback in mathematics instruction is critical for helping students deepen conceptual understanding, identify errors, and refine problem-solving strategies. Research in cognitive science emphasizes that effective feedback must be timely, specific, and goal-oriented—especially in math, where learning builds cumulatively and concepts build on one another. Mistakes in math are not just wrong answers; they offer insight into a student's reasoning. Instead of simply marking answers as incorrect, effective feedback should unpack *where* and *how* the student's thinking broke down (Hattie & Timperley, 2007). This is especially important because conceptual misunderstandings in math are often more resistant to change than factual errors, as they reflect underlying misconceptions about relationships or principles rather than isolated pieces of information (Rittle-Johnson & Alibali, 1999; Vosniadou, 2008). By targeting misconceptions—whether procedural or conceptual—teachers help students realign their thinking with accurate frameworks. When feedback explains *why* an approach was flawed and *how* to fix it, it strengthens both conceptual understanding and transfer. Task-specific feedback has also been shown to significantly improve how students approach multi-step problems, supporting the development of flexible, strategic thinking (Van der Pol et al., 2020).

Immediate, formative feedback is especially powerful in math because of its step-by-step nature. If early errors go uncorrected, they can cascade into larger misunderstandings that impede mastery of later concepts. Spacing and interleaving practice are supported by cognitive-science evidence as key components of effective learning (Dunlosky et al., 2013; Rohrer & Taylor, 2007). In addition, timely, corrective feedback helps prevent misconceptions from becoming entrenched by giving learners the opportunity to adjust before incorrect mental models take hold (Roediger & Butler, 2011). Because math requires precision, a single error can propagate through subsequent steps, leading to further mistakes. Immediate correction prevents these cognitive traits from taking hold. Over time, unaddressed errors become entrenched and harder to undo (Roediger & Butler, 2011). That's why feedback in math must focus not only on the final answer but also on the *process*. When teachers break complex problems into smaller, feedback-rich steps, they reduce cognitive load and give students the confidence to move forward as their competence grows.

Questioning Paired with Feedback and Formative Assessment

When questioning, formative feedback, and checks for understanding are used together, they create a powerful feedback loop—one deeply grounded in cognitive science and evidence-based teaching. This loop supports attention, memory, motivation, and metacognition: the core elements of effective learning. Together, these strategies foster a responsive learning environment that activates thinking through targeted questioning, surfaces misconceptions or knowledge gaps via checks for understanding, and bridges the gap between current and desired understanding with actionable feedback.

Recalling information strengthens memory, and well-crafted questions can reveal misconceptions or gaps in students' schemas, providing teachers with valuable insights. Questioning is not merely an assessment tool—it actively promotes learning (Roediger & Karpicke, 2006). When integrated effectively, questioning, formative feedback, and checks for understanding form a continuous cycle of retrieval, reflection, and refinement. This loop reduces cognitive load, supports long-term retention, and helps both teachers and students identify and correct misunderstandings in real time. Table 7.1 illustrates how this feedback loop might operate in a middle school writing lesson.

In this example, students engage several key elements of cognitive science in the learning process. First, they retrieve what they know about writing a claim, strengthening memory and supporting long-term learning (Roediger & Karpicke, 2006). Then, by generating their own responses rather than selecting from options, students increase learning because effortful generation enhances encoding and mental connections (Bjork, 1994). This also allows teachers to identify misconceptions early, preventing students from reinforcing flawed thinking (Sweller, 1988). Feedback following a retrieval attempt tends to be more effective, fostering deeper learning (Metcalfe, 2017).

TABLE 7.1 Writing Classroom Example, Middle School

Learning Goal: Students will write a clear, evidence-based argument with a strong claim and reasoning

Step	Classroom Example	Cognitive Science Link
Questioning (Activate Thinking & Retrieval)	♦ "What makes an argument convincing?" ♦ "What's the difference between a claim and evidence?" ♦ "Can someone share an example of a weak claim and why it doesn't work?"	♦ Activates prior knowledge ♦ Promotes retrieval practice ♦ Surfaces misconceptions early
Check for Understanding (Real-Time Diagnostic)	♦ Students do a quick task: Write a sample claim about a school policy in 1 minute on whiteboards. Show it when ready. ♦ Teacher scans for weak or vague claims, claims without a clear stance, and overly emotional or personal phrasing	♦ Retrieval Practice ♦ Generation Effect (Bjork, 1994) ♦ Real-time diagnosis reduces cognitive load ♦ Feedback after retrieval attempt, deepens learning (Metcalfe, 2017)
Formative Feedback (Corrective Input)	♦ Teacher selects two examples ♦ "Let's look at this one—what works well here?" ♦ "This one is unclear—how could we revise it to make the stance more specific?"	♦ Feedback is task-focused, timely, and helps refine mental models ♦ Students are not overloaded with corrections; just one or two actionable steps.

Middle school writing classroom example illustrating step-by-step instructional practices, linking questioning, checks for understanding, and formative feedback to cognitive science principles that support evidence-based argument writing.

While timely, task-focused feedback is critical for helping students act on next steps, cognitive science also shows that *how* and *when* feedback is given matter for long-term learning. Effective feedback builds on self-regulation rather than focusing solely on correctness. It should encourage students to monitor, plan, and evaluate their own work—practices shown to produce longer-lasting effects than merely correcting errors (Hattie & Timperley, 2007; Winstone et al., 2016). This process moves students from feedback dependence to feedback literacy—the ability to use feedback independently and effectively. While immediate feedback is often recommended, especially in math or high-accuracy tasks, research also shows that brief delays—for example, returning work after a day or two—can strengthen long-term retention in certain contexts, particularly for conceptual or transfer tasks like writing or science (Aljibari, 2025; Mullet et al., 2014). Delayed feedback requires the brain to re-engage with material, reinforcing retrieval. However, for novices or procedural tasks (such as early math), immediate feedback remains essential to prevent encoding errors (Kang et al., 2007; Metcalfe et al., 2009; Shute, 2008). Feedback is most impactful when tied explicitly to goals and success criteria; students need to know the learning target and what success looks like for feedback to guide improvement effectively (Carless & Boud, 2018; Hattie & Timperley, 2007; Sadler, 1989).

Once students move beyond the novice stage, feedback need not come solely from the teacher. Structured peer feedback can be a powerful tool for deepening understanding, developing critical thinking, and fostering a collaborative classroom culture. When students engage in giving and receiving feedback, they learn to analyze work against clear criteria, articulate constructive comments, and reflect on their own learning. Similarly, self-feedback encourages metacognition, enabling students to monitor their progress, identify challenges, and plan revisions independently. Teaching students how to use rubrics, success criteria, and guided reflection prompts, this process and builds their feedback literacy. Ultimately, developing students' ability to give and use feedback prepares them to become lifelong, self-regulated learners (Nicol & Macfarlane-Dick, 2006; Winstone et al., 2016).

Effective Feedback and Empowering Learning

Effective feedback is not an add-on—it is the engine of learning. When grounded in cognitive science, feedback becomes more than correction; it becomes thinking. Whether through teacher input, peer dialogue, or self-assessment, well-designed feedback supports memory, motivation, and metacognition. It helps students understand where they are, where they're going, and how to bridge that gap. Ultimately, feedback that is timely, specific, and actionable transforms classrooms into spaces where mistakes are not setbacks but steppingstones toward mastery.

References

Aljibari, S. (2025). Correction: Timing of feedback and retrieval practice: A laboratory study with EFL students. *Humanities & Social Sciences Communications*, *12*, 1182. https://doi.org/10.1057/s41599-025-05569-2

Bjork, R. A. (1994). Memory and metamemory considerations in the training of human beings. In J. Metcalfe & A. Shimamura (Eds.), *Metacognition: Knowing about knowing* (pp. 185–205). MIT Press.

Black, P., & Wiliam, D. (1998). Inside the black box: Raising standards through classroom assessment. *Phi Delta Kappan, 80*(2), 139–148.

Carless, D., & Boud, D. (2018). The development of student feedback literacy: Enabling uptake of feedback. *Assessment & Evaluation in Higher Education*, *43*(8), 1315–1325. https://doi.org/10.1080/02602938.2018.1463354

Craik, F. I. M., & Lockhart, R. S. (1972). Levels of processing: A framework for memory research. *Journal of Verbal Learning and Verbal Behavior*, *11*(6), 671–684. https://doi.org/10.1016/S0022-5371(72)80001-X

Dunlosky, J., Rawson, K. A., Marsh, E. J., Nathan, M. J., & Willingham, D. T. (2013). Improving students' learning with effective learning techniques: Promising directions from cognitive and educational psychology. *Psychological Science in the Public Interest*, *14*(1), 4–58. https://doi.org/10.1177/1529100612453266

Dweck, C. S. (2006). *Mindset: The new psychology of success*. Random House.

Hattie, J. (2012). *Visible learning for teachers: Maximizing impact on learning*. Routledge.

Hattie, J., & Timperley, H. (2007). The power of feedback. *Review of Educational Research*, *77*(1), 81–112. https://doi.org/10.3102/003465430298487

Kang, S. H., McDermott, K. B., & Roediger, H. L. (2007). Test format and corrective feedback modify the effect of testing on long-term retention. *European Journal of Cognitive Psychology*, *19*, 528–558. https://doi.org/10.1080/09541440601056620

Kluger, A. N., & DeNisi, A. (1996). The effects of feedback interventions on performance: A historical review, a meta-analysis, and a preliminary feedback intervention theory. *Psychological Bulletin*, *119*(2), 254–284. https://doi.org/10.1037/0033-2909.119.2.254

Krashen, S. D. (1982). *Principles and practice in second language acquisition*. Pergamon Press.

Lieberman, M. D. (2013). *Social: Why our brains are wired to connect*. Crown Publishers.

Metcalfe, J. (2017). Learning from errors. *Annual Review of Psychology*, *68*, 465–489. https://doi.org/10.1146/annurev-psych-010416-044022

Metcalfe, J., Kornell, N., & Finn, B. (2009). Delayed versus immediate feedback in children's and adults' vocabulary learning. *Memory & Cognition*, *37*, 1077–1087. https://doi.org/10.3758/MC.37.8.1077

Mullet, H. G., Butler, A. C., Verdin, B., von Borries, R., & Marsh, E. J. (2014). Delaying feedback promotes transfer of knowledge despite student preferences to receive feedback immediately. *Journal of Applied Research in Memory and Cognition*, *3*(3), 222–229. https://doi.org/10.1016/j.jarmac.2014.05.001

Nicol, D. J., & Macfarlane-Dick, D. (2006). Formative assessment and self-regulated learning: A model and seven principles of good feedback practice. *Studies in Higher Education*, *31*(2), 199–218. https://doi.org/10.1080/03075070600572090

Rittle-Johnson, B., & Alibali, M. W. (1999). Conceptual and procedural knowledge of mathematics: Does one lead to the other? *Journal of Educational Psychology*, *91*(1), 175–189. https://doi.org/10.1037/0022-0663.91.1.175

Roediger, H. L., & Butler, A. C. (2011). The critical role of retrieval practice in long-term retention. *Trends in Cognitive Sciences*, *15*(1), 20–27. https://doi.org/10.1016/j.tics.2010.09.003

Roediger, H. L., & Karpicke, J. D. (2006). Test-enhanced learning: Taking memory tests improves long-term retention. *Psychological Science*, *17*(3), 249–255. https://doi.org/10.1111/j.1467-9280.2006.01693.x

Rohrer, D., & Taylor, K. (2007). The shuffling of mathematics problems improves learning. *Instructional Science, 35*(6), 481–498. https://doi.org/10.1007/s11251-007-9015-8

Sadler, D. R. (1989). Formative assessment and the design of instructional systems. *Instructional Science, 18*(2), 119–144. https://doi.org/10.1007/BF00117714

Shute, V. J. (2008). Focus on formative feedback. *Review of Educational Research, 78*(1), 153–189. https://doi.org/10.3102/0034654307313795

Sweller, J. (1988). Cognitive load during problem solving: Effects on learning. *Cognitive Science, 12*(2), 257–285. https://doi.org/10.1007/s10648-010-9133-8

Van der Pol, J., et al. (2020). The effects of feedback on problem-solving. *Journal of Educational Psychology, 112*(3), 458–477.

Van Merriënboer, J. J. G., & Sweller, J. (2005). Cognitive load theory and complex learning: Recent developments and future directions. *Educational Psychology Review, 17*(2), 147–177. https://doi.org/10.1007/s10648-005-3951-0

Vosniadou, S. (2008). *International handbook of research on conceptual change*. Routledge.

Wiliam, D. (2011). *Embedded formative assessment*. Solution Tree Press.

Willingham, D. T. (2009). *Why don't students like school? A cognitive scientist answers questions about how the mind works and what it means for the classroom*. Jossey-Bass.

Winstone, N. E., Nash, R. A., Parker, M., & Rowntree, J. (2016). Supporting learners' agentic engagement with feedback: A systematic review and a taxonomy of recipience processes. *Educational Psychologist, 52*(1), 17–37. https://doi.org/10.1080/00461520.2016.1207538

8

Retrieval, Interleaving and Spaced Practice

An underutilized yet highly effective learning strategy is *retrieval practice*—how we engage students in recalling information from memory rather than simply reviewing it. The act of pulling knowledge out, as in answering a question or completing a brief quiz, strengthens memory far more than rereading notes or highlighting text. A substantial body of research supports this effect. Roediger and Karpicke (2006) found that students who studied once and then took a free-recall test remembered significantly more a week later than those who simply re-studied the material. Similarly, Agarwal and colleagues (2012) found that when teachers regularly used low-stakes quizzes and questioning, student achievement and retention improved. When retrieval is paired with feedback, its impact increases even further (Butler & Roediger, 2008; Dunlosky et al., 2013).

Contrary to popular belief, low-stakes and well-designed timed quizzes do not inherently create anxiety; rather, they can reduce it by *normalizing* retrieval and providing ongoing feedback. When teachers embed brief, no-grade, or low-grade quizzes, students begin to view testing as part of learning rather than judgment (Agarwal et al., 2014; Khanna, 2015). Research shows that frequent retrieval opportunities strengthen memory, improve transfer, and reduce the pressure associated with high-stakes exams because students experience more consistent success (Putnam et al., 2016; Roediger & Butler, 2011). The key lies in how testing is framed and practiced: frequent, short, and cumulative quizzes, coupled with immediate feedback and opportunities for correction, promote metacognition and confidence rather than stress (Pan & Rickard, 2018). Classroom routines such as daily "brain dumps," weekly mixed review quizzes, and peer explanation of answers can help students internalize retrieval as a natural and empowering learning process—turning assessment into a tool for thinking, not judgment.

The benefits of retrieval practice are part of a broader pattern in cognitive research: learning improves when students must think hard to recall, connect, or distinguish ideas. One related approach is *interleaving*, which involves mixing different types of problems or topics within a single study session rather than practicing one type in a block (known as *blocked practice*). Rohrer and Taylor (2010) compared interleaved vs. blocked practice in math and found that students who practiced via interleaving performed better on delayed tests, even though they felt less confident during learning. Kang and Pashler (2012) showed that interleaving improves the ability to transfer learning to new contexts—applying what you know to novel problems— and Samani and Pan (2021) demonstrated similar benefits in science learning, suggesting that the effect generalizes beyond mathematics to other domains. When combined with retrieval practice, interleaving further strengthens memory and helps students identify what they've forgotten. Together, these strategies improve discrimination between concepts and enhance flexible thinking.

John Hattie's meta-analyses point to similar principles behind retrieval practice, spacing, and interleaving. His synthesis of research on practice and feedback shows that students learn more when they regularly recall, apply, and connect knowledge over time—rather than simply review it (Hattie, 2023). Importantly, the value of testing lies not in grades or accountability but in using tests as *tools* for learning and feedback. Spaced practice—spreading learning over time rather than cramming—enhances problem-solving flexibility and reduces reliance on rote memorization. This is not about leaving students to "discover" solutions on their own but about providing structured opportunities to apply strategies across varied problems. Interleaving supports this process by helping students recognize when and how to use different approaches, building lasting proficiency (Hattie, 2023). Making daily review a consistent, non-negotiable part of classroom routines can also have a powerful impact on student learning and long-term retention (Swain, 2024).

Retrieval practice does not just help students remember surface-level knowledge; it actually helps to improve higher-order learning as well. Karpicke and Blunt (2011) compared retrieval practice with concept mapping and found that retrieval led to better performance on inference and application questions—not just factual recall. Because retrieval helps students organize and reconstruct what they know, it promotes more flexible understanding. Additionally, it is effective across age groups and subjects, benefiting learners from elementary school through college. Studies have shown its effectiveness in math, science, history, reading, and even complex fields like medical education (Larsen et al., 2009). Cumulative retrieval—using unit-based quizzes that include both new and previously learned material—can further strengthen long-term retention by reinforcing spacing and spiraling concepts over time (Agarwal et al., 2012).

As we'll explore further in Chapter 9, this idea connects closely to spaced or distributed practice—another powerful complementary learning strategy. Distributed practice spreads learning out over time with breaks or intervals between practice sessions, instead of cramming (known as massed practice). It is one of the most robust, well-supported principles in cognitive science. Research shows that allowing some forgetting between study sessions actually strengthens memory during retrieval—when learners have to work a bit to recall information, the memory becomes more durable (Bjork, 1994). For example, spreading the review of 60 vocabulary words across three 20-minute sessions rather than one helps deepen retention. Spaced review reduces cognitive overload and allows students to focus better during each session, strengthening long-term retention (Cepeda et al., 2006; Dunlosky et al., 2013; Rohrer & Taylor, 2006). This is especially true in math, where intentional opportunities to revisit and spiral content strengthen both retention and transfer—and benefits all learners, including those who struggle.

A Word about Math Instruction

In many math programs, particularly in secondary, there is a tendency to withhold direct, explicit instruction, assuming that discovery or exploration will lead to deeper understanding. Teachers may pose open-ended tasks without first ensuring that students know what they're doing. Some curricula avoid teaching standard algorithms until very late (or not at all), focusing instead on invented strategies. As a result, students spend weeks drawing number lines or decomposing numbers without ever mastering fluent arithmetic. This approach can lead to low confidence, poor number sense, and slow, error-prone computation. Baroody (2003) and the National Mathematics Advisory Panel (2008) concur that conceptual understanding and procedural fluency are mutually reinforcing, not mutually exclusive. They argue that quick recall of math facts and fluency with standard procedures ultimately are essential for higher-level math success. Their findings suggest that we shouldn't delay procedural instruction for fear it will interfere with conceptual learning, nor should we skip conceptual explanations to expedite procedural fluency. Instead, teaching both explicitly strengthens learning.

Unfortunately, these same misconceptions often persist into other areas of mathematics, where practices such as timed testing or cumulative review are sometimes discouraged out of concern that they create anxiety or promote rote learning. Yet, when framed as opportunities for fluency-building rather than evaluation, timed practice helps students automate foundational skills—freeing up working memory for complex reasoning and problem-solving (Sweller et al., 2011; Willingham, 2009). In recent years, many educators have pulled back from practices like timed testing or frequent quizzing, partly in response to broader movements emphasizing emotional safety and social-emotional learning (SEL). While these efforts are well intentioned—and rooted in a desire to protect students from unnecessary stress—research shows that moderate, productive struggle is not harmful; in fact, it's essential to long-term learning. This isn't to say that long periods of struggle without feedback—or struggle for its own sake—are effective. Learning requires both challenge and support, where feedback helps students calibrate effort and see growth. Decades of empirical studies have found that well-implemented SEL programs can enhance students' engagement, behavior, and even academic outcomes (Durlak et al., 2011; Taylor et al., 2017). However, their effects are *moderate*, and they depend on how well SEL is integrated into *rigorous* academic instruction. When SEL becomes detached from the learning process, focusing more on emotional comfort than cognitive growth, it can inadvertently reduce the very challenge and feedback that students need to build mastery. Effective SEL supports learning by helping students manage frustration, persist through difficulty, and take academic risks. It should strengthen, not soften, the conditions of learning. When these well-intentioned ideas about emotional support extend into math instruction, they can contribute to progressive practices that prioritize exploration over skill mastery. Teachers may avoid correcting student misconceptions, which disproportionately affects struggling learners and those with less background knowledge.

These misconceptions about mathematics and learning extend into misunderstandings of the importance of retrieval, interleaving, and distributed practice building students' conceptual and procedural understanding. The belief that conceptual must precede procedural is equally problematic. Conceptual understanding becomes meaningful only when students internalize core ideas—for example, that multiplication is repeated addition, a fraction represents division, or the equal sign signifies equivalence rather than "the answer comes next." Problem-based learning can be effective after students have developed some expertise—procedural fluency and domain knowledge—but not before. The belief that students will derive understanding solely through exploration often requires them to grapple with multiple representations of every concept, increasing extraneous cognitive load and reducing learning efficiency. Research challenges the common assumption that conceptual understanding must precede procedural fluency. In fact, studies suggest that teaching procedures first—or teaching both together—can actually promote deeper conceptual insight. When students learn efficient procedures early, they free up cognitive resources to notice underlying patterns and relationships (Baroody, 2003; Rittle-Johnson & Schneider, 2015; Rittle-Johnson et al., 2001). Conversely, delaying procedural instruction in favor of discovery-oriented conceptual exploration can leave students with fragmented understanding and slow, error-prone computation. By explicitly connecting procedures and concepts in tandem, teachers help students develop both flexibility and fluency. Yet much of the commercial curricula in the U.S. does not support this approach. Instead, conceptual understanding is often positioned as a prerequisite to fluency, leading to inefficient learning progressions that fail to meet the needs of many learners. This problem is not just curricular but systemic. Although the Common Core State Standards (CCSS) were intended to counteract this issue—focusing on depth over breadth, coherence across grade levels, and meaningful understanding alongside fluency—they have not consistently closed achievement gaps. A review of CCSS effects showed only small positive effects on math outcomes, primarily in fourth grade, with benefits varying by socioeconomic status (Bleiberg, 2021).

These instructional and systemic weaknesses are reflected in national and international outcomes. The 2022 National Assessment of Educational Progress (NAEP) scores tell a similar story—showing the steepest decline in math performance in decades, especially at the fourth- and eighth-grade levels. Between 2019 and 2022, eighth-grade math scores fell eight points, a statistically significant and deeply concerning drop. Only one in four students—about 26%—scored at or above proficient in math. While the NAEP cites learning disruptions during COVID-19 as a contributing factor, it also highlights long-standing weaknesses in math instruction: inconsistent attention to foundational skills, limited procedural fluency, and weak opportunities for strategic problem-solving. Together, these gaps leave students without the building blocks needed for higher-level math. International comparisons tell a similar story. In the 2022 Programme for International Student Assessment (PISA), U.S. students ranked below many of their global peers, with an average math score of 465, compared with the OECD (Organisation for Economic Co-operation and Development) average of 472. Only 28% of American 15-year-olds reached Level 3 or higher—the level needed to apply mathematics to real-world problems (OECD, 2023a). In contrast, students in countries such as Singapore, Japan, South Korea, and Estonia—where explicit instruction, fluency, and coherent curriculum design are prioritized—consistently outperform their U.S. peers. In Singapore, the top-performing system worldwide, the average score was 575, while 88% of Japanese and 84% of Korean students reached at least Level 2 proficiency (OECD, 2023b, 2023c, 2023d).

Strategies like retrieval practice, interleaving, and spaced practice can help address several common instructional problems in math. They counteract issues such as fragmented instruction, overemphasis on isolated subskills, and approaches that either focus only on procedures or push conceptual understanding before students are ready—problems that have appeared in some implementations of the CCSS. Retrieval practice boosts long-term retention by prompting students to recall information from memory, thereby strengthening neural connections. This approach helps students retain and apply skills and concepts across time rather than forgetting them after a test or unit (Agarwal et al., 2014; Roediger & Butler, 2011). Similarly, interleaving helps students distinguish when and how to apply what they've learned. This combats the "illusion of mastery" created by blocked practice and helps students develop conceptual flexibility (Pan, 2015; Rohrer et al., 2015). Encouraging students to recall not just steps but reasoning behind procedures helps them to build fluency and flexibility. Spaced practice also reduces forgetting and strengthens long-term retention of vocabulary, decoding, math strategies and content knowledge. This pushes students to compare procedures and problem types (i.e., multiplication vs. area problems), reinforcing both meaning and method (Kapur & Bielaczyc, 2012; Willingham, 2003).

Embedding strategies like this into core math instruction can help counteract curriculum designs that lack evidence-based instructional approaches to learning. For instance, curricular assessments often rely overly on subskill-based assessments that don't accurately capture where a student's misunderstanding lies. This often means that teachers *never* identify the deeper, conceptional misunderstandings. Retrieval practice, especially when done through open-ended prompts, provides valuable insights into student understanding because teachers get an *immediate* sense of what students know and don't know—and this can happen regularly, through daily warm-ups or exit tickets or even quick checks during class on white boards (Agarwal et al., 2014; McDaniel et al., 2011; Roediger & Butler, 2011). These approaches do not require a teacher to reinvent their math curriculum; rather, they require flexibility, support, and adequate planning time to use materials intentionally in ways that promote durable learning. Unlike multiple-choice tests, open-ended retrieval prompts allow students to articulate their reasoning. This is a crucial advantage because it helps uncover misunderstandings or incomplete thinking. This, in turn, enables teachers to make real-time instructional adjustments (Kapur & Bielaczyc, 2012).

The connection between working memory and math instruction is central to understanding both how students learn math and why so many struggle—especially under overly constructivist approaches or poorly designed curricula. Working memory is the brain's short-term processing system, and it allows us to hold information temporarily (i.e., numbers, steps in a problem) and manipulate those numbers (via calculating, comparing, or following a multi-step procedure). Working memory is limited, especially in children and novice learners. According to Cognitive Load Theory (Sweller et al., 1998), overloading working memory impairs learning especially when tasks (1) are too complex, (2) are poorly structured, and (3) require juggling too many new pieces of information at once. Math is working memory–intensive. Take, for instance, a simple enough problem like 27 × 4. To solve this problem, a student must (1) recall multiplication facts (long-term memory), (2) hold intermediate steps (working memory), and (3) perform operations without losing track of the goal. When students have not yet automatized their math facts, lack procedural understanding, or are asked to explore new methods without sufficient guidance, their working memory becomes overloaded, impeding learning. Many discovery-based math programs overlook these cognitive limits. In contrast, explicit teaching reduces working memory strain and supports gradual conceptual understanding—key factors in preventing anxiety and promoting durable learning (Gathercole & Alloway, 2008; Geary, 2011; Sweller et al., 2011). When instruction overwhelms students' cognitive resources, it can trigger math anxiety, which further diminishes working memory capacity and leads to even weaker performance (Ashcraft & Krause, 2007). Indeed, poor math instruction has a far greater negative impact on students' sense of math ability than timed tests do.

Retrieval practice, while often discussed in the context of long-term memory, plays a crucial role in supporting working memory, especially in math instruction, where working memory demands are high. Retrieval practice automates basic knowledge and skills, freeing working memory from re-processing every step of a problem. This extra cognitive bandwidth allows students to tackle complex tasks and problem (Geary, 2011; Sweller et al., 1998). Multi-step problems and word problems are of particular difficulty for many students in part because students' working memory is overloaded with too much new information (like re-learning steps or concepts in the moment of solving a word problem). Retrieval practice builds schema, and the more students retrieve connections between ideas, the more fluently they can apply them in new situations—with less strain on working memory (Karpicke & Blunt, 2011). This also helps students spot mistakes in their own work, because they have a stronger memory of what "correct" looks like, and they're less cognitively overloaded, so they can reflect more clearly. This is critical in math, where self-correction is part of problem-solving—but requires working memory bandwidth. Math instruction requires working memory, but it's easily overwhelmed. Retrieval practice (1) offloads cognitive burden, (2) automates essential skills, and (3) frees up mental space for real problem-solving. Table 8.1 offers practical, quick ways that teachers can embed retrieval practice into daily math instruction, regardless of the curriculum being used.

TABLE 8.1 Retrieval Practice in Math Instruction

Technique	Purpose	Additional Notes
Daily Cumulative Warm-Ups	Keeps key knowledge active across units	Could be 3–5 problems covering old and new concepts
Low-Stakes Quizzes	Encourages retrieval without pressure	Can be multiple-choice, short answer or open-ended
Flashcards with Self-Check	Builds fluency with math facts and terms	Include both computation and concept definitions
Interleaved Practice Sets	Requires recall of multiple strategies	Mix problem types within the same set (i.e., addition, subtraction, multiplication)
Exit Tickets	Reinforces critical concepts from the day	Quick reflection on what students learned or found challenging
Peer Teaching/ Think-Pair-Share	Retrieval through explanation	Students explain solution to peers, reinforcing memory and understanding
Whiteboard Quick-Fire Problems	Fast retrieval and immediate feedback	Can be used for skill fluency and spotting misconceptions

Retrieval practice techniques in math instruction, outlining purposes and implementation notes to strengthen long-term retention, fluency, and conceptual understanding.

Retrieval Practice and Benefits to Literacy Instruction

While retrieval practice is often aligned with math or factual subject areas, it can equally be as effective in literacy instruction, especially when applied deliberately. Just as in math, helping students pull knowledge from short-term memory, consistently strengthens long-term memory and retention. Actively recalling previously learned information, rather than rereading or reviewing it passively, can be exceptionally beneficial to students' transfer learning. Asking students to summarize a text from memory or recall vocabulary without prompts and asking questions that require inference from prior readings are all ways to engage students in retrieval practice in literacy. Actively recalling the meanings of words (rather than just rereading them) strengthens semantic memory and helps to build fluent, automatic word knowledge, which supports comprehension (Karpicke & Roediger, 2008; Tauber et al., 2015). Retrieval also helps students activate background knowledge, a key factor in reading comprehension (Willingham, 2006), and reinforces connections between texts, themes, and vocabulary across reading experiences. Just as repeated retrieval of math facts frees up working memory for complex problem-solving, frequent retrieval of sentence patterns, grammatical rules, and genre-specific structures—like argumentative organization or narrative elements—boosts writing fluency, reduces cognitive load, and helps students internalize writing conventions.

Perhaps most importantly, retrieval practice helps reduce the forgetting curve (Ebbinghaus, 1913/1885), which often impacts a student's ability to recall what was read or discussed, especially over time. Combining retrieval practice with spaced practice (revisiting texts and ideas across time), elaboration (asking why and how something works), and dual coding (combining verbal and visual recall) can further strengthen learning and improve transfer to long-term memory. Table 8.2 illustrates some ways that teachers might incorporate retrieval practice into a literacy-focused lesson. Importantly, these strategies can be applied across content areas—not just English Language Arts (ELA). Retrieval practice supports reading, writing, vocabulary, comprehension, and the ability to recall and apply knowledge in science, social studies, and other subjects. Teachers can adapt these techniques to any discipline to strengthen both memory and understanding.

The 2022 NAEP reading assessment revealed that 37% of fourth-grade students performed below the NAEP basic level, indicating challenges in fundamental literacy skills such as comprehension and fluency. This underscores the importance of retrieval practice in supporting long-term memory—exactly what struggling readers need in order to build robust skill. Combining retrieval with spaced and interleaved practice helps reverse losses and improve outcomes for students. By regularly prompting students to recall and apply knowledge—through

TABLE 8.2 Incorporating Retrieval in a Literacy Classroom

Technique	Purpose	Additional Notes/Tips
Exit Tickets	Encourage students to recall key details or ideas from the lesson.	Ask for connections to prior readings, vocabulary, or themes. Can be done verbally or in writing.
Brain Dumps	Strengthen memory of plot, characters, or main ideas.	Students write everything they remember from a text or unit. Follow up with self-check or peer review.
Turn-and-Talk Retrievals	Promote verbal recall and reasoning about concepts.	Have students explain figurative language, author's choices, or themes to a partner. Encourage elaboration.
No-Notes Quick Writes	Practice summarizing or explaining concepts from memory.	Works for main ideas, vocabulary, character analysis, or text structure. Can be revisited later for spaced retrieval.
Low-Stakes Quizzes	Reinforce knowledge and provide regular retrieval practice.	Use short, frequent quizzes on vocabulary, reading comprehension, or text analysis. Open-ended questions increase retrieval benefits.
Spaced Writing Prompts	Support long-term retention by revisiting prior topics or units.	Prompts can connect to earlier texts or themes. Useful for spiral review and building connections across units.
Concept Maps/ Knowledge Webs	Help students visualize connections and relationships between ideas.	Students recall characters, themes, or events and link them. Can be done individually or collaboratively.
Peer Teaching/ Mini Lessons	Strengthen retrieval through explanation to others.	Students explain a concept or passage from memory to a peer. Adds accountability and elaboration.
Quick Vocabulary Recall	Improve word knowledge and automaticity.	Students define or illustrate new words from memory before reviewing. Can be combined with spaced practice.
Reflection Prompts	Encourage deeper connections and metacognition.	Questions like "Why did the author choose this structure?" or "How does this theme connect to prior texts?" foster transfer and elaboration.

Strategies for incorporating retrieval practice in a literacy classroom, including purposes and practical tips to enhance memory, comprehension, and transfer of learning.

quizzes, written responses, or discussions—we help them retain vocabulary, understand texts more deeply, and apply writing skills more fluently.

Interleaving in Literacy

In literacy, interleaving means alternating between different types of reading and writing tasks—such as vocabulary practice, comprehension, grammar, and composition—rather than focusing on one skill for an extended period. This mixing of tasks forces the brain to retrieve information and make connections across different elements of literacy, which strengthens both retention and transfer. When students move between comprehension, writing analysis, vocabulary, and grammar, they must constantly "switch mental gears," which helps them remember and apply concepts in a variety of contexts. By requiring this cognitive flexibility, interleaving promotes deeper processing and longer-term retention. For example, rather than completing multiple comprehension exercises in a row, students might read a passage, switch to vocabulary practice, and then return to comprehension. Each shift encourages them to retrieve and apply different aspects of their literacy knowledge.

By mixing skills—such as comprehension, word meaning, and writing structure—students must decide which strategies are most useful in the moment, creating a more integrated and authentic literacy experience (Carvalho & Yeoman, 2018; Fisher & Frey, 2013; Rohrer & Pashler, 2007). This approach highlights the interconnected nature of reading and writing. For instance, after reading a passage, students might summarize main ideas (comprehension), identify and define key vocabulary (word learning), and analyze the author's figurative language (literary analysis). This kind of interleaved practice compels students to engage with multiple dimensions of text rather than focusing on isolated skills—a limitation of many traditional literacy programs.

While blocked practice seems efficient in the short term, it often leads to weaker long-term retention. Interleaving, by contrast, forces students to mix up what they're learning, which helps to combat forgetting and promotes a more durable understanding (Roediger & Butler, 2011). This also helps students apply multiple skills simultaneously, which is critical for reading and writing (Mueller & Oppenheimer, 2014). Effective literacy involves synthesizing information from a variety of sources: vocabulary, syntax, comprehension, and writing structures. Although interleaving increases the difficulty of learning (because students have to switch tasks), this added challenge actually boosts retention and mastery. Research shows that these "desirable difficulties" make learning more engaging and lead to deeper mastery (Bjork & Bjork, 2011).

There is substantial research supporting the effectiveness of interleaving in literacy instruction, particularly in the areas of vocabulary retention, reading comprehension, and writing fluency. When students toggle between different skills and strategies, they engage more actively with the material—enhancing long-term retention, transfer, and critical thinking. The result is a stronger, more connected literacy foundation. Table 8.3 illustrates how a secondary ELA teacher might structure a 60-minute class period to interleave concepts throughout instruction, balancing reading, writing, and vocabulary tasks in a meaningful way.

TABLE 8.3 60-Minute ELA Class Schedule, with Interleaving (Text: *Of Mice and Men*)

Time	Activity	Purpose/Cognitive Benefit
5 min	Do Now: Retrieval Warm-Up **Example**: *What are three examples of power dynamics we've seen in the novel thus far?*	Students recall key ideas, vocabulary, or themes from prior lessons to activate background knowledge. This retrieval primes working memory and prepares students to connect past learning to new material.
10 min	Close Reading Excerpt from Core Text **Example**: *Crooks' dialogue in Of Mice and Men*	Teacher models annotation and questioning, focusing on comprehension and inferential thinking. Builds metacognitive awareness and supports transfer to independent reading.

(Continued)

TABLE 8.3 (Continued)

Time	Activity	Purpose/Cognitive Benefit
10 min	Vocabulary Application Activity **Vocabulary**: aloof, fawning, liniment	Students apply target words in original sentences or short paragraphs. Interleaves reading and vocabulary practice to deepen semantic encoding and retrieval strength.
10 min	Grammar/Style Mini-Lesson Using a Sentence from the Text **Indirect Characterization through Dialogue**	Connects grammar or stylistic features directly to the core text. Reinforces syntax and rhetorical awareness in authentic contexts, supporting far transfer to writing.
10 min	Writing Practice: Analytical Paragraph **Prompt**: "How does Steinbeck show Crooks' emotional state?"	Students synthesize vocabulary, structure, and textual analysis in a short written response. Interleaves comprehension, vocabulary, and composition skills for integrated literacy practice.
10 min	Peer Review or Partner Discussion **Peer Talk**: Partner analysis of author's tone and word choice	Promotes elaboration, feedback, and retrieval through social learning. Encourages students to articulate reasoning and reflect on their writing choices.
5 min	Exit Retrieval/Wrap-Up: **Example**: *In one or two sentences, explain how Steinbeck shows Crooks' powerlessness in today's passage.*	Students summarize and retrieve key learning from the lesson. Spaced recall strengthens long-term retention and consolidates schema.

Sample 60-minute ELA class schedule using *Of Mice and Men*, illustrating interleaved activities that integrate retrieval, vocabulary, grammar, and writing to support comprehension, transfer, and long-term retention.

In this 60-minute class period, students engage in a variety of literacy tasks—each intentionally sequenced to strengthen memory, deepen comprehension, and promote transfer. Though the activities alternate between reading, writing, vocabulary, and grammar, the design is anything but random. Interleaving and retrieval practice work together to help students consolidate learning, correct misconceptions, and connect ideas across contexts.

Both strategies are grounded in cognitive science and have been shown to improve long-term retention and transfer of knowledge. Interleaving promotes discrimination learning—students learn to distinguish between related concepts, improving understanding (Rohrer & Taylor, 2006). It also reduces the illusion of mastery created by repetitive blocked practice, producing more durable learning (Kang, 2016) and enhancing transfer to new contexts (Birnbaum et al., 2013). Retrieval practice complements this by strengthening memory traces and promoting metacognitive monitoring (Butler, 2010; Karpicke & Blunt, 2011; Roediger & Karpicke, 2006). When combined, interleaving and retrieval amplify one another: as students alternate between tasks, they are repeatedly required to recall prior knowledge, compare and apply strategies, and make meaning across modalities. The result is instruction that feels cohesive and challenging—yet cognitively efficient—helping students build lasting literacy skills that transfer beyond the classroom.

SCENARIO: EIGHTH-GRADE SCIENCE CLASSROOM

In Mrs. Pero's eighth-grade science class, students are preparing to engage in a lesson on states of matter and changes of state. She begins by reviewing the learning objective: *Students will reinforce their understanding of the three main states of matter and how matter changes between states*. Mrs. Pero directs students to record the success criteria in their notebooks:

1. **Recall and describe** the three main states of matter and key phase changes without referring to notes.
2. **Explain particle behavior and energy changes** that occur during state changes using accurate scientific vocabulary.
3. **Apply knowledge** of phase changes to real-world scenarios and represent them visually (e.g., interpreting a heating curve or explaining condensation on a mirror).

After reviewing the objectives and success criteria, students engage in a 10-minute retrieval quick write, displayed on the projector:

1. List all the states of matter you can recall.
2. Describe what happens during melting and evaporation.
3. What is sublimation?
4. What's one example of a physical change?

As students respond, Mrs. Pero circulates and provides encouragement, prompting effortful recall. After five minutes, students pair up to compare responses while Mrs. Pero listens for misconceptions. Noticing several students struggle to define *sublimation*, she makes a note to revisit it during instruction. Next, Mrs. Pero transitions to explicit instruction, using a diagram to model how solids, liquids, and gases transition between states. She reviews key vocabulary, provides examples, and checks understanding by cold-calling:

"What happens to particles when a solid becomes a liquid?" While students demonstrate surface-level understanding, Mrs. Pero scaffolds responses to strengthen conceptual precision.

She then introduces interleaved practice through station rotations, telling students: "Now that we've reviewed changes of state, let's apply what we know in different contexts—and see how it connects with what we've already learned."

The three stations mix new content (phase changes) with previously learned topics to promote retrieval and transfer:

- **Station 1**: Phase changes and temperature graphs
- **Station 2**: Physical vs. chemical changes
- **Station 3**: Density and states of matter

(*This makes the interleaving intentional, not random—showing how she cycles through related but distinct content areas.*)

> As students collaborate, Mrs. Pero circulates with a clipboard, taking anecdotal notes on misconceptions and depth of reasoning. She prompts deeper retrieval with questions like
>
> - "How do you know this is sublimation?"
> - "What would happen if you increased the temperature here?"
>
> After rotations, Mrs. Pero facilitates a whole-class comparison, asking: "How is what you did here related to the graph you analyzed earlier?" Students discuss connections across stations, reinforcing integration and metacognition.
>
> To close, students complete an exit ticket explaining what happens to particles during evaporation, using either words or a sketch, and identify the type of state change. Mrs. Pero uses these exit tickets as formative data to assess conceptual understanding, identify misconceptions, and evaluate how well students are connecting prior and current learning.

Mrs. Pero's lesson thoughtfully integrates both retrieval practice and interleaving to strengthen long-term retention of key concepts (Roediger & Karpicke, 2006). Her use of low-stakes recall activities—such as the warm-up and exit ticket—builds retrieval strength and student confidence while exposing gaps in understanding early and enabling targeted feedback and responsive instruction. Her use of interleaved stations requires students to discriminate between related concepts and identify underlying patterns, which is cognitively demanding but far more effective for promoting deep learning and transfer. Research shows that interleaving helps students apply knowledge flexibly to new or unfamiliar contexts (Pan, 2015; Rohrer et al., 2015). Mrs. Pero's lesson is not simply about covering content—it is structured to build memory, deepen understanding, and cultivate adaptable thinking through deliberate use of evidence-based strategies.

The Hard Work that Makes Learning Stick

Retrieval practice and interleaving are not new ideas—but their consistent and intentional use in classrooms remains rare. In part, that's because both strategies feel harder—for teachers and for students. They require letting go of the illusion of learning that comes with "activity for activity's sake" and instead embracing practices that drive *true* learning. When we integrate retrieval and interleaving into daily instruction, we are not merely reviewing content—we are shaping how students think, remember, and apply knowledge across contexts. These strategies push students beyond passive recognition toward active reconstruction of ideas, a process that strengthens memory and understanding over time. Importantly, retrieval and interleaving transcend any single discipline. Whether students are analyzing literary symbolism, solving equations, interpreting historical evidence, or explaining the behavior of particles, they are engaging in acts of literacy—reading, writing, reasoning, and communicating about complex ideas. In this way, retrieval and interleaving are foundational tools for building not just content mastery but cognitive resilience and transfer. Ultimately, the goal is to make learning not easier but more enduring. When teachers use these strategies deliberately—like Mrs. Pero did in her science classroom—they cultivate learners who can flexibly retrieve, connect, and apply what they know. That is the heart of literacy across content areas and the essence of what it means to help students truly *learn how to learn*.

References

Agarwal, P. K., Bain, P. M., & Chamberlain, R. W. (2012). The value of applied research: Retrieval practice improves classroom learning and recommendations from a teacher, a principal, and a scientist. *Educational Psychology Review, 24*(3), 437–448. https://doi.org/10.1007/s10648-012-9210-2

Agarwal, P. K., Roediger, H. L., McDaniel, M. A., & McDermott, K. B. (2014). Classroom-based programs of retrieval practice reduce test anxiety and improve learning. *Journal of Applied Research in Memory and Cognition*, *3*(2), 131–139. https://psycnet.apa.org/doi/10.1016/j.jarmac.2014.07.002

Ashcraft, M. H., & Krause, J. A. (2007). Working memory, mathematical performance, and math anxiety. *Cognitive Therapy and Research*, *31*(3), 221–232. https://doi.org/10.3758/BF03194059

Baroody, A. J. (2003). The development of adaptive expertise and flexibility: The integration of conceptual and procedural knowledge. In A. J. Baroody & A. Dowker (Eds.), *The development of arithmetic concepts and skills: Constructing adaptive expertise* (pp. 1–33). Lawrence Erlbaum Associates.

Birnbaum, M. S., Kornell, N., Bjork, E. L., & Bjork, R. A. (2013). Why interleaving enhances inductive learning: The roles of discrimination and retrieval. *Memory & Cognition*, *41*(3), 392–402. https://doi.org/10.3758/s13421-012-0272-7

Bjork, R. A. (1994). Memory and metamemory considerations in the training of human beings. In J. Metcalfe & A. Shimamura (Eds.), *Metacognition: Knowing about knowing* (pp. 185–205). MIT Press.

Bjork, R. A., & Bjork, E. L. (2011). Making things hard on yourself, but in a good way: Creating desirable difficulties to enhance learning. In M. A. Gernsbacher & R. W. Pew (Eds.), *Psychology and the real world: Essays illustrating fundamental contributions to society* (pp. 56–64). Worth Publishers.

Bleiberg, J. (2021). Does the common core have a common effect? An exploration of effects on academically vulnerable students. *AERA Open*, *7*. https://doi.org/10.1177/23328584211010727

Butler, A. C. (2010). Repeated testing produces superior transfer of learning relative to repeated studying. *Journal of Experimental Psychology: Learning, Memory, and Cognition*, *36*(5), 1118–1133. https://doi.org/10.1037/a0019902

Butler, A. C., & Roediger, H. L. (2008). Feedback enhances the positive effects and reduces the negative effects of multiple-choice testing. *Memory & Cognition*, *36*(3), 604–616. https://doi.org/10.3758/MC.36.3.604

Carvalho, L., & Yeoman, P. (2018). Framing learning entanglement in innovative learning spaces: Connecting theory, design and practice.

British Educational Research Journal, *44*(6), 1120–1137. https://doi.org/10.1002/berj.3483

Cepeda, N. J., Pashler, H., Vul, E., Wixted, J. T., & Rohrer, D. (2006). Distributed practice in verbal recall tasks: A review and quantitative synthesis. *Psychological Bulletin*, *132*(3), 354–380. https://doi.org/10.1037/0033-2909.132.3.354

Dunlosky, J., Rawson, K. A., Marsh, E. J., Nathan, M. J., & Willingham, D. T. (2013). Improving students' learning with effective learning techniques: Promising directions from cognitive and educational psychology. *Psychological Science in the Public Interest*, *14*(1), 4–58. https://doi.org/10.1177/1529100612453266

Durlak, J. A., Weissberg, R. P., Dymnicki, A. B., Taylor, R. D., & Schellinger, K. B. (2011). The impact of enhancing students' social and emotional learning: A meta-analysis of school-based universal interventions. *Child Development*, *82*(1), 405–432. https://doi.org/10.1111/j.1467-8624.2010.01564.x

Ebbinghaus, H. (1913/1885). *Memory: A contribution to experimental psychology* (H. A. Ruger & C. E. Bussenius, Trans.). Teachers College, Columbia University.

Fisher, D., & Frey, N. (2013). *Improving adolescent literacy: Content area strategies at work* (5th ed.). Pearson.

Gathercole, S. E., & Alloway, T. P. (2008). *Working memory and learning: A practical guide for teachers*. SAGE Publications.

Geary, D. C. (2011). Cognitive predictors of achievement growth in mathematics: A 5-year longitudinal study. *Developmental Psychology*, *47*(6), 1539–1552. https://doi.org/10.1037/a0025510

Hattie, J. (2023). *Visible learning: The sequel: A synthesis of over 2,100 meta-analyses relating to achievement*. Routledge.

Kang, S. H. K. (2016). Spaced repetition promotes efficient and effective learning: Policy implications for instruction. *Policy Insights From the Behavioral and Brain Sciences*, *3*(1), 12–19. https://doi.org/10.1177/2372732215624708

Kang, M., & Pashler, H. (2012). Learning styles: A comprehensive and critical review. *Educational Psychology Review*, *24*(1), 91–121.

Kapur, M., & Bielaczyc, K. (2012). Designing for productive failure. *Educational Psychologist*, *47*(3), 234–251. 10.1080/10508406.2011.591717

Karpicke, J. D., & Blunt, J. R. (2011). Retrieval practice produces more learning than elaborative studying with concept mapping. *Science*, *331*(6018), 772–775. https://doi.org/10.1126/science.1199327

Karpicke, J. D., & Roediger, H. L. (2008). The critical role of retrieval practice in long-term retention. *Science*, *319*(5865), 966–968. https://doi.org/10.1126/science.1152408

Khanna, M. M. (2015). Ungraded pop quizzes: Test-enhanced learning without the anxiety. *Teaching of Psychology*, *42*(2), 174–177. https://doi.org/10.1177/0098628315573144

Larsen, S. C., Butler, D. L., & Larkin, R. (2009). The impact of cognitive load theory on the design of instructional materials in mathematics. *Mathematics Education Research Journal*, *21*(2), 56–75. https://doi.org/10.1007/BF03217434

McDaniel, M. A., Agarwal, P. K., Huelser, B. J., McDermott, K. B., & Roediger, H. L. I. I. I. (2011). Test-enhanced learning in a middle school science classroom: The effects of quiz frequency and placement. *Journal of Educational Psychology*, *103*(2), 399–414. https://doi.org/10.1037/a0021782

Mueller, P. A., & Oppenheimer, D. M. (2014). The pen is mightier than the keyboard: Advantages of longhand over laptop note taking. *Psychological Science*, *25*(6), 1159–1168. https://doi.org/10.1177/0956797614524581

OECD. (2023a). *PISA 2022 results (volume I & II): United States – Country note*. Organisation for Economic Co-operation and Development. https://www.oecd.org/content/dam/oecd/en.publications/reports/2023/11/pisa-2022-results-volume-i-and-ii-country-notes_2fca04b9/united-states_243107b0/a78ba65a-en.pdf

OECD. (2023b). *PISA 2022 results (volume I): Singapore – Country note*. Organisation for Economic Co-operation and Development. https://www.oecd.org/en/publications/2023/12/pisa-2022-results-volume-i_76772a36/full-report/how-did-countries-perform-in-pisa_dc514907.html

OECD. (2023c). *PISA 2022 results (volume I & II): Japan – Country note*. Organisation for Economic Co-operation and Development. https://www.oecd.org/en/publications/pisa-2022-results-volume-i-and-ii-country-notes_ed6fbcc5-en/japan_f7d7daad-en.html

OECD. (2023d). *PISA 2022 results (volume I & II): Korea – Country note*. Organisation for Economic Co-operation and Development. https://www.oecd.org/en/publications/pisa-2022-results-volume-i-and-ii-country-notes_ed6fbcc5-en/korea_4e0cc43a-en.html

Pan, S. C. (2015, August 4). The interleaving effect: Mixing it up boosts learning. *Scientific American Mind*. https://www.scientificamerican.com/article/the-interleaving-effect-mixing-it-up-boosts-learning/

Pan, S. C., & Rickard, T. C. (2018). Transfer of test-enhanced learning: Meta-analytic review and synthesis. *Psychological Bulletin, 144*(7), 710–756. https://doi.org/10.1037/bul0000151

Putnam, A. L., Sungkhasettee, V. W., & Roediger, H. L. (2016). Optimizing learning in college: Tips from cognitive psychology: Tips from cognitive psychology. *Perspectives on Psychological Science, 11*(5), 652–660. https://doi.org/10.1177/1745691616645770

Rittle-Johnson, B., & Schneider, M. (2015). Not a one-way street: Bidirectional relations between procedural and conceptual knowledge of mathematics. *Educational Psychology Review, 27*(4), 587–597. https://doi.org/10.1007/s10648-015-9302-x

Rittle-Johnson, B., Siegler, R. S., & Alibali, M. W. (2001). Developing conceptual understanding and procedural skill in mathematics: An iterative process. *Journal of Educational Psychology, 93*(2), 346–362. https://doi.org/10.1037/0022-0663.93.2.346

Roediger, H. L., & Butler, A. C. (2011). The critical role of retrieval practice in long-term retention. *Trends in Cognitive Sciences, 15*(1), 20–27. https://doi.org/10.1016/j.tics.2010.09.003

Roediger, H. L., & Karpicke, J. D. (2006). Test-enhanced learning: Taking memory tests improves long-term retention. *Psychological Science, 17*(3), 249–255. https://doi.org/10.1111/j.1467-9280.2006.01693.x

Rohrer, D., Dedrick, R. F., & Stershic, S. (2015). Interleaved practice improves mathematics learning. *Journal of Educational Psychology, 107*(3), 900–908.

Rohrer, D., & Pashler, H. (2007). Increasing retention without increasing study time. *Applied Cognitive Psychology, 21*(3), 693–700. https://doi.org/10.1002/acp.1297

Rohrer, D., & Taylor, K. (2006). The effects of overlearning and distributed practice on the retention of mathematics knowledge. *Applied Cognitive Psychology, 20*(9), 1209–1224. https://psycnet.apa.org/doi/10.1002/acp.1266

Rohrer, D., & Taylor, K. (2010). The effects of overlearning and distributed practice on the retention of mathematics knowledge. *Applied Cognitive Psychology*, *24*(6), 783–796. https://doi.org/10.1002/acp.1606

Samani, J., & Pan, S. C. (2021). Interleaved practice enhances memory and problem-solving ability in undergraduate physics. *npj Science of Learning*, *6*(1), 32. https://doi.org/10.1038/s41539-021-00110-x

Swain, N. (2024). *Harnessing the science of learning: Success stories to help kickstart your school improvement*. Routledge.

Sweller, J., van Merriënboer, J. J., & Paas, F. (1998). Cognitive architecture and instructional design. *Educational Psychology Review*, *10*, 251–296. https://doi.org/10.1023/A:1022193728205

Sweller, J., van Merriënboer, J. J. G., & Paas, F. G. W. C. (2011). Cognitive architecture and instructional design: 20 years later. *Educational Psychology Review*, *23*(2), 261–292.

Tauber, S. K., Dunlosky, J., & Rawson, K. A. (2015). The influence of retrieval practice versus delayed judgments of learning on memory: Resolving a memory-Metamemory paradox. *Experimental Psychology*, *62*(4), 254–263. https://doi.org/10.1027/1618-3169/a000296

Taylor, R. D., Oberle, E., Durlak, J. A., & Weissberg, R. P. (2017). Promoting positive youth development through school-based social and emotional learning interventions: A meta-analysis of follow-up effects. *Child Development*, *88*(4), 1156–1171. https://doi.org/10.1111/cdev.12864

United States National Mathematics Advisory Panel & U.S. Department of Education. (2008). *Foundations for success: The final report of the National Mathematics Advisory Panel*. U.S. Department of Education.

Willingham, D. T. (2003). What will improve a student's memory? *American Educator*, *27*(1), 4–11.

Willingham, D. T. (2006). How knowledge helps: It speeds and strengthens reading comprehension, learning—And thinking. *American Educator*, *30*(1), 30–37.

Willingham, D. T. (2009). *Why don't students like school? A cognitive scientist answers questions about how the mind works and what it means for the classroom*. Jossey-Bass.

9

Deliberate Practice

Practice is essential for learning. In truth, we can't accurately assess what students know until they reach the stage of independent application—when they can perform without scaffolds or guided support. Yet, despite its importance, practice is often misunderstood in ways that limit its impact. Three misconceptions are especially common:

1. that simple repetition or rehearsal automatically leads to transferable learning;
2. that practice is about getting problems correct rather than deepening understanding; and
3. that practice reflects performance instead of serving as a tool for identifying and addressing gaps in knowledge.

Each of these assumptions distorts the purpose of practice and ultimately undermines its power to build durable, flexible understanding.

The first misconception—that repetition or rehearsal automatically leads to *transferable* learning—assumes that if students simply do more of the same (i.e., re-reading the same passage, completing additional worksheets, or practicing identical problem sets), they will retain the information and apply it effectively in new situations. However, this assumption confuses familiarity with mastery. Repetition can make information feel easier to recall in the short term, but this fluency often reflects recognition rather than retrieval (Bjork, 1994; Roediger & Karpicke, 2006). Repetitive, blocked practice (as we discussed in Chapter 8, where one skill is practiced and repeated before moving to the next) fails to build transferable knowledge because transfer requires learners to *flexibly retrieve and apply concepts* under *varied conditions* (Schmidt & Bjork, 1992). Without retrieval, variation, or feedback, students experience what psychologists call an *illusion of competence*: practice that feels productive because the task is fresh, but it doesn't promote durable, flexible understanding.

The second misconception about practice is that the *purpose* of practice is to get problems or solutions correct rather than deepening understanding. In many classrooms, students equate success with accuracy—finishing a worksheet quickly, earning a score, or mimicking a demonstrated procedure. But when practice is designed or interpreted as a test of performance, it encourages students to rehearse what they already know rather than confront or refine what they don't. This shifts the purpose of practice to an exercise in *confirmation* rather than *construction* of knowledge.

Focusing on correctness promotes a performance-oriented mindset, in which learners aim to look competent rather than improve competence (Dweck, 1986). When errors are treated as evidence of failure instead of opportunities for growth, students avoid challenge and gravitate toward familiar tasks that make them feel successful. The result is shallow learning: they perform well during practice, but their understanding is fragile and context-dependent. This speaks to the third common misconception about practice: that practice performance reflects true learning. When students or teachers equate smooth, accurate performance during practice with mastery, practice becomes a test rather than a tool. Yet research shows that performance during learning often *overestimates* long-term retention and transfer (Soderstrom & Bjork, 2015). What looks fluent in the moment is often just short-term recall.

In contrast, effective practice is *diagnostic* and effortful. Its value lies in revealing misconceptions, prompting self-explanation, and requiring learners to retrieve and apply knowledge in different ways. As Ericsson and colleagues (1993) note, *deliberate practice* is not about mindless repetition or flawless execution—it is about pushing the edge of one's competence through feedback, reflection, and adjustment. When teachers frame practice as an opportunity to *think, struggle productively,* and *analyze mistakes,* students begin to engage with it as a process of growth rather than a measure of ability.

Deliberate practice is structured, purposeful repetition guided by feedback focused on improvement rather than completion. Coined by Ericsson and colleagues (1993), the concept emphasizes identifying a clear learning goal, providing expert guidance and modeling, and ensuring feedback loops that stretch the learner's current ability. It also involves repetition *with* reflection and correction, ensuring that errors become learning opportunities rather than habits. In the classroom, this means that teachers don't simply assign practice—they engineer it. Practice is intentionally scaffolded to build expertise rather than compliance. Within the gradual release model, this stage marks the shift from guided instruction to independent application, with teachers maintaining frequent, timely feedback to prevent misconceptions from becoming ingrained. Hattie (2009, 2017) identifies practice, particularly when paired with feedback and teacher guidance, as having an effect size of $d = 0.79$ on student achievement.

Knowing when conditions are ideal for success in independent practice requires that the teacher has already put a lot of explicit structures into place. These structures enable the student to perform the task with less guidance. The more clarity of expectations the teacher can provide, combined with prior opportunities for independent success, determines how well the student performs in the application phase of learning (Hattie, 2012; Schunk & Pajares, 2002). Tasks must be purposeful, avoiding busywork, and tied directly to explicit learning. Deliberate practice isn't about doing *more*—it's about doing *better*. When teachers intentionally guide students from supported modeling to successful independence, using feedback and increasing challenge, learning becomes durable, transferable, and meaningful.

Deliberate practice, when done well, is one of the most powerful drivers of learning. It is not individualized worksheets on a student's "skill level" distributed for independent work while the teacher works with small groups; this removes the teacher precisely when feedback is most needed (Rosenshine, 2012; Willingham, 2009). Effective deliberate practice targets specific, high-leverage skills tied to deep understanding. It includes teacher modeling, guided feedback, embedded knowledge, and opportunities for student reflection on what is working and what needs adjustment. While deliberate practice occurs throughout the instructional arc, it must be structured and purposeful at every phase. Figure 9.1 demonstrates how deliberate practice might begin in whole-group instruction.

Once students have demonstrated some proficiency, they continue practicing under moderate support in small groups or with partner work. Still, in this phase, teachers are circulating, providing feedback and corrections, and students are rehearsing strategies with focused intention. Formative checks—such as brief quizzes, peer review, or teacher observation—help ensure that practice remains purposeful and that misconceptions are addressed promptly. Figure 9.2 shows an example of guided, deliberate practice in small or peer groups, highlighting how teachers can monitor progress, provide feedback, and support focused, purposeful practice.

238 ◆ Teaching for Cognitive Engagement

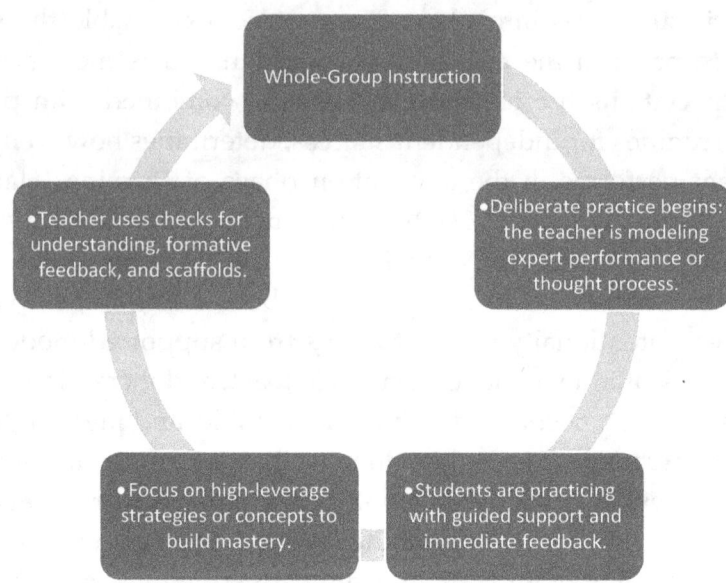

FIGURE 9.1 Whole-group instruction (initial practice phase).

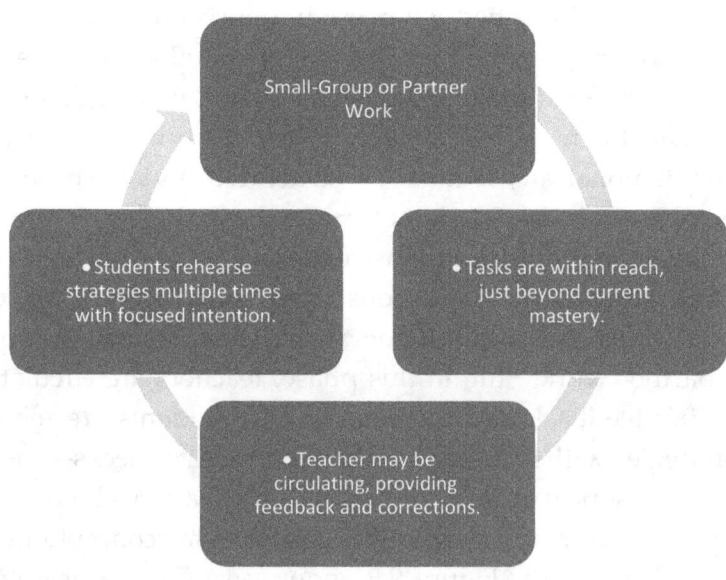

FIGURE 9.2 Small-group or partner work (guided deliberate practice).

A Word on Impactful Independent Practice

Ultimately, the goal of well-structured deliberate practice is to bring students to an independent performance stage, where they can transfer new learning to novel contexts and situations. For example, after several guided lessons on evidence-based writing, a student might independently draft an analytical paragraph about a new poem, applying previously modeled strategies to a context they haven't seen before. It is essential that teachers make meaningful time for this independent work to occur within the classroom. But what does effective independent practice look like? At this stage, students engage with new tasks presented in varied contexts, requiring them to flexibly apply what they have learned. Importantly, this occurs without direct teacher or peer support, allowing the learner to demonstrate authentic understanding. Research shows that when students practice independently after sufficient modeling and scaffolding, they develop stronger retention, transfer, and problem-solving skills (Hattie, 2017; Rohrer & Taylor, 2007; Soderstrom & Bjork, 2015).

Formative checks are critical at this stage. Brief quizzes, self-assessments, or reflective exercises provide the teacher with insight into how well students are transferring learning to long-term memory. These assessments also reveal misconceptions, informing subsequent instructional decisions. Independent deliberate practice succeeds only when students have clear learning goals, understand what successful performance looks like, and have mechanisms for feedback—whether from themselves, peers, or the teacher. Prior modeling and scaffolding ensure that students can engage meaningfully. When structured in this way, independent practice reinforces, rather than undermines, durable learning. It provides students the opportunity to consolidate skills, build confidence, and strengthen their ability to apply knowledge flexibly across contexts.

How Deliberate Practice Can Be Used Across Disciplines

Deliberate practice applies across disciplines but is perhaps most underutilized in writing instruction. As discussed in Chapter 7, writing is one of the most cognitively demanding academic tasks, requiring coordination of memory, planning, self-regulation, and attention to language conventions. Yet many teachers assign writing without providing true deliberate practice—structured opportunities for targeted feedback, revision, and reflection. Many teacher preparation programs offer minimal coursework on writing instruction, particularly for secondary educators, across disciplines (Graham et al., 2015). As a result, teachers often struggle to view writing as being peripheral to their subject (Graham & Perin, 2007). When students are assigned writing, they rarely receive frequent, focused feedback or structured opportunities to revise and reflect—the very ingredients that transform writing practice into deliberate practice. Deliberate practice in writing also emphasizes breaking down complex skills into manageable components, setting clear goals, and providing immediate, targeted feedback.

Another area that undermines effective writing instruction is the tendency to compartmentalize reading and writing, especially in elementary grades where they are often taught as separate blocks of instructional time. Research consistently shows that reading and writing should be taught *together* to build content knowledge, strengthen analysis, and reinforce language structures (Graham & Hebert, 2010; Shanahan, 2016). Writing is inherently complex, placing heavy intrinsic and extraneous cognitive load on learners. Without proper scaffolding—such as models, sentence starters, exemplars, and shared writing—students struggle to organize their ideas and sustain coherence. Deliberate practice is essential because writing is not a single skill but a *network* of interdependent cognitive and procedural skills that must be developed over time. Novice writers cannot manage multiple demands simultaneously; teachers must therefore reduce cognitive load by isolating, modeling, and rehearsing specific subskills until they become more automatic (Sweller, 1994). Effective deliberate writing practice provides immediate, specific, and goal-referenced feedback on a limited set of elements (Hattie, 2023), ensuring that students build fluency without being overwhelmed.

Many teachers shy away from assigning writing because providing specific feedback is daunting—and few manage to do it effectively. Reading and grading essays are time-consuming, and when teachers attempt to evaluate everything at once, feedback becomes diffuse, delayed, less specific, and less actionable (Hattie & Timperley, 2007). Too often, feedback is overly general or too extensive to be useful, causing students to make surface-level changes or ignore comments altogether (Shute, 2008). For example, a student might receive a note like "clarify your thesis," followed by a quick in-class mini-conference showing how to turn a vague claim into a precise argument. This targeted guidance gives the student a concrete step to practice, rather than overwhelming them with a full-page critique. Waiting until the end of the writing process to offer feedback to students is also one of the most erroneous uses of deliberate practice when, in truth, feedback should be woven throughout the process to guide improvement in real time. This approach also helps reduce the teacher's workload: by reviewing student work throughout the writing process, teachers avoid being confronted with a backlog of 90 unread papers at the end of the quarter.

Effective feedback is the cornerstone of deliberate practice, yet it is also one of the greatest challenges in writing instruction. This difficulty often stems from misconceptions about what deliberate practice entails. Some educators equate practice with mechanical repetition, undervaluing the essential role of guided skill-building. In literacy and humanities classrooms, teachers often prioritize creativity and student voice while underemphasizing the deliberate development of specific writing skills—despite strong evidence that explicit, structured instruction outperforms "free writing" or open-ended assignments (Graham & Harris, 2016). By the time students reach secondary classrooms, many teachers no longer see explicit, guided practice as necessary—particularly for skills that they believe should have been mastered in earlier grades or that they view as another discipline's responsibility (as is often the case with writing instruction). This mindset creates instructional gaps that undermine students' ability to develop writing expertise. Compounding the issue, some teachers worry that too much guidance will stifle originality, leading them to skip guided practice—the very phase that makes deliberate practice effective (Fisher & Frey, 2021).

High-quality deliberate practice requires teacher expertise: identifying the precise subskills students need to strengthen, designing scaffolded tasks that target those skills, and providing timely, actionable feedback. Yet, in many secondary classrooms, the culture emphasizes completion and grading over growth and mastery, particularly in writing. Reframing writing instruction through the lens of deliberate practice allows teachers to move beyond task completion to purposeful skill development. Table 9.1 outlines how deliberate practice can be structured to support independent application while maintaining depth, focus, and authentic engagement. These conditions ensure that students approach independent work not as a test of performance but as a deliberate opportunity to strengthen understanding, apply knowledge flexibly, and monitor their own growth.

Deliberate practice in writing instruction ensures focus, modeling, short, targeted writing tasks, timely feedback, and opportunities for reflection. Good writing isn't caught—it's taught. Without deliberate, structured practice, students rarely improve as writers. With it, they develop voice, clarity, and analytical strength over time through guided refinement and feedback. Table 9.2 provides a specific example of implementing deliberate practice in writing and can be applied across disciplines.

TABLE 9.1 Conditions for Success in Independent Application

Condition	Why It Matters
Clarity of Expectations	Students need to know what success looks like through explicit learning goals, success criteria, and exemplars. Clarity reduces cognitive load and directs attention toward the essential features of the task (Hattie, 2012). When expectations are transparent, students can self-monitor and adjust their performance effectively.
Previous Success with Support	Confidence and self-efficacy develop when independence follows guided success (Bandura, 1997). Students are more likely to persist through challenge when they've previously experienced success with scaffolds in place. This reinforces the gradual release model and prevents premature independence.
Purposeful Task Design	Tasks should be intentionally aligned to the specific skill or concept being developed. Busywork or unconnected tasks fragment learning and diminish motivation. Purposeful design ensures that practice directly supports transfer and schema construction (Kirschner et al., 2006).
Spaced Retrieval of Skill	Independent practice should revisit key skills over time and across contexts, allowing students to retrieve, apply, and refine their knowledge under varied conditions. Spaced retrieval strengthens long-term retention and promotes flexible transfer (Kang, 2016; Roediger & Butler, 2011).
Reflection and Feedback	Reflection consolidates learning by prompting students to evaluate their progress and identify next steps. Feedback—whether from self-assessment, peers, or teachers—closes the learning loop and helps students calibrate their understanding (Hattie & Timperley, 2007; Shute, 2008).
Cognitive Load Management	Complex tasks should be broken into manageable components to reduce extraneous cognitive load and prevent overwhelm. Well-sequenced scaffolding ensures that working memory is focused on learning rather than managing confusion (Sweller, 1994).
Goal Orientation	Cultivating a mastery-oriented mindset helps students see independent practice as an opportunity for growth rather than evaluation. Students with mastery goals engage more deeply and persist through difficulty (Dweck, 1986).

Conditions that support successful independent application, detailing key factors such as clarity, scaffolding, purposeful task design, spaced retrieval, reflection, cognitive load management, and goal orientation to enhance learning, transfer, and self-efficacy.

TABLE 9.2 Example of How to Implement Deliberate Practice in Writing Instruction

What to Do	How to Do It
Focus on one or two writing skills at a time	Narrow the scope: "Today we'll focus only on crafting precise, evidence-based commentary." Limiting focus prevents cognitive overload and allows for deeper mastery of a specific skill.
Model the thinking process	Use think-alouds to show how writers make decisions—e.g., revise a weak claim into a strong thesis in real time. Modeling makes invisible cognitive processes visible to students.
Use short, targeted writing tasks	Provide frequent, low-stakes opportunities to practice—e.g., "Write one paragraph that explains tone using a quote from the text." Short bursts of practice support transfer and motivation.
Give targeted, timely feedback	Comment on one element (e.g., reasoning or organization) and provide time for revision. Immediate, focused feedback enhances learning far more than broad or delayed feedback (Hattie & Timperley, 2007).
Use cumulative tasks to show growth	Ask students to revisit and revise previous work using newly acquired skills. Cumulative practice strengthens retrieval and helps students see progress over time.
Embed reflection	Encourage metacognition: "What did I do better this time? What still needs work?" Reflection promotes self-regulation and reinforces awareness of growth.

Example framework for implementing deliberate practice in writing instruction, outlining steps, methods, and cognitive principles to promote skill mastery, transfer, and metacognitive growth.

How to Incorporate Deliberate Practice in Math Instruction

Deliberate practice in math is not about doing more problems—it's about doing the right problems, in the right way, with the right feedback. It is structured, intentional, and designed to stretch thinking just beyond current ability. As in literacy, the goal is to guide students from supported practice to independent, flexible application. Incorporating deliberate practice into math instruction means moving beyond repetitive drills or procedural worksheets to create structured, intentional opportunities for deep learning with feedback and increasing challenge. A balanced approach emphasizes both procedural fluency and conceptual understanding: procedures allow students to work efficiently, while conceptual knowledge enables flexible reasoning and transfer to new contexts. For instance, when teaching fractions, a teacher might first model dividing a pizza into equal parts (conceptual understanding), then guide students through step-by-step calculations (procedural fluency), and finally ask them to apply both in a word problem about sharing ingredients in a recipe. The two are interdependent—conceptual insight supports procedural efficiency, and procedural fluency frees cognitive resources for deeper problem-solving (Hiebert & Grouws, 2007; Rittle-Johnson & Schneider, 2015). Deliberate practice in math should cultivate both through explicit modeling, scaffolded practice, targeted feedback, and gradual release toward independence.

While computer-adaptive programs such as Delta Math, IXL, I-Ready, Mathia, or Khan Academy are often marketed as tools for deliberate practice, they tend to prioritize procedural accuracy over conceptual understanding—and risk reinforcing misconceptions about deliberate practice discussed earlier, such as focusing solely on getting problems correct or over-identifying gaps in understanding. These platforms break math into micro-skills and reward correct answers through repetition until mastery. While procedural fluency is critical for developing math skills, it must be paired with conceptual understanding to ensure flexible, durable learning (Boaler, 2016; Rittle-Johnson & Schneider, 2015; United States National Mathematics Advisory Panel & U.S. Department of Education, 2008). Moreover, adaptive systems typically cannot provide the immediate, explanatory feedback tailored to student misconceptions that is essential for effective deliberate practice—feedback that students can receive only from a knowledgeable and attentive classroom teacher (Hattie & Timperley, 2007; Van de Pol et al., 2010). When used alone or merely to satisfy administrative requirements, these programs risk encouraging short-term performance and limiting students' ability to develop flexible, durable mathematical

TABLE 9.3 Deliberate Practice in Math Instruction

What to Do	How to Do It
Target Specific, High-Leverage Skills	Focus practice on key concepts or procedures that connect to larger mathematical ideas and address common misconceptions. Example: "Today, we'll focus on interpreting ratios in word problems."
Model and Scaffold	Teacher models thinking aloud, showing reasoning, strategy selection, and error checking. Scaffolded practice follows with guided questions and prompts.
Provide Immediate, Explanatory Feedback	Give feedback during practice that targets reasoning and strategy, not just correctness. Example: "You solved the equation correctly, but notice how the terms relate to the problem context."
Integrate Spaced and Interleaved Practice	Mix problem types and revisit skills over time instead of massing one skill. Example: Alternate fractions, decimals, and percentages in the same session.
Emphasize Conceptual Explanations and Multiple Representations	Have students explain reasoning, draw diagrams, or show multiple solution paths to deepen understanding. Example: Represent a word problem with both a table and graph.
Culminate with Independent Application in Novel Contexts	Students apply skills in new, unfamiliar problem types independently, using prior scaffolding and success criteria. Example: Solve a multi-step problem combining ratios, percentages, and proportional reasoning.

Framework for implementing deliberate practice in math instruction, detailing targeted steps, instructional methods, and cognitive strategies to develop skill mastery, conceptual understanding, and independent problem-solving.

understanding. Table 9.3 illustrates how deliberate practice can be applied effectively in math instruction. It highlights key components of successful practice and, importantly, emphasizes the indispensable role of the teacher in guiding learning rather than relying solely on computer-based programs. The table also provides practical examples of how teachers can structure tasks, offer guidance, and embed feedback to develop both conceptual understanding and procedural fluency.

While adaptive programs are sometimes treated as a silver bullet for addressing all students' math skill gaps from elementary through secondary, empirical evidence suggests their impact is generally modest and context-dependent. These platforms can support procedural fluency and the mastery of targeted microskills, particularly when used as a supplement to classroom instruction (Kulik & Fletcher, 2016; Pane et al., 2015; VanLehn, 2011). However, research indicates that technology-enhanced adaptive learning interventions can produce learning gains and sometimes greater benefits for students with lower prior achievement, but disparities in access, teacher integration, and support still mean that some students benefit more than others (Roschelle et al., 2016; Kulik & Fletcher, 2016). Ultimately, adaptive programs can be a valuable tool for deliberate practice, but their effectiveness hinges on teacher guidance, explanatory feedback, and integration with holistic, teacher-led instruction (Boaler, 2016; Hattie & Timperley, 2007; Pane et al., 2015; Rittle-Johnson & Schneider, 2015; Van de Pol et al., 2010).

More than in many other disciplines, the teacher's role in mathematics instruction is paramount. Research consistently shows that teacher quality—encompassing content knowledge, pedagogical skill, and responsiveness to student thinking—has a profound impact on student outcomes in mathematics (Blazar, 2016; Hill et al., 2005; Yang & Kaiser, 2022). This underscores the necessity of integrating adaptive tools within a framework of strong, responsive teaching to effectively support student learning. Many of the gaps that students exhibit in mathematics stem from ineffective instruction (Boaler, 2016), and many elementary teachers, in particular, lack the deep content expertise needed to address chronic misunderstandings. When adaptive programs replace quality instruction, they often produce lower performance or no statistically significant gains (Kane et al., 2024; Pane et al., 2017). Deliberate practice in math requires targeted feedback and scaffolding from an expert—elements that these programs typically lack. Adaptive software can also promote passive learning through over-scaffolding: students are given step-by-step hints or explanations after mistakes. While this may keep students moving forward, it reduces opportunities for independent problem-solving and deprives learners of key ingredients of effective deliberate practice, including teacher modeling, guided feedback, embedded knowledge, and reflection on what strategies are working and where adjustment is needed.

The Importance of Deliberate Practice across Disciplines

Deliberate practice is essential to the explicit teaching model because it represents the bridge between instruction and independence—where students consolidate skills, deepen understanding, and build fluency through intentional, structured effort. Without deliberate practice, explicit instruction risks becoming procedural, passive, and ineffective (Hattie, 2023; Rohrer et al., 2015). Deliberate practice should be embedded in other domains as well. In science, structured lab exercises with guided observation, hypothesis-testing, and iterative experimentation provide a framework for independent application of concepts. In language learning, targeted practice with pronunciation, syntax, and conversation under teacher guidance builds fluency. Similarly, in music or performance arts, breaking down complex skills into subcomponents, repeated practice with feedback, and reflective refinement mirror the principles highlighted in writing and mathematics instruction. Across these disciplines, the common thread is structured, purposeful repetition with feedback that moves learners from guided support to independent, flexible application.

While deliberate practice is effective across disciplines, constructivist or inquiry-driven approaches often fail to provide sufficient opportunities for it, as they tend to prioritize exploration, discovery, and student-led inquiry over structured, guided repetition with feedback. Deliberate practice requires frequent, structured practice of component skills, immediate corrective feedback, teacher guidance and modeling, and spaced, repeated exposure to core content—elements often missing in these classrooms.

When deliberate practice is infrequently used, teachers underestimate how repeated, effortful, feedback-rich practice helps students move from surface learning to deep understanding and flexible skill transfer (Deans for Impact, 2015; Hattie, 2023; Kirschner et al., 2006; Sweller et al., 2011).

References

Bandura. (1997). *Self-efficacy: The exercise of control*. W. H. Freeman.

Bjork, R. A. (1994). Memory and metamemory considerations in the training of human beings. In J. Metcalfe & A. Shimamura (Eds.), *Metacognition: Knowing about knowing* (pp. 185–205). MIT Press.

Blazar, D. (2016). Teacher and teaching effects on students' attitudes and behaviors. *Educational Evaluation and Policy Analysis*, 38(4), 508–533. https://doi.org/10.3102/0162373716670260

Boaler, J. (2016). *Mathematical mindsets: Unleashing students' potential through creative math, inspiring messages, and innovative teaching*. JosseyBass.

Deans for Impact. (2015). *The science of learning*. https://deansforimpact.org/resources/the-science-of-learning/

Dweck, C. S. (1986). Motivational processes affecting learning. *American Psychologist*, 41(10), 1040–1048. https://doi.org/10.1037/0003-066X.41.10.1040

Ericsson, K. A., Krampe, R. T., & Tesch-Römer, C. (1993). The role of deliberate practice in the acquisition of expert performance. *Psychological Review*, 100(3), 363–406. https://doi.org/10.1037/0033-295X.100.3.363

Fisher, D., & Frey, N. (2021). *Better learning through structured teaching: A framework for the gradual release of responsibility* (3rd ed.). ASCD.

Graham, S., & Harris, K. R. (2016). A path to better writing: Evidence-based practices in the classroom. *The Reading Teacher*, 69(4), 359–365. https://doi.org/10.1002/trtr.1432

Graham, S., Harris, K. R., & Santangelo, T. (2015). Research-based writing practices and the common Core: Meta-analysis and meta-synthesis. *Elementary School Journal*, 115(4), 498–522. https://doi.org/10.1086/681964

Graham, S., & Hebert, M. A. (2010). *Writing to read: Evidence for how writing can improve reading*. A Carnegie Corporation Time to Act Report. Alliance for Excellent Education.

Graham, S., & Perin, D. (2007). *Writing next: Effective strategies to improve writing of adolescents in middle and high schools (A report to Carnegie Corporation of New York)*. Washington, DC: Alliance for Excellent Education.

Hattie, J. (2009). *Visible learning: A synthesis of over 800 meta-analyses relating to achievement*. Routledge.

Hattie, J. (2012). *Visible learning for teachers: Maximizing impact on learning*. Routledge.

Hattie, J. (2017). *Hattie ranking: 252 influences and effect sizes related to student achievement*. Visible Learning.

Hattie, J. (2023). *Visible learning: The sequel: A synthesis of over 2,100 meta-analyses relating to achievement*. Routledge.

Hattie, J., & Timperley, H. (2007). The power of feedback. *Review of Educational Research, 77*(1), 81–112. https://doi.org/10.3102/003465430298487

Hiebert, J., & Grouws, D. A. (2007). The effects of classroom mathematics teaching on students' learning. In F. Lester (Ed.), *Second handbook of research on mathematics teaching and learning* (pp. 371–404). Information Age Publishing.

Hill, H. C., Rowan, B., & Ball, D. L. (2005). Effects of teachers' mathematical knowledge for teaching on student achievement. *American Educational Research Journal, 42*(2), 371–406. https://doi.org/10.3102/00028312042002371

Kane, T. J., Agodini, R., Burns, L., Cantrell, S., Domina, T., Hargrave, E., & Staiger, D. (2024). *The road to recovery: Evidence-based lessons for the next decade in education (CEPR report)*. Center for Education Policy Research, Harvard University.

Kang, S. H. K. (2016). Spaced repetition promotes efficient and effective learning. *Psychonomic Bulletin & Review, 23*(1), 1–10. https://doi.org/10.1177/2372732215624708

Kirschner, P. A., Sweller, J., & Clark, R. E. (2006). Why minimal guidance during instruction does not work: An analysis of the failure of constructivist, discovery, problem based, experiential, and inquiry based teaching. *Educational Psychologist, 41*(2), 75–86. https://doi.org/10.1207/s15326985ep4102_1

Kulik, J. A., & Fletcher, J. D. (2016). Effectiveness of intelligent tutoring systems: A meta-analytic review. *Review of Educational Research*, *86*(1), 42–78. https://doi.org/10.3102/0034654315581420

Pane, J. F., McCaffrey, D. F., Slaughter, M. E., Steele, J. L., & Ikemoto, G. S. (2015). *Promising evidence on personalized learning*. RAND Corporation.

Pane, J. F., Steiner, E. D., Baird, M. D., & Hamilton, L. S. (2017). *Continued progress: Promising evidence on personalized learning*. RAND Corporation.

Rittle-Johnson, B., & Schneider, M. (2015). Developing conceptual and procedural knowledge in mathematics. *Educational Psychology Review*, *27*(4), 587–597.

Roediger, H. L., & Butler, A. C. (2011). The critical role of retrieval practice in long-term retention. *Trends in Cognitive Sciences*, *15*(1), 20–27. https://doi.org/10.1016/j.tics.2010.09.003

Roediger, H. L., & Karpicke, J. D. (2006). The power of testing memory: Basic research and implications for educational practice. *Perspectives on Psychological Science*, *1*(3), 181–210. https://doi.org/10.1111/j.1745-6916.2006.00012.x

Rohrer, D., Dedrick, R. F., & Stershic, S. (2015). Interleaved practice improves mathematics learning. *Journal of Educational Psychology*, *107*(3), 900–908. https://doi.org/10.1037/edu0000001

Rohrer, D., & Taylor, K. (2007). The shuffling of mathematics practice problems improves learning. *Instructional Science*, *35*(6), 481–498. https://doi.org/10.1007/s11251-007-9015-8

Roschelle, J., Feng, M., Murphy, R. F., & Mason, C. A. (2016). Online mathematics homework increases student achievement. *AERA Open*, *2*(4), 1–12. https://doi.org/10.1177/2332858416673968

Rosenshine, B. (2012). Principles of instruction: Research-based strategies that all teachers should know. *American Educator*, *36*(1), 12–19, 39.

Schmidt, R. A., & Bjork, R. A. (1992). New conceptualizations of practice: Common principles in three paradigms suggest new concepts for training. *Psychological Science*, *3*(4), 207–217. https://doi.org/10.1111/j.1467-9280.1992.tb00029.x

Schunk, D. H., & Pajares, F. (2002). The development of academic self-efficacy. In *Development of achievement motivation* (pp. 15–31). Academic Press. https://doi.org/10.1016/B978-012750053-9/50003-6

Shanahan, T. (2016). Relations among reading and writing development. In C. A. MacArthur, S. Graham, & J. Fitzgerald (Eds.), *Handbook of writing research* (2nd ed., pp. 194–207). Guilford Press.

Shute, V. J. (2008). Focus on formative feedback. *Review of Educational Research*, *78*(1), 153–189. https://doi.org/10.3102/0034654307313795

Soderstrom, N. C., & Bjork, R. A. (2015). Learning versus performance: An integrative review. *Perspectives on Psychological Science*, *10*(2), 176–199. https://doi.org/10.1177/1745691615569000

Sweller, J. (1994). Cognitive load theory, learning difficulty, and instructional design. *Learning and Instruction*, *4*(4), 295–312. https://doi.org/10.1016/0959-4752(94)90003-5

Sweller, J., Ayres, P., & Kalyuga, S. (2011). *Cognitive load theory* (2nd ed.). Springer.

United States National Mathematics Advisory Panel & U.S. Department of Education. (2008). *Foundations for success: The final report of the National Mathematics Advisory Panel*. U.S. Department of Education.

Van de Pol, J., Volman, M., & Beishuizen, J. (2010). Scaffolding in teacher–student interaction: A decade of research. *Educational Psychology Review*, *22*(3), 271–296. https://doi.org/10.1007/s10648-010-9127-6

VanLehn, K. (2011). The relative effectiveness of human tutoring, intelligent tutoring systems, and other tutoring systems. *Educational Psychologist*, *46*(4), 197–221. https://doi.org/10.1080/00461520.2011.611369

Willingham, D. T. (2009). *Why don't students like school? A cognitive scientist answers questions about how the mind works and what it means for the classroom*. Jossey-Bass.

Yang, X., & Kaiser, G. (2022). The impact of mathematics teachers' professional competence on instructional quality and students' mathematics learning outcomes. *Current Psychology*, *41*(9), 1–13. https://doi.org/10.1016/j.cobeha.2022.101225

10

A Call to Action

Why Cognitive and Progressive Teaching Models Can't Cohabit

Aiming for the strongest, evidence-based impact on learning requires careful consideration of which instructional practices are most consistently supported by empirical research rather than by prevailing educational trends. For roughly 120 years, progressive, constructivist ideologies have shaped teacher education and curricular philosophy in the United States. Even amid accountability reforms and data-informed instruction, constructivist approaches continue to influence definitions of "good teaching" and educational expectations. While these approaches emphasize exploration, collaboration, and student agency, cognitive science increasingly highlights the value of explicit, structured teaching to ensure that all students achieve mastery.

Although discovery-based, inquiry, and student-centered approaches are often assumed to foster deeper understanding and transfer, empirical research suggests that their impact on long-term retention is minimal (Alfieri et al., 2011; Kirschner et al., 2006). It is therefore important to prioritize cognitively grounded, research-based practices, particularly explicit instruction and guided teaching, which align closely with the brain's natural learning processes. Ignoring this research risks employing methods that may feel engaging or look innovative but are less effective, particularly for students who need the most support. Student-led exploration and "meaning making" often postpone or avoid directly addressing misconceptions, and inquiry-heavy models that are technology-rich but substantively shallow tend to minimize the importance of clear learning goals and structured guidance. Ultimately, the goal of teaching is independence—but independence is the product of effective scaffolding, not the starting point.

As students struggle to keep pace in student-centered classrooms, schools often turn to compensatory methods—adaptive software, engagement tools like Minecraft Education, and other personalized learning interventions—to address gaps that often exist *because* of insufficient or inconsistent *explicit* teaching. This lack of clarity and scaffolding disproportionately affects learners who depend on structured guidance to achieve mastery—a category that includes most students (Belland et al., 2017; Shao et al., 2023). Crucially, constructivism, while philosophically appealing, sometimes privileges ideology over evidence, drawing more from theory than from experimentally validated models of cognition. Its appeal is deeply tied to American cultural ideals such as independence, exploration, and critical thinking. These are admirable goals, and they represent qualities we rightly value and hope to cultivate in students. Yet these ideals do not have to stand in opposition to explicit, structured teaching. In fact, well-implemented, explicit instruction provides the very foundation upon which authentic inquiry, creativity, and critical thought can thrive.

The widespread belief that secondary students no longer require guided, explicit instruction is similarly problematic. Many educators assume that by middle or high school, students have already mastered the foundational knowledge and skills that require explicit instruction. Yet this assumption overlooks the increasing cognitive demands of secondary content areas, where mastery depends on specialized disciplinary knowledge and reasoning—the very kinds of courses from which many students are often removed during elementary school for targeted intervention or strategic support (Schwartz, 2024). They often equate age with expertise, assuming that older students no longer need structured guidance. However, research shows that many adolescents—especially those from underserved backgrounds—still require explicit support to engage with complex material and to develop strong academic literacy (Shanahan & Shanahan, 2008). Maturity does not guarantee metacognitive skills or mastery. In secondary classrooms, the push to keep students "engaged" through group work, projects, technology-rich activities, and discovery learning often confuses participation with *learning*. Engagement may boost short-term motivation, but it rarely produces lasting retention or conceptual depth (Hattie & Donoghue, 2016). Explicit instruction, in contrast, benefits learners of all ages. Because expertise is domain-specific, new and complex content requires carefully scaffolded, step-by-step teaching (Kirschner et al., 2006; Rosenshine, 2012; Sweller et al., 2011). Contrary to the myth that explicit instruction stifles creativity, it actually fosters creativity by automating basic skills, freeing cognitive resources for higher-order thinking, and providing all students with a shared knowledge base.

Educational philosophies frequently advocate for progressive, student-centered approaches; however, without grounding in cognitive science, their implementation can lead to unintended and sometimes detrimental outcomes. Recent data from the National Assessment of Educational Progress (NAEP) show that, in 2024, only 35% of high school seniors achieved proficiency in reading and 22% in mathematics—the lowest levels in two decades (National Center for Education Statistics [NCES], 2024). Moreover, scores for 13-year-olds have fallen to levels not seen since the 1970s, signaling a sustained decline in foundational literacy and numeracy (NCES, 2024). We have been relying on constructivist approaches in American education for roughly 120 years. Given decades of evidence showing limited long-term retention and persistent achievement gaps, what might we gain by intentionally applying instructional practices grounded in cognitive science?

Emphasizing whole-group, explicit instruction represents a significant paradigm shift for many educators and administrators. It requires substantial unlearning to recognize that effective learning is not always noisy, visibly "active," or dependent on technology—it is purposeful, structured, and cognitively demanding. Rather than attempting to accommodate "learner variability" through continual differentiation and performative engagement strategies, explicit instruction focuses on building the shared knowledge base essential for all learners. It prioritizes uncovering and strengthening students' prior knowledge while deliberately shaping the cognitive architecture that governs how all humans learn (Kirschner et al., 2006; Sweller et al., 2011; Willingham, 2009). Explicit instruction—when paired with scaffolded supports, cumulative review, and well-defined learning objectives—serves all students effectively and promotes coherent knowledge construction (Rosenshine, 2012; Sweller et al., 2011).

Yet, even when schools strive to realign teaching with cognitive science, they operate within an educational ecosystem still governed by student-centered paradigms that dictate what "good teaching" should look like and how success is measured. Consider Cognia, an organization formed by the consolidation of several long-standing regional accrediting bodies (e.g., North Central Association Commission on Accreditation and School Improvement, Southern Association of Colleges and Schools Council on Accreditation and School Improvement, and Northwest Accreditation Commission) and now serving over 36,000 institutions in more than 80 countries (Cognia, n.d.). Its Performance Standards are explicitly described as "learner-centric," emphasizing learner agency, voice, and engagement, while positioning traits such as self-efficacy as observable indicators of instructional quality (Cognia, n.d.). Although these features appear to reflect modern pedagogical progress, they often privilege progressive ideologies—emphasizing autonomy, discovery, and the decentering of the teacher—over practices grounded in empirical learning science.

Because accreditation review tools and observational rubrics tend to reward *visible* engagement, collaboration, and innovation (e.g., technology use), schools may feel pressured to adopt strategies aligned with "learner-centeredness" even when those strategies conflict with research on how learning actually occurs. Yet research demonstrates that *observable engagement* does not reliably predict durable learning or schema formation (Clark et al., 2012; Kirschner et al., 2006). Explicit, well-sequenced instruction, on the other hand, benefits all learners—not just novices or those who struggle (Australian Education Research Organisation, 2023; Rosenshine, 2012). Ironically, accreditation systems designed to ensure educational quality may therefore perpetuate instructional myths—rewarding what looks innovative over what is demonstrably effective.

Can Constructivist and Cognitive-Science Approaches Coexist?

Many educators argue that cognitive-science and constructivist approaches can coexist—a position that appears both reasonable and diplomatic. However, in practice, this belief can be misleading, particularly when designing instruction for novice learners. Research on blended models, in which explicit cognitive scaffolding precedes or accompanies student-centered reasoning, tends to outperform purely constructivist or inquiry-based methods (de Jong et al., 2023; Guo et al., 2023; Petersen, 2022). Yet the *best*-supported blended approaches are those that emphasize explicit scaffolding combined with *guided* inquiry, not those that rely primarily on discovery learning

(Alanazi et al., 2024; Vonitasari & Amir, 2025; Kaldaras & Wieman, 2025). The fundamental challenge is that these two instructional paradigms are grounded in fundamentally different theories of learning. Attempting to merge them often results in a muddled, incoherent approach that lacks the strengths of either. For example, when phonics is "sprinkled in" to a balanced literacy program, the instruction often becomes watered down and ineffective, leading teachers to underestimate the power of systematic practice in phonics. In blended classrooms, skills may be introduced explicitly but are often followed too soon by open-ended tasks before students have achieved mastery. In mathematics and reading alike, procedures are sometimes taught in isolation with minimal deliberate practice, replaced instead by activities that prioritize engagement over efficacy. Too often, schools overemphasize small-group structures or 'innovative' tasks when, in fact, well-designed whole-group instruction—grounded in explicit teaching and strong teacher clarity—has proven to be more effective and instructionally efficient, particularly for novice learners (Rosenshine, 2012; Sweller et al., 2011; Hattie, 2023). This constant oscillation between conflicting methods creates inconsistent cues, fragmented feedback, and mixed expectations for learners.

Many educators, trained in constructivist ideals emphasizing student-centered, inquiry-based, and authentic learning, view direct instruction as overly rigid, boring, or developmentally inappropriate. This perception often leads to a misunderstanding of what effective explicit teaching actually entails and reinforces the notion that the teacher's role should be one of facilitators rather than instructor. When empirical research supports explicit instruction but conflicts with teachers' deeply held beliefs, cognitive dissonance emerges, often resulting in selective interpretation or rejection of the evidence. At its core, this raises a difficult but necessary question: If our teaching practices fail to produce durable learning, have we truly taught the student at all? Too often, what appears to be a need for intervention or

Tier 2/3 support is, in reality, a reflection of insufficient Tier 1 instruction. When explicit instruction is implemented with fidelity, many so-called "learning gaps" diminish—not because the students suddenly changed but because the teaching did.

For decades, the *Project Follow Through* initiative has been arguably the most extensive study of instruction ever undertaken in U.S. elementary education—with tens of thousands of students, dozens of instructional models, and measures of academic, cognitive-conceptual, and affective outcomes (Gersten et al., 1988; Meyer, 1984; Stockard et al., 2018). Its results demonstrated that highly structured, explicit, teacher-led instruction produced superior academic and self-esteem outcomes compared with child-centered and minimally guided models, across disadvantaged and diverse student populations (Engelmann & Carnine, 1991; Meyer, 1984). The compelling nature of these findings has made *Project Follow Through* a foundational reference point for advocates of explicit teaching—and a cautionary tale for ideologically driven instruction that ignores evidence. Moving forward, we must shift from ideology to evidence in our instructional decisions. Districts and states should invest in structured professional learning that not only presents research but models what high-quality explicit instruction looks like in practice, supports teachers through coaching, and builds shared understanding of why these methods work.

It is crucial to move beyond the misconception that explicit instruction is synonymous with "sit and get." When well executed, it is interactive, diagnostic, and cognitively rich, providing the essential foundation for higher-order reasoning and genuine inquiry. Despite decades of reform—often moving away from direct instruction toward constructivist or "balanced" frameworks—national performance data reveal minimal gains, while achievement disparities have widened. Evidence consistently shows that explicit, structured instruction yields the most substantial and equitable outcomes across academic domains, particularly for disadvantaged students (Stockard et al., 2018).

The Power of an Effective Instructionally Knowledgeable Leader

Effective leaders define quality teaching based on evidence rather than trends. They prioritize instructional clarity, coherence, and high expectations grounded in principles such as explicit instruction, cognitive load theory, and retrieval practice. These leaders recognize that every student deserves access to clear, direct, and scaffolded instruction aligned with cognitive science, where teachers explicitly model, guide practice, and incorporate spaced retrieval to enhance learning. To build teacher capacity, ongoing professional development explicitly connects cognitive-science concepts—like working memory, spaced repetition, and dual coding—to daily classroom practice, leveraging resources from leading experts to translate theory into actionable strategies. Administrators support this work by conducting walkthroughs and providing job-embedded coaching to ensure that teachers implement whole-school routines such as the gradual release model, daily review and retrieval, clear learning objectives with success criteria, and regular checks for understanding.

Leaders track instructional indicators beyond test scores, focusing on observable evidence of modeling and guided practice, authentic student engagement in cognitively demanding tasks, explicit instruction, and opportunities for retrieval or elaboration. Rather than generic professional development, coaching is feedback-driven and targeted, asking questions like: Did the teacher reduce cognitive load? Provide sufficient scaffolding? Ensure active practice? Core instruction remains central, free from fragmentation by fads or unproven methods—such as excessive technology use or over-reliance on discovery learning. Leaders critically assess how instructional practices truly align with cognitive principles. Staff meetings become forums for reviewing research briefs, discussing case studies, and analyzing student work through a cognitive lens while modeling the behaviors of research professionals. Because leadership ranks second only to classroom instruction among school-related factors impacting student learning, the influence of a knowledgeable, effective instructional leader is profound (Leithwood et al., 2004). Table 10.1 offers some "look-fors" that administrators can

TABLE 10.1 Cognitive-Science Walkthrough Tool

Cognitive Strategy	Look-Fors in the Classroom	Red Flags/What to Watch Out For
Explicit Instruction	Teacher clearly demonstrates new skills or concepts; step-by-step modeling; guided practice before independent work	Students left to figure things out alone; minimal teacher modeling
Building Background Knowledge	Links new content to prior knowledge; pre-teaches key vocabulary or concepts	Students confused due to lack of context or prior knowledge scaffolding
Clear Learning Intentions & Success Criteria	Learning goals posted/discussed; students know what mastery looks like	Goals unclear or missing; students unsure what they are supposed to learn
Teacher Clarity & Credibility	Teacher communicates instructions and explanations effectively; demonstrates expertise; maintains classroom presence	Confusing explanations; low student trust in teacher knowledge or authority
Scaffolding & Worked Examples	Gradual release ("I do, we do, you do"); support fades as students gain competence	Sudden shift to independent work; minimal support provided
Formative Assessment/Checks for Understanding	Frequent questioning; low-stakes quizzes; real-time feedback	Little or no monitoring of student understanding; misconceptions unaddressed
Effective & Timely Feedback	Corrective, specific, actionable feedback during instruction	Generic feedback or delayed correction; students unsure how to improve
Retrieval, Interleaving, & Spaced/Distributed Practice	Students actively recall prior learning; practice revisited over time; topics or skills mixed	Only passive review; cramming or repeated blocked practice

(Continued)

TABLE 10.1 (Continued)

Cognitive Strategy	Look-Fors in the Classroom	Red Flags/What to Watch Out For
Deliberate Practice	Focused practice targeting specific skills; increasing challenge; feedback integrated	Busywork or repetitive tasks without focus; lack of progression or feedback
Teacher Credibility/ Presence	Teacher demonstrates confidence, expertise, and connects with students	Weak authority, inconsistent explanations, low engagement

A guide to classroom look-fors, red flags, and instructional strategies aligned with evidence-based cognitive-science principles.

use to guide walkthroughs and assess cognitive science–aligned instruction throughout their school.

These cognitive science–aligned strategies are not limited by grade level or content area. Whether students are learning foundational literacy in early elementary classrooms, complex algebra in high school, or disciplinary concepts in science and social studies, these approaches remain highly effective. Explicit instruction, scaffolding, retrieval practice, and deliberate practice support all learners' acquisition of deep, transferable knowledge, regardless of age or subject. For example, clear learning intentions and success criteria help kindergartners understand what mastery looks like in letter–sound correspondence just as much as they guide high school students in mastering geometric proofs. Similarly, formative checks for understanding and timely feedback ensure that misconceptions are addressed immediately across math, language arts, science, and social studies. By focusing on the cognitive architecture of learning rather than grade-specific traditions, these strategies provide a coherent framework for building expertise and supporting student success across the entire K–12 spectrum.

The Problem with the Pick-a-Tool Approach

When constructivist and cognitive models are combined without a clear guiding theory, the result is a fragmented, ineffective approach to teaching. Teachers, often navigating between personal preference and popular trends, can lose sight of research-backed practices. Even the best curriculum programs falter when instruction lacks intentionality and deep understanding of how students learn. The greatest casualties are learners with less background knowledge or weaker executive functions, who are denied the structured support they need to thrive. Worse, this muddled approach leaves schools guessing why students struggle, obscuring the evidence-based solutions that cognitive science provides. To truly close learning gaps, we must abandon patchwork methods and commit to instruction grounded in how the brain learns best—systematic, explicit, and informed by evidence rather than ideology.

References

Alanazi, A. A., Osman, K., & Halim, L. (2024). Effect of scaffolding strategies and guided discovery on higher-order thinking skills in physics education. *Eurasia Journal of Mathematics, Science and Technology Education, 20*(9), em2496. https://doi.org/10.29333/ejmste/14980

Alfieri, L., Brooks, P. J., Aldrich, N. J., & Tenenbaum, H. R. (2011). Does discovery-based instruction enhance learning? *Journal of Educational Psychology, 103*(1), 1–18. https://psycnet.apa.org/doi/10.1037/a0021017

Australian Education Research Organisation. (2023, September 18). *Explicit instruction optimises learning: Explainer.* https://www.edresearch.edu.au/summaries-explainers/explainers/explicit-instruction-optimises-learning

Belland, B. R., Walker, A. E., Kim, N. J., & Lefler, M. (2017). Synthesizing results from empirical research on computer-based scaffolding in STEM education: A meta-analysis. *Review of Educational Research, 87*(2), 309–344. https://doi.org/10.3102/0034654316670999

Clark, R. E., Kirschner, P. A., & Sweller, J. (2012). Putting students on the path to learning: The case for fully guided instruction. *American Educator, 36*(1), 6–11.

Cognia. (n.d.). *Our history.* Cognia.

de Jong, T., Lazonder, A. W., Chinn, C. A., Fischer, F., Gobert, J., Hmelo-Silver, C. E., Koedinger, K. R., Krajcik, J. S., Kyza, E. A., Linn, M. C., Pedaste, M., Scheiter, K., & Zacharia, Z. C. (2023). Let's talk evidence – The case for combining inquiry-based and direct instruction. *Educational Research Review*, *100536*. https://doi.org/10.1016/j.edurev.2023.100536

Engelmann, S., & Carnine, D. (1991). *Theory of instruction: Principles and applications*. Irvington.

Gersten, R., Keating, T., & Becker, W. C. (1988). The continued impact of the direct instruction model: Longitudinal studies of follow through students. *Education and Treatment of Children*, *11*(4), 318–327.

Guo, Y., Wang, Y., & Ortega-Martín, J. L. (2023). The impact of blended learning-based scaffolding techniques on learners' self-efficacy and willingness to communicate. *Porta Linguarum: Revista Interuniversitaria de Didáctica de las Lenguas Extranjeras*, *40*(2), 253–273. https://doi.org/10.30827/portalin.vi40.27061

Hattie, J. (2023). *Visible learning: The sequel: A synthesis of over 2,100 meta-analyses relating to achievement*. Routledge.

Hattie, J. A. C., & Donoghue, G. M. (2016). Learning strategies: A synthesis and conceptual model. *npj Science of Learning*, *1*. https://doi.org/10.1038/npjscilearn.2016.13

Kaldaras, L., & Wieman, C. E. (2025). Investigating blended math-science sensemaking with historically marginalized STEM learners. *International Journal of STEM Education*, *12*, 44. https://doi.org/10.1186/s40594-025-00565-z

Kirschner, P. A., Sweller, J., & Clark, R. E. (2006). Why minimal guidance during instruction does not work: An analysis of the failure of constructivist, discovery, problem-based, experiential, and inquiry-based teaching. *Educational Psychologist*, *41*(2), 75–86. https://doi.org/10.1207/s15326985ep4102_1

Leithwood, K., Seashore Louis, K., Anderson, S., & Wahlstrom, K. (2004). *How leadership influences student learning*. The Wallace Foundation.

Meyer, L. A. (1984). Long-term academic effects of the direct instruction project follow through. *Elementary School Journal*, *84*, 380–394.

National Center for Education Statistics. (2024). *The nation's report card: Reading and mathematics assessments, 2024[Data set]*. U.S. Department of Education.

Petersen, M. R. (2022). Strategies to scaffold students' inquiry learning in science. *Science Education International, 33*(3), 267–275.

Rosenshine, B. (2012). Principles of instruction: Research-based strategies that all teachers should know. *American Educator, 36*(1), 12–19.

Schwartz, S. (2024, February 27). Social studies and science get short shrift in elementary schools. Why that matters. *Education Week.* https://www.edweek.org/teaching-learning/social-studies-and-science-get-short-shrift-in-elementary-schools-why-that-matters/2024/02

Shanahan, T., & Shanahan, C. (2008). Teaching disciplinary literacy to adolescents: Rethinking content-area literacy. *Harvard Educational Review, 78*(1), 40–59. https://doi.org/10.17763/haer.78.1.v62444321p602101

Shao, J., Chen, Y., Wei, X., Li, X., & Li, Y. (2023). Effects of regulated learning scaffolding on regulation strategies and academic performance: A meta-analysis. *Frontiers in Psychology, 14*, 1110086. https://doi.org/10.3389/fpsyg.2023.1110086

Stockard, J., Wood, T. W., Coughlin, C., & Khoury, C. R. (2018). The effectiveness of direct instruction curricula: A meta-analysis of a half-century of research. *Review of Educational Research, 88*(4), 479–507. https://doi.org/10.3102/0034654317751919

Sweller, J., Ayres, P., & Kalyuga, S. (2011). *Cognitive load theory.* Springer. https://doi.org/10.1007/978-1-4419-8126-4

Vonitasari, A. R., & Amir, M. F. (2025). The effectiveness of guided inquiry with scaffolding techniques in enhancing primary students' self-efficacy in mathematics. *Jurnal Pendidikan MIPA, 26*(1), 539–555. https://doi.org/10.23960/jpmipa.v26i1.pp539-555

Willingham, D. T. (2009). *Why don't students like school? A cognitive scientist answers questions about how the mind works and what it means for the classroom.* Jossey-Bass.

For Product Safety Concerns and Information please contact our EU representative GPSR@taylorandfrancis.com
Taylor & Francis Verlag GmbH, Kaufingerstraße 24, 80331 München, Germany

www.ingramcontent.com/pod-product-compliance
Lightning Source LLC
Chambersburg PA
CBHW061437300426
44114CB00014B/1727